Emma Newman, A Frontier Woman Minister

Women and Gender in North American Religions
Amanda Porterfield *and* Mary Farrell Bednarowski, *Series Editors*

Emma Newman (*right*) with Mr. and Mrs. Carl Emmerson,
Sierra Madre, California, 1921

Photograph courtesy of Earl Emmerson

Emma Newman

A Frontier Woman Minister

Randi Jones Walker

SYRACUSE UNIVERSITY PRESS

Library of Congress Cataloging-in-Publication Data
Walker, Randi Jones.
    Emma Newman, a frontier woman minister / Randi Jones Walker.—1st ed.
       p. cm.—(Women and gender in North American religions)
    Includes bibliographical references (p.) and index.
    ISBN 0-8156-0674-5 (alk. paper)
    1. Newman, Emma.   I. Title.   II. Series.
    BX7260.N49 .W35 2000
    285.8'092—dc21
    [B]   00-034429

Manufactured in the United States of America

To my women clergy colleagues, past, present, and future

Randi Jones Walker is associate professor of church history at Pacific School of Religion in Berkeley, California. She is also an ordained minister in the United Church of Christ and has served three congregations in Southern California. She is the author of *Protestantism in the Sangre de Christos* (1991) and several articles.

Contents

Maps

Acknowledgments

Through a decade of work on this project, many people have helped me in many ways. A few of them need to be noted publicly here. First of all, I wish to thank Virginia Renner and Mary Wright at the Huntington Library in San Marino, whose hospitality to me as I came each Tuesday to read Newman's diaries made a task of several years much lighter. The staffs of the Kansas Historical Society Library in Topeka, Kansas, the Porter Memorial Library in Machias, Maine, the Historical Society of Andover, Massachusetts, the Congregational Library in Boston, Massachusetts, the Andover-Harvard Theological Library of Harvard Divinity School, the Illinois State Historical Library in Springfield, Illinois, the Chicago Historical Society, the Chicago Public Library, and the Moody Bible Institute in Chicago, Illinois, the Osborne County Historical Society in Osborne, Kansas, and the Graduate Theological Union Library in Berkeley, California, were all unfailingly kind and helpful. In addition, I wish to thank Beth Nordbeck for her hospitality.

Lois Banner responded to a paper I gave on Newman at a meeting of the Western Association of Women Historians, and an anonymous reader for this press took time to read and suggest deeper avenues of approach. I am grateful to them.

Two doctoral students at the Graduate Theological Union served as research assistants and doggedly pursued several long searches for information; Hilary Marckx, Lorna Shoemaker, and a third student, Judy Georges, read more than one draft of the manuscript and made excellent comments. Cathy Bohrman helped enormously by typing Newman's sermons. Francesca Hughes helped with typing. Audrey Englert, the faculty secretary at Pacific School of Religion, has helped more than she will ever know with computers, formatting the manuscript, and helping me keep track of all the fussy details. Audrey also created the index.

Conversations with numerous people have encouraged me on my way, but particularly Sharon Thornton, Ardith Hayes, Mike Mendiola in a conversation on suffering, Archie Smith, Jr., Mary Donovan Turner, Tari Lennon, Eldon Ernst, Harland Hogue, and Barbara Brown Zikmund helped me to discover what I really wanted to say about Emma Newman. A final conversation with Judy and Sharon before completing the conclusion reminded me again why I thought the story was important to anyone but me.

Several long-distance phone calls to my brother, Phil Jones, helped me sort out whether or not Newman was a romantic. The person who first helped me to see Newman as a real flesh and blood person and not just a trace in the papers left from the nineteenth century was Earl Emmerson. He deserves a short story here. Earl Emmerson is the grandson of Nicholas Emmerson, the man Newman married when she was sixty years old. They had a short but happy marriage that ended when Emmerson died. Earl and Ula invited me to their farm south of Osborne, Kansas to talk about Emma. Earl was working on a family history and was interested in what I knew about her. I visited them twice. We ate chicken dinners with gooseberry pie. We visited a ninety-year-old man in a nursing home who had memories of the Dial Congregational church where both Emma and Nicholas had served as pastors. We took a long drive on a road washed out in the 1993 floods to a corn field to find the site of Dial and church. Earl found a photo of Emma and sent a copy to me. I hope to make one more visit to Ula and Earl when I have a copy of this book to deliver to them.

Earl Emmerson allowed me to use his family photograph of Emma Newman and information he shared with me in our conversations; The Huntington Library gave permission for me to quote large portions from the Emma Newman Collection. My gratitude goes also to the Andover-Harvard Theological Library for permission to use materials from the Women's Ministerial Conference papers; to the Kansas State Historical Society and the Kansas-Oklahoma Conference of the United Church of Christ for permission to use the Record Book of the Dial Congregational Church; to the Illinois State Historical Library for permission to use two items from their Federal Writers Project Files; and to the Amistad Research Center for permission to use five letters from the files of the American Home Missionary Society.

Finally, I want to give special thanks to the following members of my seminar on Women in American Religion, taught at the Graduate Theological Union in the fall of 1998. They more than any others helped me finally to give birth to this story. To these midwives, I wish they may find such conversations when they need them most: Sandra Blair, my teaching assistant for the course, Michelle Clinton, Anne D'Arcy, Kathleen Finzell, Anne Geever, Judy Georges, Rebecca Irelan, Kimberly Mazyck, Margaret McManus, and Eugene McMullan.

Introduction

Emma Newman's friends remembered her as a woman with a keen mind and a generous heart. She was "progressively inclined, had deep interest in the woman's movement," and was "intolerant of shams and often impatient with conventions" (*Townsman*, Aug. 25, 1922).[1] "She worked under conditions which would have appalled many a man, riding from charge to charge for her preaching appointments after the manner of the old circuit riders" (Abbott Academy n.d.). Though she was the first woman to be licensed to preach by an association of the Congregational Churches in 1883,[2] she was never ordained because the Home Missionary Society was opposed to the idea of women preachers throughout her career.

About fifteen years ago, I was searching the manuscript catalogue at the Huntington Library in San Marino, California, for sermons from a particular group of Southern California Protestant ministers who concerned themselves with nature and who were involved in the early conservation movement. As I searched the catalogue by place, under Pasadena, I found an entry for Emma E. Newman (1838–1921): five boxes, diary, and ninety sermons. Immediately, I put the nature sermon project on the back burner and began to explore the Emma Newman collection.

1. Abbott Academy made a file of newspaper clippings of Emma Newman Emmerson's obituaries. The newspapers are for the most part not identified. "Mrs. Emmerson Was a Pioneer for Her Sex" is clearly from a Sierra Madre, California, paper. The article "Mrs. Emma Newman Emmerson," in the *Townsman*, Aug. 25, 1922, does not contain an indication of its place of publication. The clippings can be found in the Emma Newman file of the Abbott Academy Records, Phillips Academy, Andover, Massachusetts.

2. Emma Newman was licensed by the Northwestern Association of Congregational Churches in Kansas in 1883.

At the time, I was a United Church of Christ minister serving on the staff of the First Congregational Church of Pasadena. I had recently completed my Ph.D., and although the job market for women was slim in the United Church of Christ, it was even more slim in the academic world. For the next nine years, I spent my days off at the Huntington reading the Newman collection. At first, Emma Newman was simply a companion along my way. She had done the work I was doing. She had experienced the marginal place of a woman minister in the church. She had made her own way where there was no way. She also had come to understand the churches of the West. As I moved on from the First Congregational Church to be the pastor of a small congregation in North Hollywood, I began to learn from her important and often intangible insights about the realities and opportunities of pastoral work as a woman in a small church in the American West.

From this kind of historical companionship, I began to ask some critical historical questions and began to wonder if there was material here for a biography. I was struck by the room in the American West for women's preaching. I was also struck by the relative internal ease with which Newman embarked on this career. My view had been that whenever a woman entered professional work in the church, especially in the nineteenth century, she had an external and an internal battle to fight against an institution and culture unable to imagine such a move. Not until my own generation had this ever been a peaceful enterprise for a woman. However, I realized that throughout Newman's diary I never once discovered evidence that she struggled within herself about whether this was right for a woman to do. She certainly had opposition from outside, from her family and the church, but never from within. She never doubted that she was called to these professions of ministry and medicine, and not to marriage and family responsibilities. Why was this?

The role of geography in the transition of women's leadership in the churches from voluntary societies to the church institution itself and the lack of internal conflict in Newman's assumption of pastoral responsibilities in the church proved to be easier to state than to analyze. In spite of encouragement from friends, both clergywomen and women in the academy, the anonymous reader for another press to whom I sent an early draft of this project was right to point out that, without addressing these issues in depth, the story lacked significance and even interest. For a couple of years, I let the project lie fallow.

During that time, I read three articles that began to suggest a framework for understanding the cultural assumptions lying behind the influence of gender and geography on Newman's work.[3] Essays on religion in the American West by Ferenc and Margaret Connell Szasz and Laurie Maffly-Kipp placed emphasis on the fact that people took their religion with them into the new communities of the West, and although many changed or neglected their faith traditions, those religious mind sets and values nonetheless shaped society in profound ways. This took me back to older work, such as that by Louis B. Wright in *Culture on the Moving Frontier* (1955) and Colin B. Goodykoontz in *Home Missions on the American Frontier* (1939), whose initial studies of cultural development on the frontier pointed to the religious values and traditions embedded in even secular cultural enterprises such as public schools. Both of them pointed to the Anglo Saxon or English origins of this cultural stream, and both pointed to the ways in which this culture continues to underlie the social structures of much of the Midwest and West.

A third essay radically changed my understanding of women's point of view in American religious history. Ann Braude contributed an essay entitled "Women's History *Is* American Religious History" to *Retelling U.S. Religious History* (Tweed 1997, 87–107), a recent collection of writings outlining new ways of approaching religious history. Braude's essay suggested to me that Newman's story belonged not on the margins of American religious history, but was in fact part of the mainstream story.

From 1870 to 1970, the location of women's leadership in American Protestantism changed. In her essay, Braude argues that the most useful theme for a narrative history of American religion may be found in a focus on the presence and increasing vigor of women's religious lives. Most historians agree that women were the backbone of "mainstream" American religion as well as prominent leaders in dissenting movements. Braude argues further that the story of women's roles in American religion moves from women's increasing spiritual equality with men in the colonial pe-

---

3. Two of these essays outline the most recent questions raised from the study of religion in the American West for understanding American religious history as a whole: see Szasz and Connell Szasz 1994; Milner, O'Connor, and Sandweiss 1994, 359–92; and Maffly-Kipp 1997, 127–48. The third article suggests a complete reframing of the question of women in American religion of which I will say more in chapter 1. See Braude 1977, 87–107.

riod, to the assumption of public roles in the nineteenth century because of their position as guardians of family morality and piety, and finally, in the twentieth century, to shaping public policy and serving as ordained leaders in the churches.

From 1770 to 1870, women took increasing leadership in the emerging voluntary societies organized for missions, charity, and social change. They did so from religious motives, but because leadership in church institutions was closed to them, they started organizations to one degree or another unconnected to the denominations. In the 1870s, a shift occurred. Denominations began to license and ordain women as ministers in steadily increasing numbers. The ordination movement skyrocketed in the 1970s. Emma Newman was situated in the earliest moments of this transition. By looking at her ministry as a case study we can learn something about the context in which this change was possible, and about what its roots were.

What Newman was doing and her significance lay not only in the coherence of her own personal transitions, but in the ways that they illustrate a growing movement of American religious history as a whole, the increasing involvement of women within the religious power structure. The results of that movement are, in the late twentieth century, beginning to reshape Christianity itself.

For Newman, this was not a sudden shift, but a gradual movement with an inner logic. She exercised her leadership in a constant movement toward a more primary pastoral role. Her work grew out of her evangelical Protestant upbringing. Her culture taught her that usefulness was one of the primary Christian duties, and she exercised this usefulness in her voluntary work in the Sunday School and Aid Society in Andover, Massachusetts. As she grew older, she took on responsibilities for the money of the Aid Society, its dispersal, and the organization of the charitable outreach of the middle-class Congregational Church men and women to the working poor and destitute members of the community. She taught a Sunday School class of girls who worked in the mills.

This work received a theological underpinning as she attended classes at the Andover Seminary. She began to talk about being called. Her sense of general duty to be useful developed into a belief she was called to a vocation. Her women friends encouraged her to preach; she did not resist the idea, but wondered if it was truly a sign of a call. Her first invitation to preach a sermon came closely on the heels of her friends' encouragement.

The friends also encouraged her to study and practice homeopathic medicine and mental healing, which she also began to interpret as a possible call.

Like many young women of her time, she was responsible in her early adult years for the care of her mother. When her mother died, Newman moved west. Invitations to serve small churches came as she identified herself to Congregational clergy and Home Missionary Society representatives as desiring to be a preacher and evangelist.

Thus another transition occurred as the church recognized Newman's personal sense of call. Over the course of two decades she served numerous churches for increasingly longer periods of time. From time to time she applied for regular credentials from the Congregational Church for a license to preach and then ordination. At first her authorization was irregular, temporary, and informal, then increasingly regular and more widely recognized. Without a battle and without crossing a clear boundary, she moved into pastoral ministry, preaching each Sunday, organizing the work of a congregation, and serving as pastor to a community.

Working with Newman's story proved both easy and difficult. The early part of her diary is almost all a scholar could ask. For nearly forty years, every day, Newman recorded much of what she did. In the earlier years she wrote down the minute details of what she read, who she talked to and what they talked about, what sewing she was doing, and the details of errands she had in town. She recorded her state of health and the changes in the weather. In later years, she wrote less, sometimes not even recording enough information for the reader to understand what happened. Gaps and lack of detail hamper the reader of the later part of her diary. What is easy to analyze in the early chapters of this biography became more difficult in later chapters because I was left to guess about too much.

Newman's ninety sermons are a gold mine of information about a woman's preaching in the West. However, like many preachers, she moved away from writing complete manuscripts in her later years. At first, she wrote both a manuscript and an outline. Later, she found only an outline sufficient for her purposes as she gained confidence in "extemporaneous speaking." Most of the sermons in the collection are outlines; only twenty exist in full manuscript. Although the outlines provide a general idea of her message, the lack of detail precludes any substantive analysis of changes in her theology.

Although the sources originating from her are rich, other sources are sparse. Her published writing was mostly for small Sunday School papers, and I have not succeeded in a decade of searching in finding any copies containing her articles and stories. She regularly burned her letters. The collection at the Huntington Library has only a handful of letters addressed to her. The people to whom she wrote did not keep her letters, though some of them left collections of papers behind. There are traces of her in denominational records and in newspapers. Several letters in the correspondence of the American Home Missionary Society refer to her. She is mentioned in the records of the Women Minister's Association. Her husband's family retains some memories of her. Understanding the connections that sustained her spirit or the influence she had on people is difficult in the face of the dearth of evidence, but even given the limits of the records available, the historian has more to work with than is true for many early women pastors. I found myself having to choose emphases rather than struggling to include every scrap of information.

My approach to Newman's story focuses on two categories of analysis, gender and geography. The category of gender allows me to ask how and why this woman shaped her life the way she did. It also allows me to ask why so much in her story runs against the grain of what I expected, given that she was a woman working in largely male professional territory. The category of geography allows me to ask about the development of Protestant churches in the frontier Midwest. It also allows me to ask why the life in these churches ran counter to so much of the missiology underlying the home missionary movement based in the East. Putting these two categories together helps explain what I think are significant connections between the environment and culture of the nineteenth-century West. Within this context women had unexpected but clear ways of expressive leadership in religious institutions.

Newman's transition from easterner to westerner developed through the exercise of her creativity in the face of conditions unfamiliar to her. She modified her understanding of an effective sermon as she met people whose practical concerns left them little time for formal education. In her traveling, she served as a link among scattered people and participated in forming community in places too scattered to be termed towns. She adapted her work to the western environment and she brought to it a woman's touch.

The freedom of the Anglo-American frontier worked together with new forms of women's public leadership as an outgrowth of the religious role assigned women by nineteenth-century society. Emma Newman's story allows us to see the way in which women tended to minister to the whole person, body as well as soul, the ways in which women shaped community, and the ways in which gender, geography, and the culture of the American West shaped the church and the office of minister.

The western frontier was an environment of great social change. What worked in the East did not always work in the West. Assumptions about the place of the churches in society or the role of the clergy or of women in the community changed as one moved west.

In the East, most communities held religion to be a primary concern in their founding. For example, the Puritans in Massachusetts, the Catholics in Maryland, or the Quakers in Pennsylvania had established communities in colonial times in order to enjoy free expression of their particular religious practice. Religious institutions and the clergy continued, even after disestablishment, to enjoy honored status and were consulted on important community matters. In the West, religion was of secondary importance, and to some of no importance at all. Efforts by the clergy to organize religious life in western communities were not always successful. Ministers encountered resistence and disinterest. Women had well-defined roles in church and society in the East, but in the West these roles began to change. New kinds of partnerships developed between men and women even as isolation exacerbated the traditional difficulties between them. In religious organizations, western women's roles expanded as these organizations had to be recreated to serve a new situation. The expansion of woman's roles in the West was also part of a general need for more lay involvement as the lack of clergy hampered church development. The western clergy performed the standard tasks of ministry and were among the foremost representatives of "culture" in new communities. Nineteenth-century Protestant clergy understood themselves to be the bearers of a culture rooted largely in New England, whether they were from there or not (Wright 1955). The outlines of this culture were British, marked with the confidence of the Puritan that God's chosen people should improve the world. From basic literacy to college education, the home missionaries valued the cultivation of the mind. They founded colleges and supported libraries and lecture series; they advocated for the rule and study of law; they promoted music and poetry. However, they rarely separated their vision of the Christian life from this cultural education. The clergy, along with women, were the primary promoters of this cultural vision in the western communities (Wright 1955; Riley 1988).

In his study of the clergy in the Great Plains and mountain west, Ferenc Szasz notes that Protestant clergy have remained in the background of accounts of life in frontier communities; they are rarely the heros (Szasz 1988). Glenda Riley, in *The Female Frontier*, makes the same observation about women (1988, 2). The similarities of women's work and that of clergy are remarkable. Both concern themselves with nurturing and maintaining relationships and the physical and spiritual well-being of those in their care. Although some have adopted the paradigm of "feminization" to explain this close connection between the work of women and that of clergy, I believe it is rooted in the ancient origins of the church in the *oikos* (household) rather than in the *polis* (political structure of society). In Newman's work we see the re-emergence of an old model of women's Christian leadership that helps to explain why, in the end, she faced so little internal struggle about being a woman minister.

In this study, I consider two transitions in American religious history in the nineteenth century, the transition of women's leadership from voluntary societies to the institutional church already developed above, and the transition in evangelical Protestant theology toward liberalism, especially as that is illustrated in the Congregational churches. These transitions have been evident to historians for some time; however, looking at them from the point of view of women's, particularly Newman's, experiences, I have been able to see a more complex shape to the more familiar account of them.

In addition to the two categories of gender and geography, I have chosen two frames by which to look at these transitions in American religion and Newman's life. I have chosen first to frame the study by means of an analysis of pastoral care rather than preaching, pragmatic work rather than theology. This is not to say that I do not think Newman's theology is important. I do discuss it and study its nuances, effects, and changes. However, Newman's most influential activity was her pastoral care, her relationships, visitation, and attention to her people and their lives. She transmitted her theology through her pastoral care, I would argue, more effectively than through her preaching.

Secondly, I want to frame her story by means of an analysis of the *oikos*, or household, as the basic social setting from which Christianity emerged. Newman was making a natural move, I argue, in undertaking pastoral work. She was building on a deeply embedded understanding of Christian religious leadership. The ease of Newman's assumption of the pastoral role reflects the fluidity of women's roles especially in the West, where constricting social structures were not in place.

I present this study through the cultural studies mode of "thick description." I have found it most helpful to analyze several specific situations in Newman's career, looking at them as deeply as possible, trying to understand the significance of each move and each decision she made, as well as to describe the context of her life in that situation as completely as I can. Through the analysis of Newman's career, I revisited Colin Goodykoontz's account of home missions on the American frontier, but centered the account on women because I think it is a women's story. He suggested this might be the case, but the change of point of view is a difficult one. I returned again and again to Ann Braude's insistence that American religious history is women's history. This book presents what I saw when I tried to view through one woman's life the mighty mainstream of American Christianity.

Emma Newman, A Frontier Woman Minister

1

"I Commenced on My
First Pastoral Charge"

June 11, 1873. Will took me out to Big Woods in the afternoon
and I commenced on my first pastoral charge, very sure that I
don't know anything, very sure that Christ knows everything.
                                    —Diary, vol. 7, June 11, 1873

In June 1873, Emma Newman arrived in Big Woods, Illinois, to be pastor
of the Congregational church there. She served the church for the
summer, thirteen weeks. It was a tentative situation, with an unrealized
possibility of developing into a long-term position for Newman. It was
Newman's first pastoral charge, even though she had done some preaching
in New England and in Missouri, but it was unusual to find a woman pastor
even in a peripheral rural congregation southwest of Chicago in that time.

Newman came to be in Big Woods, Illinois because it was a very small
place; few regular (male) ministers would have deemed it worthwhile.
However, in nearby Batavia there were people who had known Newman
in Andover and had heard her preaching in Missouri. On their recommendation, the Big Woods church was willing to take on an untried
woman pastor.

What the Big Woods people expected from a woman pastor was somewhat complicated. There is evidence in Newman's own writings that there
was curiosity and ambivalence about her presence. Thirteen weeks was not
long enough for her to develop a deep relationship with the congregation,
so the ambivalence probably remained prominent in the congregation's
experience.

Big Woods was a small community on the prairie about thirty-five miles west of Chicago. Batavia, less than ten miles away, was the nearest large town with railroad connections. The Big Woods church had been around for a while. Founded in 1835 by settlers from New England, it was Presbyterian at first, becoming Congregational in 1843 (*Commemorative Biographical and Historical Record of Kane County, Illinois* 1888, 855).[1] The American Home Missionary Society supplied the organizing pastor, a Rev. Young, who held the first services in a log cabin. In 1849 the congregation, in cooperation with the Baptists, Free Will Baptists, and Methodists, erected a church building for the town that was shared by all of them.

During the decade before 1855, the congregation decided that "No minister holding slavery to be right will be called, no slave holder can be a member, and it is the duty of every Christian to abstain from intoxicating drink" (Big Woods Congregational Church 1950). This decision placed the congregation in the social reform mainstream of the day. Three years earlier, Harriet Beecher Stowe had published *Uncle Tom's Cabin*. The Baptist, Presbyterian, and Methodist churches had already divided along North/South lines. The debate among Congregationalists centered on the question of whether or not war was a legitimate means to end slavery, and the temperance movement intensified among Congregationalists after the Civil War.

When Emma Newman arrived in 1873, the Big Woods church was nearly forty years old. The situation, common to so many communities in the West, was discouraging. The general Batavia community, of which Big Woods was an outlier, reported some three thousand people in the 1870 census (U.S. Department of the Interior, Census Office, 1873, 1: 114), but there were only ten members in the Big Woods church and the Sunday School had fifty members (Secretary of the National Council 1874, 108).

The Methodist church was of similar size, and like the Congregational church, had difficulty paying a pastor. The two groups also had trouble cooperating. Newman wrote, "I offered, on the part of the Congregational-

---

1. The author of the *Commemorative Biographical and Historical Record of Kane County, Illinois* suggests that the Batavia Congregational Church was known as the Big Woods Church, but Emma Newman wrote of Batavia and Big Woods as separate places, and she had to drive back and forth between them (*Commemorative Biographical and Historical Record of Kane County, Illinois* 1888, 855).

ists, that they pay a Methodist minister on their own, provided Mr. J[ohnson] would secure one to preach all the time. He seemed doubtful whether all together could support a pastor" (Diary, vol. 7, Aug. 15, 1873). However, each group insisted on its own way of doing things. Colin B. Goodykoontz listed this as a major characteristic of religion on the frontier. "To men reared in New England at a time when there was normally but one church in a town or village, the multiplicity of sects in a small Western community was a source of dismay." He cited Julian Sturtevant, one of the members of the Illinois Band of Congregational home missionaries: "When he was a boy in Connecticut the local church was not regarded as the representative of a denomination, but simply as a branch of the Church of Christ. 'If in my childhood,' he says, 'I had heard our place of worship mentioned as Congregational I would have needed to ask an explanation of the unusual term.'" Goodykoontz continued, "In each community the members of those religious groups that were strongest in numbers or faith united in congregations, so that it was not unusual to find as many as five or six struggling churches in one small town" (Goodykoontz 1939, 29–30).

In classic nineteenth-century pastoral style, Newman began her ministry with a grand round of visits to all the members of the congregation. She made her first visit on Friday, June 13, finishing them about six weeks later. She called on thirty-nine people. During her visits, she introduced herself, invited everyone to prayer meeting or Sunday service, invited the young people to form a society or circle, and ascertained, as far as she could, the state of the parishioners' souls. Her first day was typical of her visits.

June 13. Mr. and Mrs. Mandeville were not at home; I had a chat with the son. Mr. and Mrs. Macauley, also Congregationalists, I liked much, they seemed earnest Christians, but I fear they cannot come much to prayer-meeting, as they have poor health and are at a distance of three miles. I dined with Mr. Daniel Warne, a good Christian, a tremendous talker then went a mile in a field road to see a Mrs. Dunham, and her daughter and son-in-law, Mr. and Mrs. Harris. I liked them, could not stay long lest I should not get back in time with the horse . . . Went to see a good old woman, to ask if she would like to have prayer-meeting at her house; she was not at home. Called on Mr. DeWitt Brown, a prominent Methodist, but he and his wife were out; talked circle with a bright daughter. Came home at 4½ just the time agreed upon. Called on the way home, on the sick Methodist minister, not an interesting person. (Diary, vol. 7, June 13, 1873)

She made eight calls that day, seeing eleven people, including the Methodist minister who was ill, and two teenagers.

In the last month of her work at Big Woods, Newman made fewer calls. She concentrated them among the married women for the purpose of forming a Woman's Board of Missions Society. The young people's circle never got started. Newman never did relate well to children and young adults. The prayer meeting persisted, though sometimes with only two or three parishioners and herself.

This systematic visitation served a number of purposes. First, it was the principle means by which the community and congregation were informed about the time and place of meetings, changes in plans, and the news of the congregation. Visiting was the chief vehicle of social discourse. Apart from using the mail, people had to see each other face-to-face to carry on business or friendship. As it solidified social relationships, visiting also served to entertain. Conversations, reading aloud, drinking coffee, or eating meals provided pleasure as well as company. Among more isolated rural people, visiting with one another could even make the difference between sanity and madness (Riley 1988, 71).

Beyond these visible social functions, pastoral visitation was a symbolic act. An ancient tradition in Christianity, the pastor's visit represented the visitation of God to the people. Through visiting the bishop served the unity of the church, the deacons brought food and comfort to those in need, and the elders brought healing by prayer and touch. The meaning of Newman's visitation rested in this tradition, augmented by the role of visiting in Protestant pastoral care.

In the American West, an important question was how to form community among people who are new and unfamiliar with the place and with each other. This was an especially difficult problem for people who had explicitly left organized community in order to be free from its constraints and entered an environment in which dependence upon one's neighbors was necessary. Because the vast majority of immigrants to the West were part of European Christian culture, broadly understood, they shared certain expectations about who organized community and how. Religious leaders were among the key people in the creation and maintenance of community. Women, likewise, contributed important skills and concerns to community life.

Josiah Royce, an American philosopher familiar with frontier conditions, understood that for community to exist, individuals had to look beyond their own immediate needs and desires and understand that it was important to extend themselves through social activity in order to participate in a web of relationships that would sustain them in adversity. He understood religion to be necessary to community. He identified the prime virtue as loyalty, a union of longing for unity, with its active expression in deeds:

> Loyalty, whether in its distinctively Christian forms, or in any others, is a saving principle whenever it appears in an individual human life. For in the love of a community the individual obtains, for his [or her] ideally extended self, precisely the unity, the wealth, and the harmony of plan which his sundered natural existence never supplies. (Royce 1913, 2: 99–100)

As a pastor, Newman worked precisely to turn people's longing for unity into deeds of love for each other and thereby make unity a reality, symbolized by the building of a church.

Newman's visiting worked to accomplish this creation of unity as she first connected herself to each member and then began little by little to strengthen their connection to each other. In a sense, she made neighborliness sacred. Another American philosopher, George Herbert Mead, influenced by Royce but having little interest in the church, nevertheless described the work of building community in a similar way:

> In human society there have arisen certain universal forms which found their expression in universal religious and also in universal economic processes. These go back in the case of religion, to such fundamental attitudes of human beings toward each other as kindliness, helpfulness, and assistance. . . . The fundamental attitude of helping the other person who is down, who finds himself in sickness or other misfortune, belongs to the very structure of the individuals in a human community. . . . And it is out of situations like that, . . . that the universal religions have arisen. (Mead 1934, 258)

As a woman, Newman participated in the time-honored ritual of visiting, by which the social life of community was sustained, but as a pastor she brought to the activity of visiting a mystical aspect, drawing her congregation into the larger communion of saints. In her visiting she carried out tasks of physical healing, as we will see, but also of spiritual healing. She was a "bringer of glad tidings, a spiritual and psychological healer, the interpreter of the Unknown, the comforter in times of sorrow" (Smith 1982, 76). She recreated community where it had weakened or been damaged by disagreement, hard words, and neglect.

Pastoral manuals admonished the Protestant pastor to visit the sick in body and soul, and to have serious conversations with each member of the parish regularly concerning the person's spiritual state (McNeill 1951, 209–12). In addition, New England Puritan clergy used visitation to heal conflicts among members of the church thus continually reconstituting the community. Newman followed most nearly the method outlined in William Shedd's *Homiletics and Pastoral Theology,* a common textbook of the time that she had read while in Missouri. Shedd's instructions were explicit and methodical:

> We have advised a systematic visitation of the parish, by districts or neighborhoods. In case the clergyman is settled among an agricultural population, widely scattered, he will find this much the easiest, and surest way to communicate with the whole body of his people. His parish is his diocese, and he is its bishop. Let him make his visitations through the whole length and breadth of it, with the same system and regularity, with which the prelatical bishop makes his annual visitation. . . . He will find it a most genial and exhilarating service, upon his own part, and a most interesting and profitable one, upon the part of the people. Enforcing, in a common assemblage, all that he has said in the families, and to the individuals, he will clinch the nails which he has been driving.
>
> Pastoral visiting, conducted in the manner described, is a very efficient aid to the public preaching of the Sabbath and the sanctuary. (Shedd 1871, 401–2)

The role of the pastor in the creation and sustenance of Christian community was particularly important in the American West. Josiah Royce, shaped by his childhood in the gold rush era of California, emphasized the interrelationships among loyalty, community and religion in human society. His philosophy studied the difficulties and processes of creating community among migrant or immigrant people: "A true community is essentially a product of a time-process. A community has a past and will have a future. . . . A community requires for its existence a history and is greatly aided in its consciousness by a memory" (Royce 1913, 2: 37).

Pastoral visiting provided a context and a process in which individual experiences might become part of history, and thus helped the group become a community. The isolation of frontier individuals from each other was a serious problem. The systematic visitation of a pastor who carried in the act of the visit the symbolic import of the image of the church as the body of Christ incorporated the visited person into the community. This visitation was critical in the formation of churches in the West.

Visiting was also an activity closely associated with women. Gossip, the caricature of this visiting, is a word actually rooted in the Christian tradition. Its old meanings, God-kin or God-sibling and God parent, point to the necessity of informal conversation in giving depth to community relationships. Of course, such conversation could also undermine community, but that suggests part of the pastor's role was oversight of this informal community structure.

Preaching was the other anchoring point of the nineteenth-century pastor's work. In visitation, the pastor gathered the people together into a community. Through preaching, the pastor addressed that gathered community, bringing the Word of God to bear upon both the people and their situation. The shape of the Word of God heard by any given congregation depended upon the pastor's context, training, theology, and a complex system of meaning existing between preacher and hearer. The sermon was a piece of a community's interpretation of the Word, the Bible, or generally recognized tenets of the Christian faith. Although the preacher shaped the theological thinking and behavior of the congregation, the congregation's response also shaped the preaching in subtle ways.

A woman preacher in this era held an even more complex relationship to the community of interpretation. First of all, as a woman, she was simply a curiosity. People would go to hear her, but their expectations caused them to hear her differently than they heard a man. The message of a woman preacher filtered through layers of preconceived ideas about women in public roles and simple inexperience in hearing a female public voice before reaching the ear of the congregation. In other words, the surprise at seeing a woman preach might distract the audience so they did not hear what she said, or it might cause an old and familiar message to be heard and understood in a new way. Secondly, as a woman, her relationships of authority and power within the community were complicated by cultural understandings of the expected roles of women in shaping community. Whereas visiting was a pastoral task fully complimentary to women's usual social roles, preaching was not. Her congregation's understanding was often affected by ambiguities of relative authority and influence based upon their uncertainty about their own position vis-à-vis their female pastor.

In Newman's short stay at Big Woods, some of these ambiguities emerged. Turning to Newman's preaching, we can begin to see how she shaped her work in conjunction with her visitation. Newman preached thirteen sermons during her time at the Big Woods church. Full manuscripts of all the sermons exist and they can be correlated with her diary, providing a clear picture of her preaching program for the three months she spent there.[2]

Her first two sermons were of the candidating kind. The congregation's leaders invited her to preach and meet to see if she wanted to be minister there and if they wanted her as minister. In neither case did she know the congregation well enough to address any but general topics of interest to any church. Her first sermon for the Big Woods church, preached on June 1, 1873, entitled "Freedom Through Truth" (Sermon no. 4), had an American theme. It was the day after Decoration Day (Memorial Day), and a northern church, especially one with an antislavery history, would expect a sermon on American union and freedom as preserved by the North in the Civil War. Freedom was an appropriate emphasis for a congregation that had a decade before professed abolitionist views.

Her texts were from the Gospel of John 7:7, "If any man will do his will, he shall know of the doctrine, whether it be of God, or whether I speak of myself" (Authorized [King James] Version, hereafter, AV), and John 8:32, "And ye shall know the truth, and the truth shall make you free" (AV). In

2. Newman used most of her sermons on several occasions. In the text I refer to them by title, with a reference note to their number in the collection. The collection contains an index organized in this way. In the bibliography, I list the sermon numbers and titles to which I refer in this work. The date given is the one related to the particular reference.

the sermon she contrasted two ways of being a religious nation or people. One called upon citizens to observe tedious ritual, never forgiving an offender, never admitting wrong, never yielding, expecting their nation to conquer the world. Newman suggested that freedom in this kind of religion is "like the freedom of a child in a room full of knives," or of those who do things they ought not to do because they cannot help themselves.

The other way was that of Christ, where one gained real freedom by doing God's will. This was the freedom to be the best part of oneself. "We used to pity the slaves, even those who had plenty to eat and drink and wear, because they were slaves, because they knew they might be obliged to do what their master ordered when they did not want to, and it did not seem possible that they could be happy. How can a man be happy when his best faculties are not ruling?" (Sermon no. 4). Christ, she continued, does not force himself upon people. "His will is the best for us, He wills life to be joy." The sermon manuscript contains several endings, and there is no way to tell which she used in this case. In general, her closing notes suggest that God's will coincides with what is best in oneself, but that it takes time to discern the will of God.

In this sermon Newman presents a standard Protestant contrast of the "Jews" living as slaves to the law and "Christians" living in the freedom of Christ.

This sermon does not go as one might expect for a Memorial Day commemoration. Newman makes no use of the patriotic national cult that valorized the blood sacrifices of those who fought to preserve the national union. In fact, Newman admonishes her congregation to beware of a false sense of national freedom. "It is a silly boast that we are free Americans, if anything can make us do what we do not think best; where is our freedom then?" (Sermon no. 4). She reminds the people in this frontier town that they are not given freedom in this nation in order to do as they please, but to do the will of God. She implies that the American sense of Manifest Destiny is comparable to the Roman impulse to conquer the world, and is the route to slavery, not true freedom.

Whatever associations her congregation may have made, the final appeal for individual pious living according to the will of God placed her squarely in the evangelical Protestant mainstream.

Already we can see the contours of her evangelical theology. Three themes emerge that become constant over time in her preaching: individual piety, Christian freedom in contrast to slavery to religious law, and use-fulness in building a Christian society. Newman upheld an ideal of disci-plined life, seriously asking in everything whether what she did was for the glory of God. Although she worked to transmit Christian civilization to the unformed communities of the West, she did not do this for the glory of America, but because she believed it was for the glory of God. Newman constantly recognized that she was speaking in opposition to the habits of her people, what she perceived to be their individualism and self-indulgence. As we encounter more of her preaching we will see that in ad-dition to her pietism, she had a kind of theological romanticism that placed her, evangelical though she was, at a transition point between strictly orthodox Evangelicalism and the emerging Protestant liberalism of the late nineteenth century.

It was a beautiful day, and she enjoyed preaching. "I do feel like a fish out of water when I do not preach" (Diary, vol. 7, June 1, 1873). The sermon was well received, and they invited her to preach again the following Sunday.

On June 8, 1873, she returned to Big Woods and preached a sermon en-titled "True Work of Life" (Sermon no. 1). This was the first sermon she had ever written, and she had used it twice before in the last year. Her text was Colossians 3:23–24: "Whatsoever ye do, do it heartily as to the Lord, and not unto men . . . for ye serve the Lord Christ" (AV). The text fit well for a sermon beginning her ministry. It was as much a sermon to herself as to her congregation. Although she had seen them once before, she still knew little about them. The roots of the sermon lay in the years Newman spent caring for her mother instead of pursuing her dream to go west and preach. "If any one of us is weary of work that seems to bear no fruit; if the Lord delayeth His coming and our hearts are very weak while we wait for Him, for us comes the repeated idea, the assurance that 'ye serve the Lord Christ' " (Sermon no. 1).

The sermon served three purposes, according to her outline. First, she asked, though it is important to work heartily at whatever one does, "does it pay to work heartily for money?" Second, she encouraged Christians to have faith despite their circumstances, that work done for Christ has good effects. Finally, she invited the congregation to choose the best work, serv-ing Christ, for that is what is best for ourselves.

On Wednesday, June 11, 1873, she moved to Big Woods from Batavia. "Will took me out to Big Woods in the afternoon and I commenced on my first pastoral charge, very sure that I don't know anything, very sure that Christ knows everything" (Diary, vol. 7, June 11, 1873). On Friday, she began her great round of visiting the congregation, finding that she loved the work.

> I was to have a horse to-day and chose to ride him, started at 8½ and went about among the church-membership giving notice of a prayer meeting, and taking the opportunity to talk up a circle for the young people. . . . I had ridden ten miles more than I had ever done in one day, and I had enjoyed my day, though I was very sore toward the last. This thinking and talking about Christ, I love, and it does seem that I may do good. "Blessed is the man who has found his work." (Diary, vol. 7, June 13, 1873)

On Sunday, she preached her "first sermon in a regular pastoral charge." This time she could preach with some knowledge of her congregation. Her theme was "Growth in Grace" (Sermon no. 5), and she took her text from II Peter 3:18, "Grow in grace and knowledge of our Lord Jesus Christ" (AV). Here she continued the theme of the Christian life. She did not begin these first three weeks by preaching about doctrine, but showed herself a true child of the antebellum revivals, concerned with usefulness, which was the fruit of conversion to Christianity.

To know how to live as a Christian, to grow in grace, one must first have knowledge of Jesus Christ. She located that knowledge beginning in the prophets.

> We have read a few of the many things that the prophets say about Christ, for we want to know what He is, before we can know how to act so as to please Him. They tell us that He is strong and pure and very just; that He will judge those that do wrong, but will forgive and bless them if they repent; that He loved sinners so much that He suffered through an earthly life of pain to make it possible for Him to forgive them, but hates sin with that thorough hatred which only the sinless can feel. (Sermon no. 5)

To win the grace of the Lord, Newman said, one must imitate his earthly life, not only doing the right things, but doing them from the right motives. To be sure, she added, people cannot do this by their own power, but Christ promised help to everyone that tried. "Ask and it shall be given to you, seek and ye shall find, knock and the door shall be opened" (Matthew 7:7–8 AV).

"I did enjoy the service and I hope it did good, people looked inter-ested," she wrote that day. But she was disappointed when only three peo-ple other than the family with whom she lived came that evening for prayer meeting. Like any pastor, she searched for signs that her preaching had effect; measuring attendance served this purpose. Her audience the next Sunday was particularly small, but she had been warned ahead of time that there was a camp meeting in the neighborhood. The camp meeting, however, did not account for all the absences. In her visiting that week she also discovered parishioners who excused themselves because of ill health and being tired from working. "Called on Mrs. Boyd, who seemed out of health, too sick to go to meeting because she could not walk, and her hus-band was too tired with his week's work to carry her. I am selfish, I know: this incessant complaining wears on me, and I am afflicted with doubts as to whether all these people are so sick as they think themselves" (Diary, vol. 7, June 17, 1873). After her second week she began to understand the difficulties she faced and to address them in her preaching.

Her theme for the few who came to hear her that morning, June 22, was "The Coming of God's Kingdom" (Sermon no. 9). This was the only time she used this sermon. It was a sermon warning great sinners, but also the American nation that had abused its privileges. Though she did not say ex-plicitly, she probably meant to warn the people at Big Woods who had so many other things to do rather than attend prayer meetings. Congrega-tionalists understood church membership to be a covenant between the individual and the church entailing certain responsibilities. One of the du-ties of a church member was regular attendance at worship. Voluntary ab-sence from worship broke the covenant and endangered the fellowship of believers (Dexter 1880, 109).

Newman also clearly had larger national and world events on her mind. The year 1873 was one of turmoil. Ulysses S. Grant was running for a second term as president of the United States in the midst of scandals. Financial panic hit Vienna in May and New York in September, followed by a severe depression. Newman's next decade of ministry would be done in the shadow of the depression, when there would be very little money for clergy salaries.

Underlying Newman's sermon was a larger Protestant anxiety. Think-ing Protestant clergy were aware that they were witnessing the weakening and perhaps the demise of their cultural hegemony. Immigration brought a large number of Roman Catholics to the cities. The rising industrial economy and its tensions with labor threatened the Protestant notions of social order and vocation. The political scandals of both the cities and the national government pointed to the secularization of society's institutions. The Protestant clergy themselves were beginning to feel a sense of decline from the influential place they had recently held in national life. The American Home Mission Society framed a great part of its ideology as a battle against these antireligious or anti-Christian forces, particularly in the West, where people's roots in New England culture were weak.

In Newman's sermon, she located the nation's opposition to God in "scientific men who attack the Bible"; "philosophers who claim to have a better revelation"; and "men of letters who scorn to follow an example, even if it be that of Jesus." But the worst opposition to God came from those who thought Christianity to be "rather a good thing on the whole if it ever amounted to anything," but thought it had nothing to do with them. A related opposing group were those who "mean to be Christians sometime," but not yet. These, of course, were the people in her audience. So for these people, is the coming Kingdom of God a threat or a promise? Newman urgently declared that although they may not heed the threat, it was a threat to their souls. "The Earth shall be filled with the knowledge of the glory of the Lord, as the waters cover the sea" (Habakkuk, 2:14 AV). Newman pointed out that the text from Habakkuk was good and true, but it brings no joy to those who are not themselves good and true. "Live so that the promise brings joy," she concluded.

With this sermon, Newman began to engage her congregation. Disappointed by their lack of interest in the prayer meeting and young people's circle, their lateness in attending worship, and probably also wondering what her congregation's desertion of her for the camp meeting meant, the next Wednesday she wrote in her diary, "Studied on an emphatic sermon on Christ the only master, which I think is needed." She chose for her text Jesus' warning in the Sermon on the Mount, "Ye cannot serve God and Mammon" (Sermon no. 10). The core of her sermon was a story.

If a man wants to grow rich, he must give his mind to it. He must be willing to work hard, and think hard, and give up a great many pleasant things that would be good for him, because he has no time, and is too tired to enjoy them; often he must live poorly that he may save his money to make more money with. He must narrow his life to those things that have to do with money; he cannot afford to give a great deal of attention to anything else; he will not grow rich if he does. Suppose the man to have done this and to be rich, so that he has money enough and nothing to do but enjoy it at 40 years, and then to live till he is 80. I put the case as strongly as possible; we all know that very few men are satisfied with their wealth at 40, and live 40 years more to enjoy it, still it is possible. Suppose that he buys every thing that he wants, and is satisfied with those things his money can buy, feels no need of anything higher, but lives his forty years in perfect content. What is he and what has he at the end. He has seen those things that his eyes could see, he has touched those things that his hands could handle, but he has lost the power of knowing anything about those higher and better things that cannot be seen or touched. He has crowded down his whole spiritual life till the life in the body has smothered it, and only a miracle like that which called Lazarus from the grave, could make that man live again to any worthy purpose. (Sermon no. 10)

Newman reminded the congregation that Jesus spoke to working people, under the pressure of poverty, and was a working man himself. She pointed out that there is no middle ground between serving money and serving God. Neither God nor the Devil are satisfied with divided allegiance. The rewards of the god of riches are in this life only. She also pointed out that the choice to serve God or Mammon seldom seems like a grand one, but comes daily in little things. She closed by reminding the congregation that God is always available through prayer to guide a person who wants direction.

Newman noted in her diary that though she had planned to preach this sermon the previous week and deferred it to this Sunday, the camp meeting continued to draw off her congregation. Her audience numbered twenty-seven. "One or two of the families who needed it most were absent, and I felt sorry, but I know the Lord ordered it" (Diary, vol. 7, June 29, 1873).

She continued her visiting in the south neighborhood of Big Woods. At one house she met a Mrs. Hill.

At the next place Mrs. Hill told me she used to pray; but had given it all up, her husband had given up praying too; in fact there weren't no prayin' characters round there. She heard there wuz a woman a lecturin' to Big Woods and she said she'd go and hear her, but somebody said she wa'n't no good, she didn't know how to lecture and she didn't go. I told her I was the woman, and asked her to come to hear me, "Be you the woman?" said she.

"Well! If you're the woman, I'll go hear ye." Perhaps she will come. (Diary, vol. 7, June 30, 1873)

Besides Mrs. Hill, the south neighborhood was home to the Wrights, pleasant young people who did not go to church; a family with a child, a sick father and very busy mother; the Blairs, who sent their daughters to Sunday School but did not go out on Sundays themselves; and a young woman living alone with two children, who welcomed Newman's visit. Newman considered them all part of her parish, but was dismayed by their lack of interest. Newman was beginning to feel discouraged. The next Sunday's attendance was fifty. "I suppose that is what it will settle into, as Mr. Roy told me 40–60. The larger attendance at first meant curiosity." But there were signs that her work of visiting was having results. There were thirteen at the prayer meeting the first Sunday in July.

Her preaching continued on the theme of the Christian life. Her next sermon was entitled "Responsibility" (Sermon no. 11). She took for its text the story of the Good Samaritan. Her message centered on the choice to be Christian or not. This life is merely an introduction to the rest that has no end. Will we make it hopeful, helpful, and pleasing to God, or will we live it for ourselves alone, to our endless regret? When one has decided to be a Christian, one has a responsibility to live like one.

I have no words strong enough to tell the power of earnest Christian living. It is God working through us and in us. Let me tell you of one man, an ignorant man, couldn't speak grammatically, and did not appear to know more than he needed to know for his daily work. He rose to speak in a prayer meeting and not one person there did so much good by his remarks as this man; one thing he did know, that Christ had saved him from a worthless life to one full of love and good will, and that everybody else might be saved and needed to be saved. He talked as if he had seen the Lord, and I believe he had, but what good do you think his earnest words would have done, if he had not lived a good life! (Sermon no. 11)[3]

3. In this story, Newman was remembering the occasion of her first sermon, preached in Readville, Massachusetts, in March 1872. She preached both in the morning and the evening. After the evening sermon there was a time of congregational response.

"Mr. Dalrynaple made characteristic remarks; independent of all rules of grammar, punctuated with gasps, his words were so earnest as to carry weight; he spoke of 'something in your soul that you can't talk about' " (Diary, vol. 6, March 24, 1872).

The week following this sermon, Newman continued her great round of visits, seeing some people for the second time and beginning to give pastoral attention to their Christian lives in her personal conversations with them as she did in her sermons. "Agnes Porter came to spend the day. I took the opportunity to talk to her about joining the church; perhaps she was sent that I might do it. . . . Called in the afternoon on Mrs. Watson, Mrs. Mclain, Mrs. Rummage, and Mrs. Bloss; the latter I must see again, she thinks she was a Christian but is not now" (Diary, vol. 7, July 9, 1873).

The next Sunday, July 13, she had a particularly discouraging day. Attendance was small, not much over thirty. None of the young people in her Sunday School class had learned any of the lessons for the month. "I wonder if I am a failure anyway. The Lord knows all about it" (Diary, vol. 7, July 13, 1873). She might have profited by listening to her own sermon that day on "The God of Patience and Consolation" (Sermon no. 12). In the sermon, she detailed the sufferings of the early Christians, along with those in "our own quiet churches," both large tragedies of loss and change, and smaller problems as well. "When somebody calls in cross tones under your window, when the horses do not work well, and things break as you touch them, when your neighbor tries to cheat you, specially if he succeeds, when you do not feel well, and nothing goes right, when other people find fault unreasonably, then the need of patience comes in" (Sermon no. 12). Many of these details of everyday trials could come from her own diary. She was often ill, the Big Woods people among whom she boarded did not always keep their agreements, her horse was not always well, and she felt that after six weeks she was not having the effect she wanted in the life of the congregation.

Her texts for this sermon, Psalm 37, Hebrews 12, John 14, and II Thessalonians 2:16–17, with their exhortations to patience and trust, provided her with a framework for teaching patience as a cardinal Christian virtue. She assured the people of God's love, strength, help, and comfort, also pointing out that these trials come because they are best. "Those who suffer most are the brave soldiers put in the hardest places." By suffering, which comes to all people, we are fitted to help other troubled souls. She acknowledged that there were people who did not feel the help of God, but she concluded by saying that people are reluctant to ask for comfort and help. "You want to be comforted in your own way, and He knows that it is not a good way, and there's no real comfort in it."

Newman herself did not seem to find it easy to ask for comfort. Though she poured out her doubts in her diary, she rarely mentioned asking anyone for comfort and help. Perhaps in her letters to close friends she shared her sense of uncertainty about the success of her work, but the letters are lost. Certainly she never turned to her congregation for comfort and seldom to the neighboring pastors or the mission superintendent.

The following week she became ill. The weather was hot and she had trouble sleeping for several nights. By Saturday, July 19, she was suffering "with an attack half-nervous, half-bilious." That Sunday she preached but did not teach her Sunday School class or go to the prayer meeting. "They heard one of my best sermons, but I am afraid it was poorly delivered" (Diary, vol. 7, July 19–20, 1873).

She had preached this sermon, "The Touch of Christ" (Sermon no. 3), four times previously, and it is an expression of key aspects of her theology. The text was a passage from the Gospel of Luke (8:43–49 AV), the story of the healing of the woman with a hemorrhage. Related texts listed by her in the manuscript come from the first chapter of Deuteronomy, the assurance that God is with the people of Israel as they enter the promised land; the eighth chapter of Matthew, Jesus' healings and the calming of the storm; and the fourteenth chapter of Numbers, assuring the people of Israel that God is slow to anger and abounding in steadfast love.

The sermon had two parts. The first was a list of the ways in which people touch Christ. If they touch in carelessness, they gain nothing. If they touch in curiosity (and how many are in the congregation out of curiosity to hear a woman preach?), they may or may not feel anything. Some touch with enmity because Christ condemned evil. Some touch with cool friendliness, especially in America, because it is convenient. But for those who touch with faith, the quality of the faith does not matter; they will find their highest needs answered.

In the second part of her sermon, she claimed that Christ was present in the nineteenth century even more clearly than in Jesus' own day. Christ passes by every day, but what are people gaining from him? "Is there one soul here that is satisfied with the days as they come, glad at night that every word and thought and action has been just what it has been, willing that the next day shall be the same? Then I'm not speaking to that man; but I speak to the common human experience of failure, and of sorrows for failure, and of wish to do better, and I ask, 'Do we not all need help? Can we get it anywhere else?' " (Sermon no. 3). Newman viewed her society as one that was religious only when it was convenient, and she assumed that most of the people in her congregation had not committed themselves to faith in Christ. She believed that each person was responsible for making such a commitment, and that even those who were in church from simple curiosity could benefit from the invitation to faith. Those evangelical Protestants who grew up influenced by the revivals of Charles Grandison Finney[4] received a clear message that one's conversion was demonstrated in living a useful life. I will discuss Newman's own deep appropriation of this principle in the next chapter.

Newman continued to work on her sermons and make her calls on the people of the parish even though she was suffering from an inflammation of the liver and a high fever. She took only three days in the next two weeks to rest and consult a homeopathic physician. On Saturday, July 26, she gave a preparatory lecture for a few of her congregation in anticipation of the communion service the next day. On Sunday, July 27, Mr. Partridge, a neighboring pastor preached and gave communion at the Big Woods church while Newman preached in the South neighborhood, an outlying community even smaller than Big Woods, where she had been so discouraged in her visiting. "I was moved to write just this sermon 'Every good gift and every perfect gift is from above' etc. for that godless 'South neighborhood' and I should not have felt that I had done my best if I had not done so" (Diary, vol. 7, July 26, 1873). She had a small congregation. "Mr. Blair whom I specially wanted to reach, was out, but I do not know what he thought of the sermon" (Diary, vol. 7, July 27, 1873). Blair seldom went to church, though his daughters did. Newman had paid him at least one visit, as noted above. She reluctantly agreed to drop the prayer meeting in the afternoon because one leading member of the congregation was in a rush to get to his chores.

The sermon itself, "Good Gifts, God's Gifts" (Sermon No. 13), was the first in which she used farming and farmers as illustrations for her points.

4. Emma Newman was born at the end of the great evangelical awakening that occurred in the first part of the nineteenth century. Charles Grandison Finney was one of the foremost revivalists of that awakening. His method of conducting a successful revival continues to be influential to this day. His insistence that a converted life manifested itself in useful work inspired many to participate in the bourgeoning voluntary movements of the day.

"The broad fields full of bright corn or wheat, and the fine horses, and the great loads of hay are good to see—all this is very good to have, but do these things belong to those perfect gifts of which the apostle speaks?" (Sermon no. 13).

She talked about farm tools that look good but are not good quality and break when they are put to use. She used rain as a metaphor for God's gifts of honesty, truthfulness, purity, helpfulness, gentleness, and courage, but suggested that unlike rain, one could take action to secure these virtues by taking trouble to practice them, taking trouble to imitate Christ. "But I want to know if you think it is a rational performance to spend one whole life on things that are of no use in the future life, and to try to forget the time, which you know must come, when every one of these things must be dropped? You wouldn't use such bad management, with so little fore-thought, about your farms. Do you think it is sensible to do it about your souls?" (Sermon no. 13).

Colin Goodykoontz, in his analysis of the theology of the home mission movement in the American West, observed that the missionaries tended to preach a conservative kind of Protestant doctrine. "It was practical rather than mystical; it put emphasis on individual righteousness and personal salvation after death rather than on social righteousness and community salvation now" (Goodykoontz 1939, 425). He also characterized the theology of the movement as nationalistic, Trinitarian, and prone to a literal interpretation of the Bible. This conservative Christianity has colored the religious ethos of the American Midwest ever since.

Newman shared this theology to a large degree. She certainly understood the Christian faith as a personal thing. The transformation of society would come, she thought, only when every person made a commitment to Christ. Just as certainly, her theology shared the practical emphasis Goodykoontz discussed. One's commitment to Christ always involved a visible change in behavior and values.

The home mission movement was deeply suspicious of the new immigrants from Europe, especially those who were Catholic. The movement believed that the Protestant churches held the key to maintaining the democratic and religious traditions of the American republic. The home mission movement's characteristic nationalism was clearly displayed in Newman's sermon for August 3, 1873. This was her third comment on national life in seven weeks.

The connection of the home missionary movement with the United States was clear in Newman's mind. "God has made America the hope of the world" (Sermon no. 14). Many people were drawn, even called to come to America. It was the responsibility of the "natives of the best country under the sun" to undertake to teach the newcomers the true faith and right way of life.

> As surely as the most of these newcomers are bringing to us the strength we need to work our country, they are bringing a weight of ignorance that threatens to swamp us. Their votes count as much as if they knew anything, and it is our business to see that they do know something. Some of them bring heathen rites and superstitions, it is our affair that they shall be taught the truth and the beauty of a better religion. We are responsible for doing all that we can do to christianize these new-comers to our soil. (Sermon no. 14)

She reminded the people that they had at hand a good way to take to their responsibility, by supporting the home mission effort.[5] "A cool clean air. . . . Enjoyed my sermon, too, though a small audience, about 40, was depressing. Am I running it down? . . . This was a good Sunday for me, though I felt sorry that the collection for home missions was only $3.00. Wrote to Mr. Roy sending $8.00" (Diary, vol. 7, Aug. 3, 1873). The extra five dollars she added to the collection represented about a week's salary for her. Whether she was embarrassed by the small collection or she believed in the cause of home missions to the extent of making a sacrificial gift is not easy to tell. Certainly the amount would be publicly recorded, so she made her congregation and possibly herself look better. "If we cannot go ourselves to tell them we must give our money. Lest we be ashamed when the Lord calls us to account," she concluded (Sermon no. 14).

Her text for the home missions sermon was taken from the Book of Revelation. It was a reference to the coming of Christ at the end of the age.

---

5. In this sermon Newman followed Lyman Beecher in his *Plea for the West* (1835). American civilization was, according to this theology, to be an evangelical Protestant civilization. The anxiety she presented in the sermon centered on the waves of immigration from Europe and Asia that threatened to overwhelm the older Protestant majority. But the anxiety that lay behind the sermon centered on the other home missionary enterprise, that of maintaining the evangelical Protestantism of the members of her own congregation and others like it in the frontier settlements.

That Christ would appear in the United States was the New England Puritans' firm belief. For their nineteenth-century descendants, America was still a new land, but it had grown fast and needed to be brought back to its calling as the holy city set on the hill. The home mission movement had in mind the preparation of the whole country to receive the coming Christ. This sense of destiny pervaded the home mission movement in the nineteenth century, giving it a sense of purpose in creating the moral conditions necessary for Christ's return. Part of the motive for the missions to the West lay in an anxiety that this project of moral improvement was not progressing well there, threatening the "heavenly" destiny of America.

For Newman, however, the primary home missionary task was not to reach the immigrant from another culture and religion, but to retrieve those who left the church behind when they moved west. "The religious element in the country, specially in the western part of it, is not strong enough to make much impression upon the tide of irreligion that rushes in, unless it is re-inforced by the help of those who have the sober thought and right feeling to work on the Lord's side at this turning point in our national affairs" (Sermon no. 14). The next Sunday, she preached directly to these prodigals. Among those in her congregation, she had a particular young family from the south neighborhood in mind. "Went to take tea with Mrs. Henry Wright. Those Wrights are bright, and they like me, I ought to be able to do them good, but I can only touch the wife and Mr. W. has the strongest nature" (Diary, vol. 7, Aug. 6, 1873). Her sermon for August 10 took as its text the story in Luke of the prodigal son. As it is one of the most well-known Bible stories, she hesitated to say anything to injure the effect of the story itself, but she did use it as an allegory for the individual spiritual journey, casting parishioners like Henry Wright as the wandering son. However, Wright was not in church that morning to benefit. That week Newman had also been occupied helping to care for a dying infant. Perhaps the imminence of death had made her feel an urgency that Wright did not share. If they did not take thought for their spiritual well-being, where would the prodigals find comfort in time of need?

In the afternoon, she and others in the congregation visited with the family whose baby had died. "After S. S. and service, we trailed slowly in the hot sun, two miles to Mr. Harris' with friends of the baby. At the house, there were two hymns sung and a prayer offered. I had opportunity to speak a few words to the mother, then came home. Of course there could be no prayer-meeting, and I think the whole was easier for me than the usual routine; I had more time to rest" (Diary, vol. 7, Aug. 10, 1873).

After working in big Woods for two months, Newman knew the people well enough to begin to encourage those who were lukewarm toward more commitment. She continued to press Mrs. Bloss. "Mrs. B. says she has been a Christian and is not, but does not seem roused to feel what that means; can seldom get out to church on account of 3 little children" (Diary, vol. 7, Aug. 22, 1873).

By the middle of August, Newman had finished most of her time at Big Woods. Joseph Roy, the Home Mission superintendent for Illinois, had hoped she could stay there, but the congregation was not able to raise a large enough salary to pay her, and the Home Mission Society would not pay for the support of a minister "not having ministerial papers" (Diary, vol. 7, Sept. 12, 1873). On more than one occasion, the same Home Missionary Society officials who so appreciated her work in one of their most difficult churches failed in their public advocacy for her to have proper credentials.

Newman tried two plans for getting the Big Woods people a pastor. Her negotiations with the local Methodist people about sharing the salary of a minister for both churches came to nothing, and her effort to recruit an older minister living some way off to come and preach occasionally was also discouraging.

On August 17, she preached a sermon entitled "Kindness and Forgiveness" (Sermon no. 16). Her congregation was somewhat smaller than usual, only thirty-four, which she saw as a very small group. An event in a neighboring town had attracted people. "Everything seemed discouraging to-day, yet I am not discouraged; perhaps I ought to be and decide to stop" (Diary, vol. 7, Aug. 17, 1873). By the next Sunday it was clear that things would not work out for her to stay. She did not know where she would go next, though she received encouragement from Roy. Her sermon "Trust in God" (Sermon no. 17) seemed directed as much at herself as at her congregation. The text came from Exodus 3:17, the Israelites crossing the sea and venturing out into the wilderness, and from John, "What I do thou knowest not now; but thou shalt know hereafter" (John 13:7 AV).

With the question of failure resting in her mind, she preached about Jesus' defeat and death, and about the disciples who could not know what was going to happen, but who had to trust God's love "to do all things well." "I should be happy and satisfied over my summer, if I knew I had done any good," she wrote in her diary (vol. 7, Sept. 3, 1873). Her growing sense of failure rested on the same indexes any home missionary would have used to judge the results of their work. She had made no converts (that she knew of); attendance at worship had declined (though not by much); and the prayer meeting and Women's Missionary Society did not meet in a regular, organized way. Furthermore, though the church had oversubscribed their originally agreed salary for her, they could not raise enough salary for a minister to live on.

> With every experience of defeat and disappointment, the words of Christ to His disciples gain a new meaning of rest and comfort. What if we do not see that our work is really worth anything? If we work in obedience to Him, that work is part of His plan for His world, and He is using it to produce results that stretch beyond our knowledge, we are part of a whole so large that we cannot see it now, but He accepts the efforts that we count as failures and says to us, lovingly, "What I do thou knowest not now, but thou shalt know hereafter." What we do may fail, so far as we know anything about it; what He does with us and our doing can never fail, while we trust in Him. (Sermon no. 17)

Her final sermon in Big Woods was addressed to herself, and to those in the congregation who wanted the church to succeed, to Deacon Manville who thought it was a hopeless case, to the three women who joined the Women's Board of Missions Society, and to the others of her congregation who attended worship, taught Sunday School, visited each other, and generally worked to sustain the church. She left Big Woods in the middle of September. Roy had not yet found another place for her to go.

Though at the moment it was difficult for Newman to imagine she had influenced the church at all in so short a time, their next year was highly successful. The pastor was E. D. Bailey, a licensed minister. Church membership increased to eighteen, almost doubling. Twelve members were admitted on profession of faith and six by adult baptism (Secretary of the National Council 1875, 109). These were not members simply transferring membership from another congregation, but people who had made a new or renewed commitment to be a church member. Although Bailey received credit for this work because his name appears in the *Congregational Quarterly*, Newman's pastoral visits and preaching cannot be dismissed as contributing nothing.

Emma Newman's thirteen weeks in Big Woods, Illinois open up several questions for us that we will explore more deeply in later chapters. Her case illustrates the geographical issues facing clergy and their congregations in the American West. Distance between people and between towns forced changes in the customary forms of ecclesiastical life. Newman rode over ten miles in one day to visit eleven people. Simple communication among the members of a congregation challenged the energy of pastors. Though distances between churches of the same denomination often prohibited ministers from meeting each other for mutual support, churches from different denominations often competed with each other in small towns for the souls of a few people. The newness of community in the West and the rapid and unsettled movement of people made it difficult for ministers to establish or count upon the kinds of sustained effort it took to build strong congregations. Still, in her work in Big Woods, we can see the method Newman followed and begin to understand its theological and sociological underpinnings.

Newman's case also opens up the gender question in showing us both the novelty of a woman preaching in rural Illinois at this time and the confidence with which Newman undertook the work. We can also discern the importance of women in the Protestant congregations. Newman spent her last few weeks organizing a Women's Mission Society, an important component in the stability of a church, as well of the fund-raising efforts of the home missionary societies that supported most of the congregations founded in the West. Newman's work illustrates the conflicts, ambiguities, and style of female religious leaders.

In the thirteen sermons she preached in Big Woods, we see the main outlines of her Evangelical and romantic theology. The two theologians she read most often, Horace Bushnell and Henry Ward Beecher, were both evangelical and romantic in their theologies. Bushnell was among the first to introduce the ideas of Coleridge and Schleiermacher into American Protestant theology.

In the mid–nineteenth century, Congregational theologians fell into two broad streams of thought. One stream was based in Scottish Common Sense philosophy and followed the Enlightenment in its respect for reason and the discoveries of science. The other stream, the romantic, into which both Bushnell and Beecher belonged, took a more pietist turn and followed Schleiermacher's location of religion in feeling and intuition. Both

streams honored human experience and emphasized the practical application of theological truth to ordinary human living.

The first stream was well represented at Andover Theological School
when Newman attended lectures there. Evangelicals considered this theology to be solidly orthodox. The romantic stream took them by surprise.
Bushnell and Beecher both faced controversy over their theological points
of view, yet they persisted, and the romantic theological view became a
common underpinning of later nineteenth-century liberalism. Newman
began her preaching career just as the Congregationalists began to consider the newer ideas. In the next chapters we will explore further the question of whether Newman was clearly a romantic and how that theological
view found expression in her preaching.

The titles of Newman's sermons, "Good Gifts, God's Gifts," "Kindness
and Forgiveness," "Trust in God," "Responsibility," "Cannot Serve God
and Mammon," "Growth in Grace," "True Work of Life," "Patience," and
"Touch of Christ," suggest an evangelical theology interested especially in
the character of the Christian life in the world. Newman presented a sense
of urgency in encouraging her congregation to make a Christian commitment, but does not emphasize God's judgement, rather God's forbearance
and patience and love. In her Big Woods sermons, the themes of piety,
unity, and the necessity of decision show that she stands primarily in the
broader pietist movement, clearly respectful of the older Calvinist orthodoxy, but also finding the emphasis on feeling in religious life and its impli-
cations for her theology important.

The same theological themes lie behind her pastoral care. In fact, her
most effective theological work may have been done in the context of
her pastoral visits. There she could tailor her message to the individual
and be certain of their response to it. In her visits, as in her preaching,
she pressed for an individual decision to live a Christian life to those
she thought had not made the commitment; to those who had, she
pressed a higher standard of Christian behavior and commitment to
Christian work. In all these cases, "Christian" meant placing the life
of the community before one's personal life, not for the purpose of
creating a good opinion of oneself or even the community, but for the
sake of the glory of God. She located the source of both inspiration and
ability to do this Christian work in the sensibilities, intuition or feelings.
That her culture associated these feelings primarily with the feminine is

important for understanding how women came to be accepted in American pulpits.

In the next chapter, I will further develop the discussion of gender as a category for understanding Newman's experience and the larger story of Protestant leadership in the American West. To do that it will be necessary to take a close look at the New England Protestant culture in which Newman was raised and that itself has a long history in the larger context of Christianity. In addition, I will explore the construction of gender in that culture and the ambiguities of woman's roles that both closed and opened doors for Newman and other women like her.

"Situated to Receive
the Highest Christian Culture"

I was strongly influenced, while at school, by the literary and religious atmosphere of Andover. I have always thought it an ines-
timable blessing to have been so situated as to receive
consciously and unconsciously, the results of the highest Christian culture, and I am sure that what I took in at the pores, has
been quite as valuable to me, as what I deliberately learned.
                                        —Philena and Phoebe McKeen,
                                         A History of Abbot Academy [1]

Emma Newman's Formative Social Situation

I have often been curious as to why women's entrance into pastoral ministry in the nineteenth century provoked much less internal conflict in the
women than one might expect. There was external opposition, and most
women who made this move found obstacles visible and invisible in their
way. We usually think of what Emma Newman and her New England Congregationalist contemporaries considered the "highest Christian culture"
as solidly conservative with regard to women's place in society, even
among its liberal branches; however, few experienced much internal struggle over their own fitness for the work.

There was ambiguity in this culture about the role of women. The ambiguity was there for all women, but middle-class women felt it particularly

---

1. This letter was Emma Newman's response to the inquiry from Abbot Academy asking
for information from alumnae for this volume.

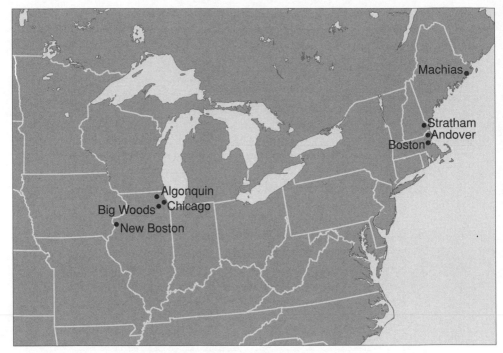

Emma Newman's Early Life and Preaching

keenly. Upper-class women could ignore the ambiguities because they seldom had to earn their living. The women in the lower classes felt no economic ambiguity; for them the burden was solid and unavoidable. Emma Newman's social location among the middle class, but with relatively few financial resources, made the dilemmas clearer. On the one hand, she could preach hard work, temperance, and church-going as necessary to a respectable, economically secure life. On the other hand, her own economic situation was precarious. Without a husband, she had to work for a living. Because of her education and connections, that work was interesting and respected but hardly settled or continuously sustained. In many ways she was simply lucky. She could continue to earn a small living and enter the male, public world while still maintaining her status as a respected woman by playing society's prescribed roles in that sphere. However, her salaries in small churches, despite her hard work, barely allowed her to live.

The ambiguity of women's roles had deep roots both in ancient models of Christian leadership drawn from Greco-Roman household organization and in the new cultural changes of the nineteenth century, particularly the emphasis on intuition and feeling as primary sources of religious truth. In the nineteenth century, these ambiguities eased women's way into a religious profession that called upon a great many household skills, such as teaching, healing, compassion, and management of a family-like community. Emma Newman's life allows us to view these ambiguities up close, and helps us to put into focus the various cultural pressures shaping the beginnings of women's professional religious leadership.

William Newman (1812–1850), Emma Newman's father, was born in Andover, Massachusetts. The Newman family was one of the town's important families. Mark Newman, Emma Newman's grandfather, owned a bookstore, was a trustee of Andover Theological Seminary, and had been the preceptor or principal of the Phillips Academy for fifteen years. Mark Newman's nephew Wendell Phillips, the famous abolitionist, remarked that "Most men thought Newman too easy and contented in his mood."[2] He was influential in starting the Abbot Academy for young women. His daughters, Margaret Wendell and Hannah Fay, were well connected in Andover society. Hannah Fay was particularly closely connected to the Andover Theological Seminary.

William Newman graduated from Yale College and Bangor Seminary, was ordained in 1836 in Stratham, New Hampshire, and married Caroline Cooper the same year. Cooper grew up on a farm some miles outside Machias, Maine, where a cluster of houses and a small church formed her town. Her parents were children of the earliest Machias families, migrants from the Massachusetts Bay Colony in the eighteenth century. One of Caroline's brothers, James S. Cooper, was a lawyer in Calais, Maine. Another attended Phillips Academy in Andover, but died a year later. A third kept the farm ("The Cooper Family" 1889, 46; 1886, 40–41). Emma Newman was born March 8, 1838, in Stratham, New Hampshire, during her father's second year as pastor there.

William Newman was the fifth pastor of the Stratham Congregational Church. In 1842, he presided over a revival in which thirty or forty people were admitted to membership by professing their faith. After twelve years,

2. Quoted in Allis, Jr. 1979, 100.

in May 1849, he was dismissed or resigned. "The cause of his removal is said to have been a conviction on his part that some individuals were disaffected" (Lawrence 1856, 143). He accepted the pastorate of the York Congregational Church in Maine in 1849, but died in Andover, Massachusetts, in 1850, at the age of thirty-eight. His daughter Emma was twelve years old. William and Caroline had one other child, a son, Arthur, who died some time in childhood. One can only imagine the weight of her father's death upon Emma Newman's life. She did not leave any record of her memories of the event, except noting on the day of her mother's funeral that her father was buried during a wild March storm (Diary, vol. 5, Sept. 5, 1871).

In her teens, Emma Newman attended the Abbot Academy in Andover for three years, 1853–1856, while her mother lived in Maine. Emma was fifteen when she began and just under nineteen when she graduated. Established in 1828, Abbot Academy was one of the earliest women's high schools established in the United States. At a time when few people thought women needed higher education, Abbot's constitution declared its objective:

> To regulate the tempers, to improve the taste, to discipline and enlarge the minds, and form the morals of the youth who may be members of it. To form the immortal mind to habits suited to an immortal being, and to instil principles of conduct and form the character for an immortal destiny, shall be subordinate to no other care. Solid acquirements shall always have precedence of those which are merely showy, and the useful of those which are merely ornamental. (Lloyd 1979, 453)

The curriculum included arithmetic, grammar, ancient and modern geography, ancient and ecclesiastical history, botany, mineralogy, poetry, drawing, algebra, physiology, philosophy, rhetoric, geometry, chemistry, geology, astronomy, Latin, Greek, French, Italian, and German, and other courses as the faculty could provide (Lloyd 1979, 50–51).

Newman attended the school at a time of transition in its history. Throughout the 1850s there had been a series of changes in the office of principal and in the faculty after a relatively stable early period. The year after Newman graduated, Phoebe McKeen became the new principal, serving in that capacity for at least two decades. Newman did have a close relationship with one of her teachers, Miss Blair.

In 1856, the year Newman graduated, Abbot was "blessed with a revival of religion, and quite a number became Christians. . . . A citizen remarked of one of the converts that he would know by her walk on the streets that a change had taken place" (Lloyd 1979, 80). Years later, Newman wrote this short account of her coming of age.

> Came out of school in 56. Failed in a county school in summer of 57, joined the church in Cooper Sept. 57. Visited Stratham, York, and Andover in summer of '58, not interested ever to return to Machias which I had always disliked as the climate was bad for me. The visiting was very pleasant to me but I could not find my place in the world and suffered intensely because I could not. God had work for me, the last work I should have chosen. When I reach Heaven I shall know why it was best. My selfishness and impatience called for a severe discipline and they had it. There was little improvement in the moving to Andover in May 1865. The Machias fogs had kept me two thirds sick all through those hard years and cough and catarrh haunted me for years in memory of them, these yielded after years of a good climate.[3]

For the time being her work was taking care of her mother.

Emma Newman's Diary

In 1852, the year Newman graduated from Abbot Academy, she began a diary that now serves as the main source of information about her life. She made the first entries just as she finished her education, kept it sporadically for a decade, and then wrote every day for at least thirty years. In her diary she recorded her correspondence, her reading, her work, studying, writing, visiting, preaching, sewing, mental healing, her health, and her feelings about what was going on around her.

The diary may have been meant for other eyes than her own, but she does not say so. Diaries were part of the vestiges of the Puritan spiritual

3. Except for this attempt to give an autobiographical sketch, she never gave any other shape to an account of her life. She wrote the sketch on the back of a program for a meeting that took place in Illinois, probably Chicago. The most likely year for Emma Newman to have written this is 1879. On Friday, October 3 of that year, she was in Chicago for a meeting of the American Board of Commissioners for Foreign Missions (Diary, vol. 11, October 3, 1879).

struggle. In earlier days, New Englanders kept diaries, scrutinizing each day's events for evidence of the saving work of God, looking for God's will, seeking meaning for every event. In the nineteenth century, diaries still served this primary spiritual role, but they served other purposes as well. Though Newman's diary has elements of the search for God's will within it, it is not often self-consciously introspective.

She recorded one rare example of introspection on June 28, 1869. She was thirty-one years old. "I should be a very different person if I had not such one-sided development; the sensibilities give me so much pain that I let them lie dormant mostly, and had almost forgotten they were so powerful; yet I am responsible for their use and I have been rather deliberately ignoring them to spare myself; selfish and cowardly—a noble character to judge others" (Diary, vol. 2). The context for her writing this was a quarrel with a male friend, Fred Stone, the husband of a very close friend, Mary. Though Newman had a few male friends in her youth, she never revealed any particularly close relationship to them. She reserved the word passion for Mary Stone.

> I have gained the passion power, and paid for it of course: I fell in love with one of my lady friends, she thought that she returned my love as long as she needed me, but, as soon as her husband returned from the army, concluded that it had been a mistake, and she had never loved me; I think she was right, for she had been occasionally paining me, even when we were nearest to each other, in little careless ways, so that, had it not been for her continually repeated assurances of love, I should have decided that she did not care for me very deeply. . . . I am thankful for the experience, it has given me more intensity, more power, and I think I have been more useful for it; pain is nothing compared with development. (Diary, vol. 1, Jan. 2, 1866)

Newman also had friendships with men but never passionate ones. In her Andover years these were with seminary students. Several men courted her, read aloud to her, brought her books from the library because women were not allowed access to it, and allowed her to critique their preaching. In later years, her male friends were usually colleagues in ministry or temperance work. She was close enough to one man in New Boston, Mr. Roberts, to cause talk among the people of the town. Late in life, she married Nicholas Emmerson, with whom she had corresponded for years.

Clearly she valued her passionate friendships. In this regard she was a woman of her times. Not only did the romantic poets and philosophers place a high value on emotion as a source of truth, evangelical Protestantism held the heart and the feelings to be the most reliable means for reaching God. From the point of view of the late twentieth century, feeling and thought have become dissociated, but in Newman's time, the sensibilities, particularly for women, were the seat of understanding. Without cultivating the sensibilities women could not hope to fulfill their duties to society. Newman regarded this duty as important, and recognized the power and contribution of feeling and thought to her moral development.

Newman's diary was primarily a daily memoranda of the events she experienced and some of her thoughts about them. Whether she kept this kind of diary to aid her memory, to help in soul searching, or for some other reason, it is impossible to know. Primarily, I believe, it provided her with a place and an accepting reader (herself) to whom she could reveal her experiences. Marion Yeates, studying the function of diaries in women's lives, concluded, "women created an imagined audience to substitute for lack of personal contact, to combat isolation, and to provide safe space for expression denied them in the public sphere" (Yeates 1994, 153). Newman's diary also allowed her to keep an account of her life in which she might discern the working of divine grace. It further allowed her to structure her sense of self in the context of the common attitudes of her society.

The daily entries, like beads held together with an invisible string, are the only thing available to us. To some degree her readers can say we understand her life through it, but our reading of her diary also reveals ourselves as much as it reveals her to us. Patterns and the "plots" of events stand out more sharply for the diary reader than for the diary writer. For me, my understanding of this history is a collaboration between Emma Newman as she wrote her diary and myself as I read it, clearly colored by my own experience as a pastor.

The question of how individual identity is portrayed in a diary is a difficult one. Perhaps the best way to look for the author behind the words of the diary is to seek the multiplicity of contesting unstable selves manifested in the text and begin to see how they are related (Nussbaum 1988, 136). Prompted by the tensions between her familial duty and her sense of call or vocation, Newman's diary served as a receptacle for emotions and observations. Living in a boarding house, caring for her mother, she was careful about her confidants. She became an observer of her own life, and her diary became a means of keeping herself emotionally healthy.[4]

Newman's diary begins with this account of her spending Christmas Day, 1857, alone. "I know how Thoreau came to take to the woods as he did, he happened to be alone for a day or two, and finding how delightful solitude is, concluded to take one long holiday from all tiresome conventionalities and to rest. I want to see his book now more than ever" (Diary, vol. 1, Jan. 5, 1857). The entry introduces her life for us. Its themes of solitude sought outside in nature show her already to be torn between her duties to other people and her longing for quiet to pursue her own thoughts and chosen work. Usually she was surrounded by other people and their demands, almost never alone, and seldom in company with someone who did not need her.

Though Newman never terms herself a romantic, I think she was one. The solace she found in nature, along with her emphasis on the necessity of feelings even when they are painful, mark her as sharing Romantic ideals. In addition, her theological reading of Coleridge, Bushnell, and Beecher, as well as Thoreau and Emerson, suggest she had a lively interest in their ideas.

In 1858, Newman moved from Andover, Massachusetts, to Machias, Maine, to care for her mother who was going blind. "The last two years have taken away pleasant dreams, I was longing for action, certain of success, now I am a tree maimed by lightening" (Diary, vol. 1, June 1858). Whatever her plans, this family burden seems not to have been among them. As the only daughter, unencumbered by marriage, she was expected to assume this duty. She expected it of herself.

The Burden of Usefulness

Newman's transformation from dependent daughter to caretaker of her mother was swift. As a single daughter and only child, Emma's first responsibility was to her parents. Daughter was a prime vocational identity for women, married or single. With no other provision available for aging peo-

---

4. Two other works that have been particularly helpful to me in understanding the nature of nineteenth-century diary literature are Culley 1985 and Kagle 1988.

ple, families performed the necessary nursing functions for their elders. The biblical imperative to honor one's parents, the love daughters had for their parents, and the expectation of society that women would find their chief vocation in the domestic arena all combined to make it difficult for a daughter, especially a single, only daughter, to extricate herself from these responsibilities. In addition, the evangelical theology of the day, especially in Andover, shaped as it was by the revivals of the early 1800s, called upon Christian people to be useful. Newman's first vocational call was to be useful to her mother (Chambers-Schiller 1984, 106). Even so, her vocation as caretaker was for Newman "the last work I should have chosen."

In 1865, Newman and her mother moved from Machias, Maine, back to Andover. There they boarded with her paternal aunt, Hannah Fay. She, like Newman's mother, had married a minister, but was a widow when Newman and her mother came to Andover.

Newman lived in Andover until her mother's death in 1872, boarding most of that time with her Aunt Fay, though she later moved to another house. Newman wrote positively on the subject of boardinghouse life, although living with other people was not particularly easy.

> I have never had a home since I was child, and, finding all the work waiting for me that I was able to do, without expending my vitality on the important matters of the table, have always been glad to board. I feel sure that the work in which I have accomplished most and taken most satisfaction, would have been crowded entirely out of my life, if house-keeping for which I have no natural faculty, had been forced into it. The pleasures and uses of a home may be more than counterbalanced by the care and work of it, unless there are little children whose well-being must be considered.
>
> But I am thinking specially of the other side of the unpleasant juxtaposition involved. It is not always unpleasant. I have met delightful friends in those same boarding-houses, and have found that any case of sickness or distress called out a generous helpfulness. Those on whom the sufferer had no claim but that of our common humanity were ready, eager, to lavish time and trouble to give the needed aid—and they would never have known it was needed, had it not been for the composite family. (Newman, "The Other Side of the Boarding House Question," n.d.)

Hannah Fay was difficult to live with. "She boarded us for less than the current Andover prices, but I paid her the difference in running all her errands, doing much of her sewing, and furnishing a safe object for her temper. Sewing for my mother and myself and often for my aunt: called upon for errands at any distance at any time and never having any opportunity to be still, however sick, while anybody wanted anything" (Diary, vol. 1, Nov. 30, 1868).

Fay was apparently not pleased at having to provide shelter to her brother's widow and daughter, but viewed it as her duty. Webs of duty surrounded all of these women. Some of it was personal duty to family, some of it was a matter of social duty, all of it was religious duty, tasks laid upon them by God. It was not always easy for Emma Newman or Hannah Fay to take such duties with grace.

For seven years Newman lived in Andover. These were her young adult years. Because of her mother's illness, she could not marry, and she was not trained for housework. The proximity of the Andover Theological seminary, her family's interest in the church, and her necessary care of her mother shaped her future work. Preaching and medicine became twin roles in her career.

The church was of central importance in Newman's life. It was the source of her categories of meaning, and her family was among the leaders and shapers of Congregational church life in Andover. As was expected of all young people when they took up adult responsibilities, Newman joined the Congregational Church in Cooper, Maine, when she finished school and began to teach school.

In 1871, Newman decided to transfer her church membership to an Andover congregation. Athough it was common for a Congregationalist who moved from one place to another to retain his or her membership in the original church, most did eventually transfer their membership to a congregation nearby. Newman's decision, supported by her disinterest in returning to Maine, seems to signal that she had decided to make her home in Andover. Of the churches in Andover, three were close enough for her to attend on Sundays. The Free Church was formed in 1846 by antislavery people and had no creed to which its members subscribed. The preaching in that church tended toward the liberal, even radical, side of contemporary theology. The South Church was her family's church. Her grandfather had been a deacon, and her father was buried in the churchyard. It was the largest church in Andover, with over three hundred members. However, the pastor, Rev. Smith, did not preach to Newman's liking.

The Seminary Church was the one she could attend most easily. The seminary professors preached, and it had a congregation of about seventy-five members and a Sunday School attendance of over two hundred. Newman had been going to this church most regularly, it being closest to Hannah Fay's house. "Went to communion in the afternoon, and heard a sermon on the love of Christ from a Mr. Abbey: I don't care to hear the love of Christ proved. Prayers at communion very good: I enjoyed it more than usual. I am coming to have a home feeling in the old-fashioned chapel; it is a home where Christian hearts are, all over the world" (Diary, vol. 2, Nov. 7, 1869). The decision to commit herself was difficult. Her choice of the Seminary Church was a step away from her family, an assertion of independence. She waited until she no longer lived in her Aunt Fay's house. "Went out to see Prof. Thayer, who was very kind and cordial, gave me a copy of the church creed, to which I am very ready to assent, and made himself agreeable generally. I do feel relieved the first step is taken, for I dreaded it" (Diary, vol. 3, Feb. 20, 1871). Newman was formally received into the Seminary Church on March 5, 1871, a few days before her thirty-third birthday. She was beginning to feel at home in the community, and not just temporarily living there while taking care of her mother.

Church work engaged most of her free time. She taught in the Sunday School, both in Andover for the children of church members,[5] and in neighboring Abbott Village for a class of mill girls one evening a week. She was active in the Home Relief Society, providing charity for the people in her assigned section of Abbott Village.

Though Newman was a dependent relative of Hannah Fay's, she was shaped by a middle-class family. Their evangelical theology called for every person to be of use to society. Newman's usefulness to her mother was not enough. Her family of educators and clergymen expected her to participate in the great enterprise of preserving and expanding the New England Protestant culture they considered the highest and best.

The mill workers in Abbott Village were the nearest threat to that culture. Recent immigrants, on the margins of the economy, and many of them Roman Catholics, they aroused both the worries and the charitable spirit of the leading families of Andover. The Andover Congregationalists

5. Diary, vol. 2, April 25, 1869: "Took Mrs. Pierson's S. S. class; such theological nine-year-olds never were heard of; their minds seemed fully decided, after mature consideration, on all points, and I believe they would have discussed original sin and federal headship indefinitely: Frankie Phelps was the least theological of the three."

sought to aid their new neighbors out of their deep belief in individual effort, education, temperance, and thrift. Newman's charitable work focused on individual reform, such as persuading Mr. Goodwin to quit drinking, or Annie Farnham to associate with more respectable men. The Andover Church Aid Society gave clothes and food, but worried that these gifts fostered dependency. The society did not at this time consider the larger social and economic systems that placed them in the middle class and kept the Abbott Village people in poverty to be beyond the remedy of individual temperance and hard work. Society members were optimistic about the power of education and Christian conversion to better the lives of the poor. They were situated comfortably in the mainstream of New England Christian culture and believed that those who adopted this culture, it values, and practice would prosper.

The Shape of New England Christian Culture

Here we need to take a closer look at the New England Christian culture itself, especially that of Andover during the years of Newman's youth. This culture formed Newman, and she in turn participated in it until she was thirty-four years old. The years in question, the 1840s through the 1870s, were a watershed time for New England culture. In the space of these thirty years, New England Congregationalism in particular moved from being the dominant intellectual force in American Christianity to being one of many options, and not the most influential among them. No one moment of cataclysmic change explains this, but rather many small changes accumulated toward this result. Protestant church people increasingly had to either defend the faith or try to adjust it to new ways of thinking. Immigration was fast making Roman Catholicism the dominant religion in New England. Science and the churches' inability to engage the scientist in meaningful conversation conspired to secularize thinking people. Reformed Protestantism lost its initiative in shaping American culture.

Many scholars have described New England culture in detail.[6] Rooted

6. A helpful discussion of this Yankee culture, especially as it traveled west with American society, is found in Wright 1955. See also McLoughlin 1978, which discusses some of the connected patterns of American life as the New England religious culture made itself felt in shaping secular society.

in Reformed Protestant theology and shaped by Puritan concerns for individual responsibility for community, a high regard for the Word and intellect pervaded all aspects of New England life. The Reformed understanding of the Word of God found in the Bible, and the principle that each Christian had the ability to interpret it using simple common sense, created several related characteristics of this culture. First was the high value of literacy, making the Bible accessible to everyone. Second, the concern that everyone's interpretation might differ led to a tendency to value a literal reading of the words. The great awakenings of the eighteenth and early nineteenth century also produced a characteristic emphasis on the useful Christian life, the duty to shape a society fit for the expected millennial return of Christ.

The New England culture was also an Anglo culture, shaped by English literature and philosophy. It shared British optimism about its own place at the pinnacle of civilization. The Enlightenment thought of John Locke shaped its political organization and produced a democratic form of government modeled on the traditions of the English parliament, but including new ideas about natural rights and the covenant or contract between the government and the people. New England culture also embraced the Enlightenment idea of reason and optimism about the ability of human reason to address the problems of the day.

The people of this New England culture set for themselves the task of transforming America, making it a truly Protestant nation that would in time transform the world.

The primary institutions they used in undertaking this work were not established government or church bodies, but newly organized voluntary societies specializing in various aspects of reform. The projects of home and foreign missions, antislavery, Sabbath observance, Sunday schools, temperance, and later women's rights each had their local and national organizations. In addition every town had its relief society for the material, educational, and spiritual needs of the poor. Christianity in its common sense meaning came to be identified with those who, by professing their faith and sometimes also by convincing the church they had experienced a conversion, had joined the church. In making this profession, they determined to alter their lives, outwardly conforming to a set of behavioral standards including abstinence from alcohol and tobacco, keeping the Sabbath, regular attendance at the services of the church, and working to better the world.

During this period a growing division in New England theology profoundly shaped the "highest Christian culture" of Andover, Massachusetts. New England Congregationalism was strictly Calvinist in its origin, the doctrine of predestination serving as a key mark of orthodoxy. In the seventeenth century Jacobus Arminius softened Calvinism by removing its emphasis on predestination. Many Protestants followed him in this, especially John Wesley and the Methodists. As a consequence of the revivals of the two great awakenings, one in the mid 1700s and another in the early 1800s, splits developed in Congregationalism between the liberal parties who embraced an Arminian emphasis on the importance of human will in conversion, and the Calvinist parties who continued to emphasize predestination and the freedom of God. Andover Theological Seminary upheld the Calvinist orthodoxy, but many of its students and faculty were interested in the success of the Methodists with their Arminian theology. Both the Calvinist and Arminian groups appreciated Enlightenment rationality in the face of religious intolerance. Both groups rejected the more extreme emotional expressions of revivalism. Other liberal Congregationalists, in contrast to both the Calvinists and the Arminians, began to differentiate themselves from the more strictly Calvinist parties in their optimism about human nature and human reason, their view of the benevolence of God, and their movement away from Trinitarian theology. They were among the first in North America to become interested in the new German critical historical work on the Bible. Many became Unitarians. In Andover, Newman was exposed to all three options and positioned herself theologically in the middle between the strict Calvinists and the openly Arminian.

Beyond these differences, the liberals and orthodox Calvinists, at least in Congregational circles, did share some traits. Both valued congregational independence. Both went along with the established tax-supported church until it was finally ended in Massachusetts in 1833. Both saw America as the birthplace of the new humanity. Both emphasized theological truths and moral duties in their preaching, valuing an educated clergy and intellectual sermons. This put distance between both groups and those who could not afford the education necessary to appreciate such preaching, creating a class divide in New England religion.

Nonetheless, in the 1830s, there was a brief moment of broad consensus in New England about Yankee values. New England people based their consensus in a largely Calvinist world view, though with room for many variations, including the rationalist and the revivalist. New Englanders understood themselves to be a new people of God. Expanding upon that vision they embraced the idea that they had a "manifest destiny" to inhabit and convert the entire continent to their way. This national sense of divine purpose pervaded American rhetoric in the nineteenth century.

This national covenant with God protected individual freedom and called for community life based broadly on the Ten Commandments and the Sermon on the Mount. Americans steeped in this New England culture believed society was made up of free, morally responsible individuals with inalienable rights, though public respect and economic success were reserved for those who worked hard. People were free, in both the Calvinist sense of free to follow God's law and the Enlightenment sense of free to pursue happiness, though few discussed the dilemmas posed by this double understanding.

Although there was a national mythology of unity, celebrated in the Birthday of George Washington and the Pilgrims' Thanksgiving Day, it was never clear that all human beings living within the bounds of the country were equally part of this covenant. Immigrants from Europe could assimilate by learning English and converting to Protestantism, but most New Englanders assumed that the Native Americans could not fit into this scheme and would have to move on. The question of the place of African Americans was tabled for a future generation to resolve—a consensus sustained as long as the question of slavery was not introduced and the slowly growing urban tensions were swept under the rug. This consensus ideology fueled the Congregational Home Missionary Society in its effort to convert the West to Protestantism.

The good Congregationalists of Andover fought to maintain this cultural ideal through the decades of Emma Newman's youth, and she "took it in at the pores." It formed a framework for her world view and the organization of her life, but by the time she entered school, this consensus had been broken and the Civil War had torn the country in two.

We know then that Emma Newman was educated and began her work during a period of transition in New England religious culture. The "highest Christian culture" she valued suffered attacks, and even grew defensive. It contained within it ambiguities that allowed for both theological and practical innovation, as well as for increasingly strict legalism. Its ambiguities regarding the place and role of women in church and society are particularly significant if we are to fully understand Newman's formation as a minister.

Ambiguities about Women's Role in Church and Society in New England Culture

New Englanders held two ideals that, on the surface, are not contradictory, but when applied to women opened important questions. The importance of biblical moral tenets and the Bible as a model for Christian life, including the organization of Christian institutions, led people to search in the text of the Bible for women's proper role. They also looked to the principles of Enlightenment political theory.

The Biblical text is itself ambiguous in dealing with women. There are prohibitions of women's participation in church leadership found in the Epistles, particularly those with Paul's authority attached to them. Like most interpreters of the story of the Fall in Genesis, early Christians placed blame on the woman who ate the fruit first. However, there are signs that some biblical writers considered women equal to men. Women were clearly leaders in the early church—preachers, heads of house churches, and missionaries. Biblical writers such as Paul appreciated the work of women. The verse in Galatians reading, "There is neither male nor female, for ye are all one in Christ," (3:28 AV) does not bear the weight of the whole argument for women's leadership, but it is a powerful affirmation. The Gospel writers' insistence that women were first to proclaim the resurrection is another example of Biblical support for women. Following either stream of thought as the authoritative biblical judgement on the matter required that one ignore material that nineteenth-century evangelical Protestants regarded as equally the word of God: either they ignored suggestions for women's roles, or suggestions against.

The Greco-Roman culture out of which the early church and its scriptures emerged had its own ambiguities regarding women. The idea of separate spheres of life was fundamental to its structures (Torjesen 1993, 65–76).[7] Both *oikos*, the household, and *polis*, the public space, were

7. Torjesen (1993) discusses the historical literature on women in the Greco-Roman culture and the relationship of this literature to the matter of women's leadership in the early church.

spheres of activity for men, but only *oikos* was the proper sphere for women. However, within the *oikos*, women had a great range of authority and responsibility. Women as *materfamilias* or patron handled the management of large numbers of people, financial transactions, business decisions, and the education of the household. Business roles took them into the *polis* from time to time, where they appear to have been accepted when performing the economic duties of the *oikos*.

Religion was also a proper reason for a woman to enter the *polis*. In the religions of the region, women were accepted as leaders: they served as leaders in the synagogues (Brooten 1982, 5), and in pagan religions they served as high priestesses and prophets, their duties to the deities equally important to those of men. Although women were officially subordinate to men, they nevertheless exercised a sizable influence in society. The Christian church began in the private realm of the *oikos*. Within that sphere, society accepted women's leadership, so women played a large role in the spread of Christianity.

At the end of her book on women in classical antiquity, Sarah Pomeroy summarizes the philosophical underpinnings of Greco-Roman culture, and therefore also to a large degree our own. From Aristotle's systematic account of women's inferiority, to the Stoics who confined women to marriage and motherhood, Pomeroy writes, "The argumentation is brilliant and difficult to refute. And this rationalized confinement of women to the domestic sphere, as well as the systematization of antifemale thought by poets and philosophers, are two of the most devastating creations in the classical legacy" (Pomeroy 1975, 230). Ironically, this very confinement provided the environment in which women's leadership developed in the early church. Unlike the nineteenth-century idea of the home as a refuge from the public arena, the household in classical antiquity was the political arena in microcosm. For males, the household served as a training ground for the state; the one who desired public office must show the ability to manage the household.

The early church offices described in the New Testament and other literature—bishops, elders, and deacons—all derive from offices of household management that women as well as men could hold. Bishops had the task of oversight, elders contributed their wisdom as teachers and presided at meals and family ceremonies, and deacons managed the everyday care of the members of the household. The small community of the house church allowed for the participation of women in all of these roles, if not in all of the formal offices, in developing Christian identity and institutional structures (Klauk 1981, 101).

The kind of community Emma Newman tried to foster in the church and create in the raw society of the American West has its origin in the earliest Christian house churches as well. The small size of the house churches made interpersonal relationships between leaders and members possible and, indeed, necessary (Aguirre 1984, 27–51). Even when the churches grew much larger, the ideal of the pastor or elder who presided at the communion table knowing and caring for each member of the congregation prevailed. Newman followed in this ancient form of pastoral care.

The house church was also prone to the difficulties of division that Newman found in the frontier churches she served. The existence of several house churches in a single city in the early years of the church was the result of divisions as much as the confinement of the congregation to the limited space of the house. "Christians of a certain tendency grouped together and thereby were confirmed in that tendency. Separation from Christians of somewhat different background, views, and interests must have operated to prevent the growth of mutual understanding. Each group had its feelings of pride and prestige. Such a physically divided church tended almost inevitably to become a mentally divided church" (Filson 1939, 110).

From the beginning male leaders were nervous about the influence of women on the course of Christian development. Especially as Christianity moved into the public sphere, Christian writings show increasing hostility to women's leadership. Thus in early Christian writings, including the New Testament, there are contradictory messages regarding the place of women in church and society.

The developing theology in American Reformed Protestantism contained its own ambiguities. Emphasis on feeling and intuition as a source of religious truth made a place for so-called feminine ways of thinking. The romantic movement countered the cold reason of the Enlightenment with the experience of the heart. Though in every era some women were preaching and writing, women found their voices anew in the nineteenth century. Catherine Breckus ably documents the female preaching of the antebellum period (Breckus 1998). The first ordinations of women were justified by the authority granted by virtue of women's experience and the community's experience of their preaching, rather than rational deduction from the principles of scripture.

In addition to biblical moral teachings, a second ideal can be found in the political theory of the Enlightenment, and it also provided ambiguous guidance on the role of women in society. On the one hand, the Enlightenment's egalitarianism emphasized the rights of all human beings, and provided philosophical justification for arguing that those rights be restored to women as well as men. On the other hand, Enlightenment philosophers had in mind only free white males when they referred to "all men" being created equal. The newly organized United States lumped women, children, and slaves into the same legal category of dependence and subordination (Myrdal 1944, appendix 5).

Out of these ambiguities arose a peculiarly nineteenth-century theory about women, called by some the cult of domesticity, or true womanhood. Evangelical Protestant women particularly forged an ideal that supported not only the wife and mother in the sphere of the household, but also supported the single woman teacher, missionary, social worker, and, I argue, minister. Making (probably unconscious) use of the household models of leadership in the church, these women took on a priestly role within the home and outside of it, though apart from the institutional churches that they also supported wholeheartedly. This priestly role included the pastoral role of shepherd, keeping the family together, and serving as the focus for communication and care. The sacraments of sacred meal and healing were central responsibilities of the woman head of the household. Women kept the family religious traditions, attended church, prayed for husbands and sons, and taught their daughters to do likewise. In order to accomplish these priestly tasks in a wider sphere, they organized useful societies, financing them independently of their husbands or fathers, often by selling the products of their own hands. Within these societies evangelical women provided charities, healed the sick, taught religion, and built new churches.

After the Civil War, the problem of single women and their appropriate roles in society became acute. The demographic trends, particularly in the eastern cities, showed increasing numbers of single women compared to the numbers of single men. A great many men had been killed in the Civil War, but many more were moving west. Immigrants also were more often single men rather than single women. In addition, young people were marrying later in life.[8]

Newman was part of a cohort of women who grew up and came of age in New England during or shortly after the Civil War. They remained single and entered the professions at a rate unprecedented for their time and in numbers unmatched until the present. Many of these women had identifiable vocations—teaching, sewing, writing, medicine—but they rarely made an adequate living. Most, like Newman, lived at home with family. They shared their parents' middle-class Protestant ambitions for achievement, recognition, and self-improvement, but their independence was circumscribed by duty to aging parents (Chambers-Schiller 1984, 4).

Lee Virginia Chambers-Schiller concludes her study of single women in this period by describing four desires these women shared: desire for a life of high purpose, desire to expand the intellect, desire to cultivate the self, and desire to be free and independent (Chambers-Schiller 1984, 4). This required an independent income, a room of one's own, and collegial company in which to expand the mind. Newman had all these things, though in meager supply. The necessity of self-dependence fostered the desire for independence, but independence was difficult to attain. Emma Newman lived out her desire—barely self-reliant and self-sufficient— never needing to marry to survive. She cultivated her intelligence, had a good education, and continued to improve herself by reading and attending lectures.

I have avoided the term "domesticity" thus far because, although it clearly categorizes most of what Newman did, it is not helpful in analyzing the transition in her form of leadership. She herself did not value domesticity for its own sake. Though she did study church history, Newman was probably unconsciously adapting the household model of the earliest churches in order to shape her frontier congregation. The Greco-Roman householder with responsibilities for healing, money, organization, and the religious practice of the family served as a template for Newman's ministry.

8. The number of single women in the post–Civil War era was surpassed only in the last quarter of the twentieth century. Nationally, of the women born in the period 1835 to 1838, just over 7 percent were never married. Of those like Newman, northeastern white women, 14 percent were never married (Smith 1974).

Though the ideal of true womanhood called for marriage and child rearing, for increasing numbers of young women this was not possible. How then did they find a place in society? Several scholars, among them Barbara Welters, Nancy Cott, Katheryn Kish Sklar, and Anne Boylan, have ably addressed this question. Boylan focuses on the models of womanhood among evangelical women. Her thesis is that these women "self-consciously developed an ideal of womanhood which stressed self-sacrifice but permitted women to adopt active social roles in areas such as teaching and moral leadership" (Boylan 1978, 63). These women, like their ancient Greco-Roman sisters, considered entry into the public sphere justified if it involved self-sacrificial service to home and humanity. Voluntary societies focused on various aspects of social reform provided one of the most popular venues for this service.

These voluntary societies were middle-class organizations because middle-class women had the resources of time and money to spend on them. Until later in the century, very few of the women involved recognized or understood the social and economic systems that affected the people they desired to help. Consequently, their work focused on charity and the conversion of individuals. Only in problems of personal morality, such as drinking alcohol, did they seek systemic solutions to individual problems. Even there, they generally failed to recognize the ways social systems supported the very behavior they were trying to eradicate. In their efforts, transmission of religion was closely tied to transmission of culture. The poor, those destitute of the Christian gospel, would gain the full benefit of Christianity only if they also worked hard, practiced thrift, pursued education, and learned to live a respectable middle-class life.

Emma Newman's Concern for Healing, Spiritual and Physical

Newman's earliest sense of vocation grew out of her day to day care of her mother. Although her interest in medicine originated in the practical necessities of life, she recognized within herself an interest and ability that could flower into a useful life's work. Because her own health was not good she had an additional reason to be interested in healing. Her early studies in medicine coincided with her early studies in theology. We will consider her theological education later.

Newman was not alone in her interest in both medicine and preaching. Many of the woman ministers of the time had similar interests. Anna Howard Shaw attended medical school and became a physician after her ordination. Dr. Clisby, with whom Newman studied mental healing in Boston spring 1875, was a member of the Association of Woman Ministers.

In addition to homeopathy, Newman studied animal magnetism and mental healing. James Howarth was the homeopathic physician she consulted regularly in Andover for her own and her mother's ailments. He began training her in the preparation of medicines for herself, suggested books for her to study, and taught her his view of homeopathic principles. Howarth treated both her physical symptoms and her spiritual state as he saw them.

> It occurred to me that Dr. Howarth would go into Boston tomorrow and that I wished to consult him about this deafness, so I walked down again and was fortunate in finding the doctor at home: he told me that the difficulty was caused by a rush of blood to the brain and neighboring parts and I must equalize the circulation, leave off coffee and take wine, and he gave me a mystic discourse on the power of God to compensate for deprivation, and the duty and beauty of serving Him by cheerful submission to His will, where one has not done anything to bring on sickness. (Diary, vol. 4, Dec. 27, 1870)

Newman's care of her mother was exhausting her. Howarth's strategy for healing relied first upon locating the spiritual difficulty. Newman, in doing her duty, had not brought on her illness, so she need not feel guilty about being sick. However, her duty was God's will, and part of her cure lay in cheerful submission to it.

Newman received more practical instruction in the art of prescribing by consulting another homeopathic doctor in Andover, O. L. Bradford. The principles of homeopathic medicine required that a medicine be prescribed that in a large dose would cause the same symptoms from which the patient suffered. In its diluted form, the medicine stimulated the body's own powers of fighting the disease. While mixing the medicines Bradford prescribed and following the changes he made in them as her condition changed, Newman learned first-hand the effects of the basic homeopathic remedies, using pulsatilla, aconite, nux, macaria, china, alum, conium, iron, and sulfur on her headaches, colds, neuralgia, and deafness (Diary, vol. 5, July–Dec. 1871, and vol. 6, Dec. 1871–June 1872).[9]

With two friends, Miss Anna and Miss Harris, she read several books on homeopathy between October 1871 and February 1872, including Lutze's *Manual of Homeopathic Practice* and Burt's *Comparative Materia Medica*.[10] She participated with a group of young women in Andover who were interested in homeopathy, exchanging information about various remedies and illnesses, reading homeopathic journals, and building up kits of homeopathic medicines. They encouraged each other in study and practice.

Newman also studied mental healing for a few months in Boston after her summer preaching in Big Woods, Illinois. She studied with two women, Dr. Spettigue and Dr. Clisby, and with Warren Evans, who wrote about the theory of mental healing and Christianity. Both women were experimenting with mental healing, and from them Newman learned to treat various illnesses without medicines at all. Newman retained a critical view of mental healing, and she insisted on a scientific presentation of it (Diary, vol. 8, Jan. 26, 1872).[11] Clisby and Spettigue maintained a charitable practice among the poor in Boston, and in assisting them, Newman learned the limits of mental healing and magnetism. "Went with Dr. Spettigue to see one of her patients; we went about among the poor sick colored people, who seemed really to do their best at being jolly under difficulties; but my patient was beyond me, cancer and inflammation of the bowels are not at all amenable to my strokings, and I wonder that Dr. S. should have thought they would be" (Diary, vol. 8, Dec. 5, 1872).

Much of Newman's interest in mental healing and homeopathy was nurtured by people related to the Swedenborgian movement. Howarth was, according to Newman, a "semi-Swedenborgian" until he converted to

9. Newman's recipe for homeopathic medicine called for a first dilution of the medicine in a solution of one part medicine to ten parts a mixture of one-third water to two-thirds alcohol. Then one-tenth of this mixture would be further diluted in ten parts of a solution containing more alcohol than water, and then diluted again in alcohol only. By the time the patient received the dose of medicine, the solution was mostly alcohol. The patient was likely to sleep well in any case (Recipes to Cure Certain Illnesses).

10. I have not been able to locate further information about these titles.

11. Diary, vol. 8, Jan. 26, 1872: "Finished 'Mental Medicine' in the evening. I have copied many of the directions which seem really scientific, and shall see if I can do anything with them. I fail entirely on Lucy."

Roman Catholicism. Clisby was also Swedenborgian. "Dr. Clisby seems to believe in those Swedenborgian emanations"(Diary, vol. 7, Dec. 18, 1873 and vol. 8, Jan. 31, 1875).

Both homeopathy and magnetism attracted the interests of Swedenborgians. Swedenborg shared with Hahnemann, the founder of homeopathy, an interest in the theories of Paracelsus, a sixteenth-century alchemist and physician whose studies of the action of chemicals on human physical functions led him to think of disease as a disorder of the spirit. Hans Gram, the doctor who introduced homeopathy in the United States, became a Swedenborgian. Warren F. Evans, whose books Newman studied, was a Swedenborgian.

Evans was healed by Phineas Quimby, who influenced several healers, most notably Mary Baker Eddy. Both Evans and Quimby were interested in homeopathy as well as in the effects of animal magnetism (Ahlstrom 1976, 588). Evans became the founder of the New Thought movement. The thought and practices of these groups, whether churches like Swedenborg's Church of the New Jerusalem or Mary Baker Eddy's Church of Christ, Scientist, or informal networks of practitioners and followers, interested a broad range of American Protestants. Sidney Ahlstrom, in his discussion of these movements, suggests that they reveal a "fundamental kind of religious uneasiness" in response to the threat of modern science to faith, with their quasi-scientific way of addressing mystical or occult phenomena (Ahlstrom 1976, 588–89).

Newman remained an orthodox Congregationalist, interested in the practices of homeopathy and mental healing, but not completely subscribing to the theologies that were often associated with them. But many former orthodox Protestants were persuaded that mental healing offered a more effective framework for understanding disease than that provided by the mainline churches. Newman retained, throughout her mental healing practice, an orthodox view of the divine role in healing. With a line of reasoning derived from Calvin ([1559] 1950, 4.19.5), she emphasized that it was God who healed, not her ministrations. Calvin dismissed healing ceremonies, urging the sick to accept the will of God rather than trying to change their circumstances. He desired a return to the practice of laying on hands in blessing; anointing the sick or dying was a ceremony too easily misunderstood by the superstitious. We can put Newman's practice of magnetic healing and rubbing (massage) in this category of laying on hands in blessing, but she regarded it as also physically therapeutic.

Emma Newman's Theological Education

In a setting other than Andover, Newman's culture might not have opened to her the idea of preaching. She would probably have followed the medical track if she became interested in a profession at all. The particular circumstance of her family's location and connection to Andover Seminary opened the means of discovering this religious call within her.

Andover Seminary was in many respects still a theological center of the New England culture. In 1803 and 1804, the deaths of two professors at Harvard University, including the president, left openings that the overseers filled with liberal scholars. In dismay, Jedadiah Morse, one of the orthodox party of overseers, drew together a group of like-minded ministers and scholars and founded an orthodox seminary in Andover in 1808. Within five years, Harvard was solidly liberal, and Morse called for orthodox Congregationalists to cut off communion with those he considered to be Unitarians. The orthodox maintained the essentially Calvinist theology of the Puritans, reinterpreted by Jonathan Edwards and his disciples. This New Divinity theology protected the sovereignty of God above all (Ahlstrom 1990).[12]

12. The Andover Seminary creed was based on that of the Phillips Academy, written in 1778. "Whereas many of the students in this seminary may be devoted to the sacred work of the gospel ministry . . . it shall be the duty of the Master, as the age and capacities of the scholars will admit, not only to instruct and establish them in the truth of Christianity; but also early and diligently to inculcate upon them the great and important doctrines of the existence of One true GOD, the FATHER, SON and HOLY GHOST; of the fall of man; the depravity of human nature; the necessity of an atonement, and of our being renewed in the spirit of our minds; the doctrines of repentance toward God and of faith toward our Lord Jesus Christ; of sanctification by the Holy Spirit, and of justification by the free grace of God, through the redemption, that is in Jesus Christ (in opposition to the erroneous and dangerous doctrine of justification by our own merit, or a dependence on self-righteousness), together with the other important doctrines and duties of our HOLY CHRISTIAN RELIGION" (Ahlstrom 1990, 30–31).

The creed was printed Woods 1885, 228; it was quoted in Ahlstrom 1990, 30–31, where I first read it. Ahlstrom points out that it was a defensive, apologetic creed opposed to Unitarians, Universalists, Atheists, Jews, "Papists," and "Mahometans" (Ahlstrom 1990, 44).

Though the New Divinity theologians were uncomfortable with the notion of original sin, they redefined it only so far as to remove God's responsibility. Joseph Bellamy emphasized God's permission of sin as necessary to achieving the greatest good. Samuel Hopkins equated sin with human self-love, not inherited but inherent in every person. Hopkins also tried to reconcile popular Arminianism's view of human freedom with Calvin's certainty of human total depravity, arguing that the first step in salvation, regeneration, was a work of the Holy Spirit and imperceptible to the person; conversion rested wholly with the person as an exercise in human will, but was impossible without the prior work of regeneration. Hopkins expected, as Edwards had done, that conversion would lead to growing holiness in life. This reconciliation with Arminianism allowed the orthodox Evangelical Protestants to accept revivals without compromising their Calvinism.[13]

The ambiguities of New England thought on the place of women in the church allowed Emma Newman a place to slip through the barriers this orthodox Protestantism placed before women. She had advantages as the granddaughter of a famous trustee. She was known and respected. She was also careful, apparently, about revealing her intentions. The seminary trustees and faculty guarded the knowledge they dispensed; not all professors welcomed women. Theological knowledge was the preserve of the male gender. Still, although Andover Seminary forbade the admission of women students, it was too much a creature of its own culture for the ambiguities of women's role in the church not to have their effect. The door was left open just a crack. "I am continually annoyed by the fact that Prof. Phelps is delivering exquisite lectures on style within a quarter of a mile, to which I don't quite dare to go alone, and I can't rouse the least interest in aunt; it is very tantalizing" (Diary, vol. 2, May 19, 1869). Austin Phelps, professor of sacred rhetoric, was one of those who allowed women to audit his lectures. However, propriety forbade a woman to attend lectures alone. At first Newman avoided being the only lady in class, but gradually she broke through that tradition.

I have been alone two mornings, and there has never been any other lady except Mrs. Downs; the students are civil when they are anything and it is

13. A good recent study of these theological developments can be found in Toulouse and Duke 1997.

very much less awkward to have my own place and go to it at once. Mr. Pratt told me one morning that I was the opening wedge for the admission of ladies to the seminary: I answered truly, that I did not think Prof. Phelps would have me there, if it were not known that I do not intend to preach. (Diary, vol. 3, Apr. 23, 1870)

At least she did not preach while her mother lived.

In Emma Newman's notes on Austin Phelps' lectures, we have important confirmation of the shape of New England culture as it was spread by the Congregational and Presbyterian home missionaries in the American West. The pastor, in Phelps' view, was responsible for transmitting better culture to the people, along with Christian truth. The New England middle-class anxiety about the immigrant poor, especially those of another culture (the Irish in Andover's case) showed clearly in his lectures. The responsibility of the preacher was not only religious conversion, but cultural conversion as well.

> The ministry has great influence over the practical usage of the people. The clergyman of a parish is usually the model of refinement to his congregation in literary matters: this we are in danger of forgetting, and may be led by the people instead of leading them; having the power we ought to use it. It should be regarded as one of the incidental duties of the clerical office to elevate the literary usage of the people, it is one way of elevating their minds, it tends to refine their thought if they are helped to express thought in refined language. (Notes on Austin Phelps' Lectures on English Style)

In his third lecture on homiletics, Phelps gave a long list of authors who provided models for the preacher, all English or American preachers and theologians from the fourteenth through the mid-nineteenth centuries (Newman, "Notes on Austin Phelps' Lectures on Homiletics," 164). Of them, Emma Newman read only two, Horace Bushnell and Henry Ward Beecher. Her reading tended to be more modern and more diverse, including Italian, German, and ancient Greek authors, and she read fiction. She was more likely to read a poem or story by Elizabeth Stuart Phelps, Austin Phelps' daughter, than she was a book from his list.

Still, Newman read extensively. In addition to regular reading in the religious journals of the day, especially the *Independent*, she read short fiction, history, and theology. Bushnell, Henry Ward Beecher, Emerson,

Wendell Phillips, and Frederich Max Müller were her favorites. She often read Beecher's sermons from the *Plymouth Pulpit* aloud to her mother. This reading provided her with a foundation in the emerging Protestant liberalism grounded in feelings and intuitions of the spiritual rather than logically deduced from the Bible. It was tolerant, open to new intellectual currents, and stressed Christian responsibility for society. Her sermons, though not as polished as Beecher's, have the same tone of spiritual pragmatism. Williston Walker traced the rise of liberalism in Congregational circles to this period. Bushnell, influenced by Coleridge and Schleiermacher, first introduced the liberal ideas in the middle of the century. They were controversial at first, but by Newman's day had become less alarming. By the end of the nineteenth century, liberalism had become characteristic of Congregational theology (Walker 1906, 204–18).

More influential for Newman was the theology of Edwards Amasa Park, the last of two generations of Jonathan Edward's disciples, who would not allow women to attend his lectures. As she finished Prof. Phelps' course of lectures, she became interested in taking the theology course from Park. "As I went to the P. O. Mrs. Park asked me to take their mail, and we chatted awhile: I seized the opportunity to ask the professor's idea on the subject of ladies' attending on his lectures: she answered that the professor said he 'could not lecture to the students, as he wanted to, when ladies were present.' Is theological truth essentially masculine, or is anything the matter with these lectures?" (Diary, vol. 3, July 26, 1870).

Edwards Amasa Park was the leading theologian in Andover during Emma's time there, having become Abbot Professor of Christian Theology in 1846. Park was educated at Andover under the theologian Leonard Woods, a Hopkinsian Calvinist, and Moses Stuart, who introduced biblical criticism to the seminary (Vanderpool 1971, 350).[14] After a short time as a parish minister, his health broke down and he spent some time in Germany recovering. There he was exposed to new currents in theology. He

14. See Vanderpool 1971, 350. Stuart's first use of biblical criticism was to support New England orthodox theology against the Arminians. The second step was a proof of orthodox positions from Biblical texts. Also, it was shown that some of the points of the Westminster Confession were not in scripture any more than Arminian theological points. Therefore, it "became a platform for lessened loyalty to every creedal formulation" (Vanderpool 1971, 350).

returned to Andover as a professor, but the questions of critical study of the Bible and doubts raised by his study of Charles Lyell's geological discoveries and Charles Darwin's *On the Origin of Species* shook his faith for a time.

Other orthodox Congregationalists struggled with similar issues. Horace Bushnell, in his New Haven church, was attempting to frame a theology that would speak to the people of his congregation who were familiar with the changing thought of the times and questioning the Calvinist orthodoxy in which they had been raised. Henry Ward Beecher was similarly engaged in reframing traditional evangelical Protestantism for a post–Civil War generation.

In 1850, Park elaborated his idea of a twofold theology, that of the intellect and that of the feelings. He wanted to remain within the school of Jonathan Edwards, but to take account of the ideas of the mid-Victorian age in which he taught.

Park's "humanitarian Calvinism" or "progressive orthodoxy" defined a new turn in orthodox Congregationalism that influenced more than one generation of Andover students. Newman was in Andover absorbing Park's mature thought when his students thought of him as an "aging high Calvinist" (Vanderpool 1971, 353), but before controversies began to rage between the conservatives, some more conservative than Park, and more liberal younger faculty. Park was thus, T. H. Ahlstrom argued, the first of the Andover liberals (Ahlstrom 1990, 74). The liberals eventually led Andover Seminary back to Harvard a century after it had split off to preserve orthodox Calvinism.

T. R. Ahlstrom, in his thesis concerning the Andover theology, linked Park's thought with that of Bushnell and other contemporary theologians in several ways. First, they shared the catalyst of the new learning in science and critical study of the Bible. They generally accepted such new thinking, but determined not to relinquish valued points of orthodoxy. They had to deal with contradictions in their thought and to resolve the contradictions they elevated sentiment and experience over deductively discovered truth. In the end they concluded it was more important to be a Christian in one's heart than in one's head (Ahlstrom 1990, 78–99).

Newman's embrace of this theological perspective during her years in Andover is evident from her response to sermons. Here lay Newman's objection to Mr. Abbey's sermon noted above in which he tried to prove the love of Christ. The deductive, purely intellectual theology characteristic of eighteenth-century Congregationalism began to break down in the middle of the nineteenth century. As the century progressed and the Andover expression of Calvinist orthodoxy evolved, two things remained constant: emphasis on the uniqueness of Christ for the salvation of humanity, and a passion for missions both home and foreign (Ahlstrom 1990, 104).

By the final quarter of the nineteenth century, the period in which Emma Newman received her education and did most of her ministry, Protestantism reached the height of its hegemony in American culture and began to divide and decline. The Protestant churches confidently continued to move west, but two intellectual problems were surfacing, in ways Park and Bushnell could not have imagined.[15] The question of evolution at first seemed not to have an impact on Protestant faith, but the idea of human rise from a primitive origin undermined the idea of a sudden human fall from a time of superior morality and grace. If the Bible's account of the Fall was not historically true, was a redeemer necessary? The question of the critical historical study of the Bible began to separate clergy and academic students of scripture from the laity in the churches. Though the ideas were not necessarily troubling to the laity, they sought more emotional support from the churches at a time when the clergy were engrossed in intellectual quandaries. Perhaps these very quandaries made Professor Park reluctant to develop his theology in the presence of the ladies. It was a theology that if pursued to its logical ends supported the ministry of women, credited in this society with having especially acute emotional sensitivity, a sign of higher evolution.

Situated in the aftermath of the pietist movements and in the growing romantic century, New England Congregationalists looked for religion that touched the heart. Although their primary religious experience was communal in the worship, educational, and missionary work of the church, they valued solitude and personal converse with God as well. Newman in particular loved solitude. We have seen that she had romantic

15. Works that discuss this problem at length are Schlesinger Sr. 1967, a reprint of an essay written by Schlesinger for the Massachusetts Historical Society in the 1930s; Szasz 1982; and Turner 1985.

leanings; she also lived with constant pressure from the demands of others. Although she accepted her duty, she was not a martyr. Whenever possible she went into the woods, to Pomps Pond or to Sunset Rock. She was sentimental about nature; she filled her diary books with pressed leaves and made miniature moss gardens for her room.

Newman's theology was evangelical, but since the early twentieth century, definitions of "evangelical" have shifted. In the late nineteenth century, evangelical simply meant a broadly mainline orthodox Protestantism enthusiastically concerned with spreading its churches and its culture across the world, converting individuals to its particular way of life. Today it has come to mean a more narrowly conservative version of the same project, both in terms of its interpretation of the Gospel and in its view of morality.

In addition to being the bearer of an Anglo New England culture, Newman and the other ministers educated at Andover seminary at this time became bearers of a progressive but still orthodox Protestant theology, centered in an understanding of religion as fundamentally a matter of feeling more than intellect. They were hopeful that they could contain the apparent damage done to faith by science, by allowing science to take over the realm of natural history and keep the life of the heart for religion.

Emma Newman's Decision to Preach

In August 1871, Newman was vacationing in Stratham, New Hampshire, where she had been born. A letter arrived saying that her mother was very ill and she was needed at home in Andover.

On reaching Andover, I found mother in a profuse perspiration, but thoroughly wild: she knew me, but informed me at once that our lives were in danger, and heard noises and invented people worse than ever before. No one had ever known before of her powers in this respect, and she had frightened people pretty effectually. Of course I took command, sat up giving medicine till 12 and slept fitfully in the hammock, rousing to give "two spoonfuls" occasionally. Equally of course mother objected violently to my leaving the bed, but the doctor said that no one ought to sleep with her so I insisted. Mother was tolerably good about her medicine at night, though she always represented to me forcibly that it was very weak-minded of me to insist that she should take medicine, when we should neither of us be alive by morning. (Diary, vol. 5, Aug. 24, 1871)

She tended her mother for eight days, with the help of friends and relatives, particularly the Davises who also boarded at Mrs. Beards' house. Her mother died quietly, on the morning of September 3. "That soul so long hampered and tortured by the body was free" (Diary, vol. 5, Sept. 3, 1871), and so finally was Emma. At least she would soon be free. The day after the funeral, she had to move out of her room in Mrs. Davis' house. "Providence treats me just as my mother did. If I said I was sick and could not get up, she said 'You shall' and just so I was forced through this day" (Diary, vol. 5, Sept. 6, 1871).

Her cousin Mary, who had managed the financial affairs of Newman and her mother since the death of her uncle James Cooper, assisted her with the funeral arrangements.

I was thankful that the day was pleasant, remembering the pitiless beating of the wild March storm in which my father lay down in the tomb. Cousin Mary went down town and got one or two things I wanted, a piece of bristol board for the foundation of a cross of geranium leaves, which I wanted to make myself, and a pair of black gloves. . . . Mr. Davis cut my cross and I arranged geranium leaves for it, the last thing I could do for my mother. . . . I gave myself a severe extra strain by going too early into the room, after my last look at mother's body: it did not look like my mother, and I could not enjoy seeing it. . . . Prof. Smyth read and offered one of his touching, trusting prayers full of thankfulness and confidence, and the students sang *very* well. . . . Then we rode down to the South Church cemetery and walked in among the trees to the Newman tomb, where Mr. Eldridge prayed again: he prayed for me that I might have heart and strength to do God's work: may He grant the prayer. . . . I directed that my mother's casket should be placed beside my father, looked into the tomb where I should like to lie sometime, then had to turn away: I think that was the hardest thing. . . . They sang Whittier's "With silence only as their benediction", and "Let saints below in concert sing with those to glory gone." I wanted Charles Beecher's "New Jerusalem" for the last, but there was a difficulty about the tune. (Diary, vol. 5, Sept. 5, 1871)

For Emma Newman, securing her independence involved asserting her right to manage her affairs herself. Even more than before her mother's death, she was now head of the household. The process of securing her rights to handle her own money was complicated. As a woman, even though known by the lawyer, the banker, and her relatives, she had to ask two men to guarantee her responsibility (Diary, vol. 5, Sept. 28–Nov. 9, 1871). Newman had stock certificates from the Boston and Maine Railroad, the Calais Bank, and the St. Stephen's Bank. She sold the St. Stephen's Bank shares for a little over $217.50. The Boston and Maine and Calais Bank dividends gave her a small income for many years that made her able to live in spite of the tiny salaries paid by the churches she served.

The day after her mother's funeral, Elizabeth Stuart Phelps began to urge Newman to preach. "She thinks I could manage my bad voice, but I can't tell yet" (Diary, vol. 5, Sept. 6, 1871). Both Miss Harris and Miss Phelps made plans on behalf of their friend as to what she should do now that she was free to be professionally useful. "Miss Phelps suggested that it would be a great advantage to me to have a license to preach, and planned about getting one. I should like one, but am rather hopeless about getting one from the Congregationalists" (Diary, vol. 5, Sept. 24, 1871). There were other women preaching at the time. Newman's friends in Andover knew Julia Ward Howe and the women preachers invited to preach at her house on Sunday afternoons. Her friend's proposal that she preach was not an entirely new idea. Elizabeth Phelps and Miss Harris (whose given name Newman never recorded) were daughters of Andover professors. Single and inclined to intellectual work, they were part of Newman's circle of friends. They tended to be much more liberal on questions of woman's participation in the church than their fathers. Indeed, Phelps and her father were often directly at odds with each other on the matter. Phelps earned her living writing; Harris practiced homeopathy. Although not sharing Newman's desire to move west, they insisted that she not simply go to visit relatives, but go with some useful work to do. They even encouraged her to seek a license to preach before she left, though the conservative Andover professors would be likely to fight such a move in the local association. Newman was a pragmatic woman. She was careful not to request credentials unless she had some hope of success and on more than one occasion was glad not to have been the cause of divisions among her colleagues.

In addition to urging her to preach, her friends encouraged her to study homeopathic medicine formally. Newman immediately declined that idea because of the necessity of spending three years in study.

Newman began work on her first sermon, "True Work of Life," in early October 1871, though she did not use it right away. She preached it in June 1873, in Big Woods, Illinois. It was a sermon encouraging Christians to live as if all they did was in Christ's service. She suggested that work for Christ was at hand wherever providence placed a person.

Quite apart from the audience she might address, it was a sermon reflecting on her own situation, serving to encourage her along an uncertain path. It illustrated a major component of her spirituality in its emphasis on Christian work. The Calvinist emphasis on living life to the glory of God is present in every word.

While she was working on this sermon, Elizabeth Phelps told her of a church in Alton Bay, New Hampshire that was ready to welcome "a lady preacher." Newman considered it. "If I had two sermons and a voice, I'd go, though I do not wish to settle in one of those discouraging little New England towns" (Diary, vol. 5, Oct. 25, 1871). Newman's only concern about preaching was her voice. She did not say whether her voice was weakened by her many respiratory illnesses or just naturally soft. In the same way that she had been preparing herself to write sermons and serve as a pastor by attending the seminary lectures, she prepared herself to preach by studying privately with John Wesley Churchill, the seminary's elocution professor.

Her second sermon, "Exhortation to Leave Wrong and Turn to the Right," which she preached four months later, also showed signs of her recent experience.

How many of us have watched through long, cold, dreary nights by dying friends! We know how heavily the hours move on, how sad forebodings press thicker and darker in the silent chill of midnight, how fears grow strong and faith droops, and God himself seems far away in these darkest hours before the dawn. The soul feels the langour of the body, and, life longs for the sun. Life and death seem alike sad. But the dawn begins to brighten in the east, and little glad clouds come to show where the day will soon appear. (Sermon No. 2)

She used this experience as a metaphor, locating darkness of the soul in ignorance.[16]

Light, by contrast, was contained in the lost arts of beauty in Greek culture and in the free schools of the United States. This light was especially in the spirit of Christ and in Christianity. "Faulty as we are as a nation, we are yet the beacon light for the oppressed and the suffering all over the world, because of so much of Christ as we have in us. . . . Whatever hinders the progress of His kingdom and Prevents His rule in the hearts of His creatures, does just so much to keep back our day, and make the night more gloomy" (Sermon no. 2). However, she continued, it is not enough to stop hindering the light; one must help it along. The armor of light is necessary for this, and it comes from God, not from ourselves. Newman ended the sermon with a call to faith. "Today He offers it to you. He may never offer it to you again. Will you come to Him and receive His gifts? Think of it. For you the night is far spent. Is the day at hand?" (Sermon no. 2).

This sermon would have been typical for one preached to an unknown congregation. It contained the basic message of Christianity as the mainline evangelical Protestants saw it. The whole gospel could be boiled down to the warning against darkness, ignorance, and sin, and the promise of light in Christ, and the necessity of deciding, today, to receive God's gifts.

---

16. On several occasions, Newman wrote sermons that seemed to address her own situation as much as that of her congregation. In this case, she writes a few weeks after the death of her mother, framing her experience as a dark night of the soul. Another examples of such sermons are her "Trust in Christ," and "Patience," discussed in the first chapter. Those who study suffering point out that giving voice to the experience, telling about it, and possibly finding meaning in it are part of the process of recovery. I am grateful to Michael Mendiola, professor of Ethics at Pacific School of Religion, for a conversation on his work on suffering in giving me some insight into Newman's incorporation of her own suffering into her preaching and pastoral work. Problems lie in the use of other people's suffering to explain or give meaning to one's own; however, Newman seems to have done that only rarely. "We think of human suffering not as a storehouse but as an arable field, on which some do the difficult work of plowing and planting, and others arrive just in time to enjoy the harvest. This metaphor highlights the ambivalence humans seem to have about suffering: it is dirty work, but sometimes there are spiritual profits to be gained" (Spelman 1997, 172). Newman's theological foundation rests on understanding that there are spiritual profits in all suffering, that God gives meaning to every experience, and that suffering leads to compassion in those who would truly understand the Christian experience of sacrificial love.

The sermon contains the cultural connections of this message with the United States. Though it is an imperfect nation, nineteenth-century evangelicals optimistically maintained that the light of God was manifested in the United States earlier than in other places. The sermon's conclusion would serve either Calvinist or Arminian theology. Newman included both God's free choice in giving people faith and the necessity of the believer's choice. The equation of ignorance with sin was in one sense a legacy to evangelical Protestantism from the Enlightenment, an optimism that a properly educated individual would understand. Enlightenment came through education. Early evangelical liberalism embraced this claim before the liberals and evangelicals parted company in the twentieth century over the issue of teaching Darwinism in the public schools. Still, American Protestantism has a high view of the value of a proper education in developing a Christian society.

Newman's first invitation to preach was on the way, arranged by Mr. Davis, her fellow boarder. "Mr. D. asked if I would preach at Readville where he supplies which I at once agreed to do. He said he would go and propose it and see how it would work: He thought it would be well received, and in that case, he should like me to go this vacation. This invitation, coming as soon as I am able to go anywhere, seems to me a providential indication of the way to go. May I be strengthened to walk in it" (Diary, vol. 6, Mar. 3, 1872). On Saturday, she set out for Readville, Massachusetts, to deliver her first sermon.

> I found the lecture-room a cozy little place, nearly filled with an audience of about 100. I wonder if I preached in a pre-existent state; no sense of unfitness or newness disturbed me. . . . It was all the most natural thing in the world: it was the Lord's servant who prayed for His strength, read His word, spoke His truth very simply and quietly. I had selected my simplest sermon, text Romans 13 ch 12 v. One lady came up and congratulated me, telling me that I had great reason for encouragement; I was introduced to several of the people. I asked Mrs. D. about the comparative size of the audience and she said "Sometimes they's more, and sometimes they isn't so many." One lady evidently found me funny as she smiled amusedly through the service. I was sorry that I could not do her any good, but she did not disconcert me in the least: was I not the Lord's servant? . . . In the afternoon I took off my bonnet; in the evening, as I should speak so short a time, I kept it on, but did not like it so well. (Diary, vol. 6, Mar. 24, 1872)

Here Newman describes a typical Sunday in a small New England town. The people gathered for a sermon in the morning, and a prayer meeting with a second shorter sermon in the afternoon. If there was a Sunday School it would also have been held in the afternoon. She recorded her nervousness while packing, but experienced no stage fright while preaching. She seemed remarkably self-assured for a woman in her situation. This was not an earth shattering event for Newman, but a logical outgrowth of her previous roles in society. Once she believed her call came from God, her question to the church was only where she might preach. She did not first seek permission to do it. Consequently, though she was never officially, fully recognized as a minister, she seldom lacked an opportunity to preach.

Newman's confidence was shaken the next week when she asked Mrs. Davis what the people thought of her preaching.

Found an opportunity to get Mrs. Davis' report from my sermon and found it very unfavorable. "No argument—sounded like a composition," "some good things in it," "Didn't like to hear a woman preach." One lady spoke of "such a want of humility and spirituality", another objected to my reading, yet another said that I looked round, as if to say, "Didn't I do that pretty well?" It is very clear that I failed badly; not so much it appears because of their criticisms, as because, if they had been touched with the meaning of the truth spoken, they would not have been thinking of sharp things to say about the speaker. God knows I must attend to that about my manner: I drove my own personality into the background probably too much: something was very wrong, if I made an impression like that. Surely God is strong enough to work with a very poor tool, and, as I never thought He would take me into service on any other theory, I don't think I ought to hang back because of a serious failure: it is not I but He that is to do the good, if any good is done through me. (Diary, vol. 6, Apr. 5, 1872)

A notice in the *Woman's Journal* read, "Miss Emma E. Newman, who is an Orthodox Congregationalist, preached her first sermon in Readville, Mass., on Sunday March 24th. It was well accepted" (April 6, 1872, 109). Newman commented, "I am afraid that was imagination on somebody's part" (Diary, vol. 6, Apr. 5, 1872). *Woman's Journal*, founded by Lucy Stone in Boston, regularly carried news of women preaching, as well as articles arguing in favor of woman ministers. It also carried news of woman physicians and lawyers. Newman had stopped in at the office of the journal in Boston on her way to Readville to preach. Lucy Stone greeted her, and introduced her to two other women preachers, Mary Graves, with whom Newman corresponded for many years, and Charlotte Burleigh. Stone also accepted an article from Newman, published in the same issue that carried notice of her preaching.

Emma Newman's family had their own opinions of her preaching. Her aunts in Andover laughed about it. Newman wrote, "Aunt Fay said I'd better pick up somebody to do my preaching for me, but she did not say ugly things as I had expected. It is a blessing to be perfectly independent of her" (Diary, vol. 6, Apr. 11, 1872). Her cousin Mary had no sympathy with her project of preaching and declined to help with her move west. Another cousin, Lizzie Cooper amused Newman with her comments. "I did not know that I had got to be disgraced in my own family. My Goodness! my goodness! my goodness! I have heard of things before, but—well! Cousin Emma's preaching! I think its horrid! I should think that, with doing your own sewing and the things that every lady has to do, that's sphere enough. Not such disgraceful labors as that. I should think you could find enough to do without doing *that*" ("Things in General"). Her friends were more charitable. "Miss Chickering says that, in preaching I have turned my back on my habits and followed my true nature" ("Things in General").

The transition of women's leadership in the context of the American West and the reappropriation of the household model of authority from the early church are clear patterns in the life of Emma Newman. Ann Braude's sketch of the history of women in American religion is helpful here.

> The story shifts . . . as women move toward spiritual equality with men in the colonial period, as they assume public roles because of their positions as guardians of private morality and piety during the nineteenth century, and, in the twentieth, as women exercise public moral authority first as voters and as shapers of the welfare state during the Progressive era, then as members of the ordained clergy following the rise of feminism in the 1970s. (Braude 1997, 88)

Newman's life spans both the transition to public roles in the guardianship of private morality and the transition to ordained leadership in the churches, though she personally did not receive ordination.

Emma Newman's Move West

In January 1872, Newman began to inquire into the possibilities of going west to work. She had friends in several places in the west, particularly Lizzy Emerson Humphrey in Chicago and Julia Newcomb in Missouri. Both were schoolmates of hers and both had married men in the ministry.

> The morning was enlightened by the coming of a letter from Julia, enclosing one from a leading Congregationalist of Missouri to whom Mr. Newcomb had written at my request, saying that, if I would go out there to make myself a name and character on the spot, there would be no obstacle in the way of my ordination, and adding that "the influence of such a woman for good would be just boundless." My heart was very glad, but I did want strength to start at once. (Diary, vol. 6, Jan. 3, 1872)

During June 1872, Newman packed her things preparing to move to Missouri. Toward the end of the month she traveled to Maine to visit family. The boat from Portland to Machias traveled through a thick fog. She noted her impressions in her diary. "Rose at six and found that same fog surrounded us, but it was luminous and hopeful. If I must pass my life in the fog may it be like this, luminous with the presence of the sun" (Diary, vol. 6, June 29, 1872). She had no clear view of her life in the West. She was going with no settled guarantees, trusting that God was leading her. This metaphor of the fog expressed both her reality and her hope. Still having trouble with deafness and headaches, low on money, uncertain of her reception in Missouri, she left for the West on October 14, 1872.

From October 1872 to April 1873, Newman lived with her friend Julia and Julia's husband Earle Newcomb in Missouri. She nursed Julia through an illness and looked after the Newcomb's young children. She preached for a few weeks in a town nearby and made inquiries of the home missionary superintendents for more settled work.

The issues of gender we have explored in this chapter, the roles of women in New England society, the logic of women's leadership in the church with its roots in the most ancient days of the church, and the background of romantic Evangelicalism and the new liberal theology that left cracks in the determined resistance within Congregationalism to women's preaching help in understanding the significance of Emma Newman's life. However, gender is not the only issue shaping her experience and work. The geographical difference between the West and the East is also a factor. This issue will be our next focus.

"Algonquin Needs the Gospel"

I am glad to hear that you have gone to Algonquin, and I hope
that the Providential indication may be such as will induce you
to remain there. As you say the case is not at all hopeless.
—Thain to Newman, Oct. 26, 1875

In the first chapter we looked at Emma Newman's first pastoral charge, as
she termed it. We looked closely at her work during those thirteen weeks
in the summer of 1873, and opened up several questions concerning categories of gender and geography for analyzing the experience of women
moving into the leadership of the churches in the nineteenth century. In
the second chapter we looked specifically at the category of gender, and
how the ambiguities of New England constructions of gender affected
women's self-understanding and their choices of leadership roles in the
churches. In this chapter, we will see how the freedoms and constraints of
women's lives based upon their gender in the nineteenth century inter-
acted with geographical issues in the American West to further help us understand the experience of women ministers. We will also look at ways
concepts of dependence and independence can be used to analyze the
forms that both women's lives and the churches took in the West. Finally,
through Newman's sense of her call to preach and her work in the Algonquin church,[1] we can begin to elaborate the household models of pastoral care discussed in the earlier chapters.

1. The most extensive description of Algonquin in the 1870s is found in *History of
McHenry County, Illinois* 1976, 390–95.

Geography of the Mind

In her diary entry for April 3, 1867, written at the age of twenty-nine, Emma Newman records her desire to move west some day, even as far as California. Many of her friends and relatives were making that journey. She regularly read the *Overland Monthly*, a literary journal published in San Francisco, carrying the work of Bret Harte, Mark Twain, Jack London, Mary Austin, and other western writers. Bret Harte's short stories about Gold Rush California were Newman's favorites. Already she was exposing herself to a particular geography of the mind, before she ever saw the land that gave rise to it.

In using the term *geography of the mind* here, I am combining two ideas from both older and more recent historiographical traditions. By "mind" I mean what the French *Annales* school of historiography meant by *mentalité*, that is, "mental structures that defined an array of thoughts and concepts available to a group at a certain time, delimiting the possibilities of what could be thought and understood in a culture at a certain time" (Breisach 1994, 375). Connected to this array of mental structures characteristic of the group is the power of place or geography in their shaping. A geography of the mind, then, is the constellation of the physical experience of a place, the relative ease or difficulty with which people can live there, and the roots cultural symbols have in the physical place in which they develop. Here I employ concepts of cultural region or regional state of mind from the sociological and psychological study of American culture. Raymond Gastil, in his *Cultural Regions of the United States*, outlines several criteria for defining a region, including geographic criteria of rainfall, elevation, soil type, and mineral availability; socioeconomic relationships; political boundaries; and most important in his analysis, the culture of the area from which the settled population comes (Gastil 1975, 19–37).

Newman's experience of growing up in New England in the heart of evangelical Congregationalism shaped what she expected to happen in Big Woods. A growing mythology about the American West further shaped these expectations. Like others in the home missionary movement, she had to come to terms with the discrepancy between her expectations formed in New England town life and the realities of church life in the rural Illinois frontier in order to do effective work there. Other discrepancies appeared in the shift of Congregationalism from center to periphery in the life of western frontier society. The movement from East to West called for a corresponding shift in the geography of the mind.

The two geographies of mind that are relevant for understanding Emma Newman's situation are the New England mind and the western, or specifically midwestern, mind. I mentioned the New England mind above, as Newman saw herself to be an ambassador of that culture. It was shaped by the Puritans, the Yankee merchant, and the institutions of politics and education that came to characterize the public life of the United States. New England culture rested on three pillars, according to Raymond Gastil: the town, the school, and the Congregational Church. Characteristics of the mentalité of New England included sobriety, hard work, order, self-reliance, emotional reserve, and practicality (Gastil 1975, 144–47). This was a geography of the mind born of poor soil and easy access to the sea. The seasons were sharply delineated and used in making meaning of human life.

This mentalité manifested itself in three projects: to Christianize and control the West, to reform the South, and to industrialize and capitalize the East Coast. In some measure these projects, according to Gastil, were responses to a sense of decline, or being outnumbered. The New Englander's three projects aimed at preserving the economy and way of life they had determined to be the best on earth. The home missionary movement was part of these projects.

The three pillars of New England society were found in diluted form in the West. People from New England settled Illinois in the 1840s; however, replicating these central institutions was a difficult matter (Gastil 1975, 205–20). In the Midwest, the characteristics of New England take a practical and optimistic turn. The soil is better. Rural life and family farms flourished. An additional shaping reality of the midwestern mentalité was the relative absence of Jews, except in the cities, and even fewer Southerners, except in southern Illinois and Indiana. Xenophobia became part of the midwestern mentalité, with the large influx of mostly Catholic immigrants in the nineteenth century.

A good climate for agriculture and business in the Midwest strengthened New England pragmatism. Economic success was the measure of life. Midwesterners placed a high value on technology and the consumer culture. In contrast to New England, though, larger farms scattered people over a wider area. Towns were more spread out, less unified. People moved

frequently and were less inclined to put down roots lengthening to generations. Schools, churches, and other institutions suffered from this rootless-
ness, developing necessary financial bases slowly and exiting in weakened
forms. However, as Cynthia Tucker points out in her work on the women
ministers in Iowa, the western states offered a freedom to women not found
in the East. Westerners were willing to try new ways, they gave women
more rights, and with the chronic shortage of men in the professions
needed for stable community life, women enjoyed opportunities not available to them elsewhere (Tucker 1990, 3–4). Kansas, where Newman did
most of her ministry, was among the most progressive states for women.

Newman understood her task to be shaper of New England life in the
unshaped frontier. Lyman Beecher, in his *Plea for the West* (Beecher 1835),
outlined what New Englanders considered to be grave dangers to the
American republic if the institutions of town, school, and Protestant
church were not planted as soon as the people arrived in the new western
territories. The fear of Roman Catholic influence was uppermost in the
minds of Beecher and other New Englanders, but the reputation of the
West among orthodox Congregationalists for loosened moral standards
was almost equally alarming. In addition, Congregationalists found the
spread of Unitarianism a dilution of the Puritan faith. The home missionary movement, which dotted the Midwest with Protestant churches and
fundamentally shaped the evangelical piety of the people, was a response
to this anxiety on the part of New England for these future states
(Goodykoontz 1939).

The discrepancy facing Emma Newman in Big Woods lay in the difference between the energy of this anxiety at the intellectual level in New
England and the reality of the paucity of support for its solution in the
frontier towns. Although the New England mentalité might in principle
agree to the home mission project, the vast distance between those who
decided where money would be spent and those who were doing the work
diluted the appeal. Newman herself did not recognize the difference in her
attitudes and those of the midwesterner until she arrived on the scene. The
difference in mentalité had a practical and negative effect on her work.

Newman also carried with her certain assumptions about church life
that pertained to town churches. She expected that people would be at
church twice on Sunday and in the middle of the week for prayer meetings
and aid society meetings. In a town where people lived blocks from the

church and where daily work did not depend on weather or deal in animals, this was easy. In rural churches, people traveled some distance to church and did not usually make more than one trip unless they could comfortably walk. The nature of farming made it necessary to attend to animals and crops respecting season and weather rather than the artificiality of the Sabbath Day.

One of Newman's great disappointments was the lack of educated conversation available in these rural towns. The move west diluted New England culture. Though Chicago boasted a university and several Congregational schools existed in the area, few of the parishioners in her small rural church read books. The two people essential to the New England project to civilize the West were the school teacher and the Congregational minister. In some cases, there might be a school teacher but no minister. In the situations where Emma Newman served, there was sometimes no school teacher; in those cases she carried the civilizing burden alone.

Mircea Eliade noted that "when possession of a territory begins, rites are used which connect it to the beginning of creation," so that civilization can be seen as an act of creation, an organization of "chaos into cosmos, giving it form and norms" (Eliade 1954, 9–10). This was precisely the project the Home Mission Society set for itself. The home missionary movement was part of an act of conquest as well as civilization, though Emma Newman framed the project solely as one of civilization.

The establishment of a Congregational church, like planting a cross in the ground, marked the territory of the New Englander. They saw the West as a wild land to be tamed by church and school. But in the West, Newman was dealing with people who, like her, were not well rooted in the place. The importance of place in the development of a mentalité is discussed with depth and imagination by Keith Basso in his book *Wisdom Sits in Places: Landscape and Language among the Western Apache*. "The most estimable qualities of human minds—keen and unhurried reasoning, resistance to fear and anxiety, and suppression of emotions born of hostility and pride—come into being through extended reflection on symbolic dimensions of the physical environment" (Basso 1996, 146). Whether she knew it or not, Newman or any other home missionary had to connect the people to the place in order to build an effective community—or to civilize them. Part of her sense of failure came from being unable to do this. People saw the land simply as a resource for making a living. Newman's people had not lived in their place long enough for the process of memory to do its work. Basso shows that the memories associated with place constitute the history that gives identity to the people. The recognition that memory is the source of hope places the future of a people in their mentalité, but the recognition that people's mentalité is shaped by the geography in which they live points to an additional aspect of the task of "civilization." Missionaries like Newman sought to root the constantly moving population of the West by recreating a New England soil. The school, the Congregational church, and even place names such as Andover, New Boston, Cambridge, Matherville, and Bradford in northwestern Illinois indicated the settlement of New Englanders. In a different geographical context, people hoped these features would make them feel at home. Just as they hoped to put their mark on the geography, it as surely reshaped them. Geography was not a conscious part of the home missionary's ideology, but it shaped the missionary as much as it shaped her congregation.

In this shift of geography of the mind, the move from East to West, Newman shared the experience of her male colleagues. Like them, Newman's evolution as a westerner came slowly, yet she began to feel at home in the West because it offered her freedom to carry out her vocation, and freedom from the "stifling New England town" (Diary, vol. 5, Oct. 25, 1871).

As a woman, she had an additional measure of freedom in the West. In New England, the extension of her roles as caretaker and aid society organizer into the pastoral ministry of the church would have been difficult. In the West it came naturally. There was space and need for such an extension. Because she began in the West, Newman did not seek permission to do what she did. She simply asked for a place to work, and there were many places that needed her.

Though she carried her New England presuppositions with her to the West, she adapted and stayed. The home missionary movement of which she was a part shaped the midwestern culture to a remarkable degree. Colin B. Goodykoontz in his study of home missions concluded that the Midwest has become a stronghold of fundamentalism and shows the strongest traces of Puritanism of anywhere in the country. New England individual practical piety, orthodox theology, a conservative interpretation of the Bible, and a sense that people attain goodness by the observance of certain rules of behavior all continue to be characteristic of the Protestantism of the region (Goodykoontz 1939, 425–26).

The Politics of Women's Presence as Ministers in the West

Joseph Roy, the American Home Missionary Society superintendent for Illinois, had encouraged Newman to return to Illinois when she left Big Woods in 1873. His message to her had been that "he could not tell about a place for me so far in advance, but presumed some community would have sense enough to do so good a thing as to get you" (Diary, vol. 7, Nov. 26, 1873).[2] Newman temporarily settled in Boston, pursuing further studies in homeopathic medicine and studying oratory with Wendell Phillips.

> He was everything charming as he always is and there I sat for an hour while the prince of orators talked to me concerning oratory. Sometimes in Missouri I wasn't sure whether it was I or my dog, but here I'm certain it is *I*. Mr. Phillips advised me, as his own plan, to learn extracts and be in the habit of repeating them to myself, especially long sentences requiring a variety of intonations and skill at taking breath at the right time, of which he gave me an example. . . . He said my voice ought to fill a house capable of holding 1000, advised me against outward excitement with the subject, and gave me many hints for forming extemporaneous style. . . . If I did not leave delighted, I do not know the meaning of the word. (Diary, vol. 7, Nov. 28, 1873)

In May 1874, she moved to Andover for nearly a year, living with her aunts and attending lectures at the seminary on ecclesiastical history and practical theology.

Throughout the spring and summer of 1875, Newman searched for a place to resume her pastoral work in the West. She faced a difficult task for several reasons. First were her gender and her resulting lack of clear professional credentials. Second were the economic difficulties of the time; a nationwide depression had hit Illinois farmers particularly hard. Third were the cumbersome placement structures of the Congregational churches. "Wrote to Dr. Thurston Sec. H. M. S. for Maine asking him to give me

---

2. Awkward change of person in the original. Diary, vol. 7, November 26, 1873.

work for the summer. . . . Mr. Thurston wrote me that he had already more applications for missions than fields occupied by the society; and had already been obliged to refuse sundry young men; he did not go into the vexed question at all; the facts gave him a good excuse" (Diary, vol. 8, Apr. 1, and Apr. 7, 1875). She also wrote to the home mission secretaries for Rhode Island and New Hampshire. "The H. M. S. secretary of R. I. wrote that he had no place for me, want of fields, want of funds" (Diary, vol. 8, Apr. 12, 1875).

By August 1875, even Joseph Roy's hopeful tone had changed. Newman, planning to attend a missionary conference in Chicago, had written to him letting him know she was coming. "Mr. Roy wrote, rather curtly, that he knew of no place for me" (Diary, vol. 8, Aug. 30, 1875). She tried other home mission people in the West. "Wrote to Dr. Edward Beecher, who had offered to help me when I was at Big Woods, asking his advice about coming out" (Diary vol. 7, Sept. 1, 1875). Beecher replied "with sympathy and good wishes—and no help—no fault of his but he knows of no place for me, poor me" (Diary vol. 7, Sept. 8, 1875). She also wrote to the home mission superintendent for Minnesota, "offering her services for that frozen region" (Diary vol. 7, Sept. 8, 1875). "Rec'd letter from Mr. Cobb, Superintendent H. M. for Minnesota detailing the condition of four unoccupied fields, two, however on the 'cold blast frontier' and offering to refer the question to one of them for decision *if I had received a license*. Sat down and wrote Mr. C. copying my certificate, and protesting against condition of the license" (Diary vol. 9, Sept. 17, 1875). Newman's search for a place reveals much about the West and about the official prospects for women. We will consider the economic factors later, but the issue of professional credentials needs discussion at this point, and requires that we go back in Newman's story to the months before her invitation to preach in Big Woods for the summer of 1873.

The certificate Newman had to copy for Cobb, the Minnesota Home Mission superintendent, was a letter from three members of the Chicago Association, given to her when she was called to the Big Woods church for the summer, stating that they did not mind if she preached. It was not an officially recognized license, because the association had not voted approving her work. The story of the meeting in which the letter was granted reveals the beginnings of a change in thinking in the Congregational churches regarding the role of women in the church. In several American

Protestant denominations, most notably the Universalist, the Congregational, and the Christian, the West provided a venue for early debates regarding the licensing and ordination of women. Though little in the formal discussions of Newman's status showed consciousness of the geographical factors, the results have the telling marks of geographical concerns. Issues of gender and geography met in these denominational discussions and are hard to separate.

In April 1873, Emma Newman was in Chicago visiting her friend Elizabeth Humphrey, whose husband was an official of the American Board of Commissioners of Foreign Missions. On Sunday, April 20, the Humphrey's invited Joseph Roy to call after church. "Mr. Roy H. M. Sec. for the state . . . walked home from church with me, and talked over my plans a little. He advised me to apply for license and I suppose it is best for me to do so" (Diary, vol. 7, Apr. 20, 1873). Roy, as home mission superintendent, was responsible for supplying the Congregational churches in this rapidly growing state with ministers at the least expense to the Home Missionary Society. Newman was an attractive candidate, willing and not requiring a large salary. "He came in, later in the day with Mr. Huntington, pastor here, who urged me to preach in the evening, but my cold absolutely prevented, had there been no other reason" (Diary, vol. 7, Apr. 20, 1873). Newman pondered for several days whether or not she should apply for a license when the Chicago Association met later in the month. She preached at Mr. Huntington's church the next Sunday and studied Edward Amasa Park's theology, as she said, "getting my own theological notions in position for an examination, in case I should apply for license" (Diary, vol. 7, Apr. 24, 1873).

The sermon she used was one we know to be one of her favorites, "The Touch of Christ." She preached it for the third time here in Oak Park, and we discussed her fourth use of it in chapter 1, when she used it in Big Woods on July 19, 1873. It contained the basic outlines of her theological point of view, and would have been a good sermon to use when it might be judged by an association thinking of licensing her. Huntington's Oak Park church was one of the largest and most influential in the Chicago Association. Newman's themes of covenant, healing, the love of God, and the need of the individual for a decision to respond affirmatively to God's offer of healing and help were basic themes in orthodox, evangelical Congregationalism in the 1870s. The association could have no argument with her theology.

She consulted other acquaintances regarding not only her own qualifications, but also the possibilities for acceptance or rejection.

Went in to Chicago on the early train to see a Mrs. Smith, wife of one of the city ministers, hoping she would be able to tell me about the different members of the Chicago Association so that I could decide on my prospects. Mrs. S. was very cordial and pleasant, but she did not know the people well enough to tell me what I wanted to know. . . . Called on Mr. Huntington and wife. Mr. H. advised me to make the application for license, said that the association would license a man in my place.[3] Mr. H. went over with me for an interview with Mr. Roy, and the two gentlemen checked off names of the members of the Chicago Association so far as they knew them, and came to the conclusion that the majority would probably be against me. In that state of things, I declined to apply. (Diary, vol. 7, May 6–8, 1873)

But she did continue to think about doing so. The Chicago Association met in Blue Island, about twenty-five miles south of Chicago, on May 13, 1873. The people assembled included clergy, seminary professors from Chicago Theological Seminary, and lay people. On the way to the association meeting, Newman had favorable conversations about her application and left it to Roy to decide whether to present it.

Mr. Huntington proved to be chairman of [the business committee], and my application approved in its report: nothing of special interest came before it except a case of a student who had been licensed a year ago by the association: the professors coolly asserted that he was not a proper person to receive a license which sounded impudent towards that body. Mr. Huntington moved that I should be examined, motion seconded by Mr. Smith followed by a speech in favor by Mr. Roy, who as well as Mr. H. spoke in praise of my sermon at Oak Park. Mr. Bascom, an old gentleman, said he felt like the Jews when they heard that the spirit had been poured out upon the Gentiles also; his habits of thought were against the new movement, but we need workers, and it is only a question of formal sanction of what is being done. Prof. Fiske said we could not shirk the question: the scripture argument is against it, he

3. Although formal education in a theological seminary was quickly becoming a requirement for ordination, it was not yet a universal practice among Congregational churches. Licenses are still granted to men and women who have not completed formal educational requirements and yet are called as pastors.

would not license wife or sister, yet thanked God for what women do (in spite of him). He introduced an amendment "In the judgment of this association it is not well to enter on examination of the candidate." Prof. Boardman agreed and said he would as soon vote to abrogate the ten commandments as to license a woman; did not want the motion voted on at all. . . . A middle-aged man thought the movement unwise; the professors did not like it (!): it introduces a divisive element. Mr. Smith asked which is more divisive, free discussion or the action of several brothers who invite women into their pulpits—a private approbation. Prof. Fiske said that action was irregular. . . . (Mr. W. observes that if his women have anything to say in meeting, they speak; if they haven't, they keep still): somebody adds sotto voce "That's more than the men do." . . . Chamberlain said there was no logic on the part of the opposition, no reason for stopping a woman at any one point, no reason for not licensing one whom they would all allow the 3 gentlemen to indorse: still could not vote without consulting his church, which he thought himself to represent. . . . Mr. Holyoak (a small man fussy like a humble-bee) said he would not be connected with an ecclesiastical body that voted to license a woman (Mr. Roy observed in the evening that that was a big speech from a man whose wife was the better man of the two.) Mr. Packard said we are not opening the door to an extensive inroad, the exceptions will be those that preach: why will we not license as ministers, those whose sermons we approve as men: there is an anachronism in obeying Paul's direction to the early churches. Mr. Wm. A. Bartlett says the day is too far gone to carry out simple sex-distinction: Paul worrys him, he never established S. S.: Theological seminaries are the baggage-trains and must move up to the van of the army: it is time for the professors to reconcile Paul with facts: We have the approval of God on women's preaching down to date, the latest bulletin, and they must tinker Paul to suit that. . . . Vote on Prof. Fiske's amendment; tie in the association 11 to 11, moderator's vote killed the amendment. There was an attempt to put off the vote till the last of the afternoon checked by Mr. Huntington who knew I was anxious to return at night. Prof. Boardman tried to stave off the question as revolutionary and was answered by Mr. Smith and Mr. H., then introduced a resolution laying it on the table for 6 months, till the next meeting, which was carried, some of my friends voting for it. . . . Profs. Boardman and Fiske spoke courteously to me and were anxious to show that they had no prejudice against me: indeed the whole discussion had been kept on the broad ground where it belonged, and there was very little personal in it, nothing unpleasantly so. It was a fair discussion, and I like my fellow men of the Chicago Association, had a pleasant chat with some of them coming back in the cars. (Diary, vol. 7, May 13, 1873)

Newman was apparently left with the letter from Mr. Roy, Mr. Huntington, and Mr. Humphrey.

The practical question raised by Mr. Bascom, "whose habits of thought were against the new movement, but we need workers," and echoed in Moses Smith's comment that there was "no harm in sanctioning what she has already been doing," indicate that important issues were at stake and were not all theological. Geography became a critical factor in their decision whether or not to abrogate a traditional prohibition in Christianity. Few men were willing to serve marginal frontier churches where the salaries were small and the future uncertain. The decline of male population in New England (the center of these men's religious tradition) after the Civil War and the continual exodus of men to the West left plenty of eastern pulpits available for male ministers. Those men who were turned away from the home mission fields in Maine or New Hampshire did not have to look far for work in fairly comfortable situations.

In Illinois it was a different story. Male ministers avoided the marginal situations in the West. The fact that Newman had not actually completed a degree from the Andover Theological Seminary was not a difficulty, either. In this era, Congregationalists expected a pastor to be well educated, but a person could acquire that education by wide reading and private study. The Chicago Association was reluctant to discourage a willing and able worker too much, but neither did they want to be the first to license a woman.

Two aspects of the discussion were indicative of the theological developments of the 1870s, the debate about interpreting Paul and the argument that women should be licensed because they are needed. Until the mid–nineteenth century there was a broad consensus among the orthodox (read Trinitarian) evangelical churches in the United States regarding the interpretation of the Bible. In the 1870s, the consensus began to break down as historical criticism and the evolutionary theories of Darwin took their toll on the easy literalism of the early nineteenth century.[4] The call among some present at the meeting to be up-to-date in thinking about the matter was evidence of their basic agreement with the modern interpretation of the Bible.

However, there was another, older, layer to the discussion. In this de-

4. An especially helpful work on this subject is Marsden 1980.

bate among people of a Calvinist tradition, Calvin's views on the Bible and cultural forms were evident. That Calvin viewed certain parts of scripture, particularly certain matters discussed in Paul, as culturally conditioned and relevant to Paul's time but not necessarily other times, was known to most present. The debate was simply over whether Paul's prohibitions of women speaking in church were to be considered a matter for Paul's time but not our own, or applicable to all times. Calvin placed women's public preaching in the realm of human governance, leaving the question open (Douglass 1984, 172). Eventually, the ordination of women became a marker signaling a denomination's position in the debates over modernism.[5]

Actually, a Congregational woman had been ordained before this, as had a few women in other denominations. The Quakers and Universalists were particularly open to the ministry of women, and most women ministers belonged to one of these groups. The Unitarians[6] also had a few women ministers. Methodist churches licensed women but did not ordain them. Exact numbers are difficult to determine because not many of these churches kept detailed records, and some left women off the official lists. The United States Census reported a few female "clergymen" in each census, but it is impossible to tell anything more about them than that they understood and reported themselves in this way.

The South Butler Church, an orthodox Congregational church in New York, had ordained Antoinette Brown in 1853, the first known Congregational ordination of a woman. They acted on their own authority as a congregation, without the usual approval of the local association of churches. Although in Congregational church polity the congregation authorizes and can ordain its own ministry, that ministry is not recognized by any

5. In his concluding statement of this sociological study of formal denominational policies regarding women's ordination, Chaves (1997, 192) points out that "rules about women's ordination largely serve as symbolic display to the outside world, and they point to (or away from) a broader liberal agenda associated with modernity and religious accommodation to the spirit of the age." Chaves also points out that a denomination's official policies regarding the ordination of women often have little to do with the actual practices within that denomination.

6. The Unitarian and Orthodox Congregational Churches shared a common history, but by the 1820s had parted theological company sufficiently to be considered separate denominations.

other church unless the authorization is approved by a larger body of neighboring churches.[7] Brown's ordination was never approved by any wider body. From 1853 to 1873, the Congregational church had not officially authorized any other woman's ministry, though Newman and a few other women did some preaching.[8]

In neighboring Iowa at about the same time, the Unitarians faced a similar debate over women who presented themselves as candidates for ordination, and geographial factors proved to be important in the decision. "As the general missionary officer, [Jenkin Lloyd] Jones had cause enough to encourage these eager women in the 1870s, when it was almost impossible to get any male clergy to come to work in his district" (Tucker 1990,

7. Antoinette Brown's ordination actually followed an irregular pattern, but it was not contested by the association to which her church belonged. It was simply not recognized as valid outside her own congregation. Henry Martin Dexter, whose manual on Congregational procedure set the standard for the process of ordination during the last decades of the nineteenth century, explains the reason why congregations normally did not act as the South Butler church had acted on its own: "Extraordinaries excepted, the neighboring churches should first of all be invited to constitute this Council [to ordain a pastor], because from their position they must bear the chief weight of the new fellowship. This Council, when assembled will look over all records and correspondence of church and pastor-elect, with any further documentary or other facts bearing upon the regularity of action thus far taken. If satisfied as to this, the Council will next examine the candidate: (1) as to his good standing in the Christian church, and his intention to become a member of the particular church which has called him—if he have not already become such; (2) as to his approval as a preacher of the gospel at the hands of some competent body; (3) as to his evidence of past fidelity and present good standing, if he has already served in the ministry of the Word; (4) as to his religious experience and the purity of the motives for his entrance upon, or continuance in, the sacred office; and (5) as to the soundness of his theological faith, the sufficiency of his literary culture, and the reasonable probabilities of his success in the position to which he has been called" (Dexter 1880, 99). The ordination of a woman would have been an extraordinary occasion, and the openness of Congregational polity to this kind of exception allowed it to be among the first American Protestant denominations to ordain women, though it did not officially declare itself open to such ordinations until the latter part of the century.

8. By 1873, six American Protestant denominations had ordained at least one woman: the Congregationalists and the Universalist Church of America, 1863; the Christian Church (General Convention) 1867; and the American Unitarian Association, 1871, all ordained women first by a congregational action alone, though unopposed by any formal action. The Adventist Christian Church, 1860, and the Salvation Army, 1870, included provision for the ordination of women in their founding documents (Chavez 1997, 16).

21). In 1875, again seeking a church where she might preach, Newman asked an association to consider her for a license, this time the Elgin Association. She visited her Big Woods church and obtained from them a paper giving her a reference about her work there. "Big Woods voted to join the Elgin Conference,[9] and Mr. Coffin thinks I might have a chance for a license, if I were to apply for one there. . . . Mr. C. had tried two of the ministers on the woman question, found both on the fence, but, on the whole, advised my going—decided to go" (Diary, vol. 9, Oct. 10–11, 1875). The association meeting was held in Huntley, about forty-five miles northwest of Chicago.

> Pres. B. [Blanchard of Wheaton College] had told me that he could not vote for me, but would not oppose; he moved the reference of the whole matter to a special committee: he was made one of the committee, but, Mr. Coffin being also on it, I have some hope. The committee brought in a report declining to express opinion on the main question, but recommending me personally, and the case was quashed for this time. They asked me to speak, wishing to know whom they were recommending, and I just spoke wretchedly, I was vexed with myself for doing so badly. However, I carried my audience: they cried, and they would have given me the license in a moment if I had had any one to put the motion. Pres. Blanchard is wise in his generation: he rose at once and began to praise me and my work at Big Woods; he called me, "this *dear* child", with melting emphasis, he said that he could hardly keep the tears out of his eyes when he looked at me, and he told the association that it would be an act of positive cruelty to put me, so frail, delicate and nervous, into the pastorate. The report of the committee was accepted. The moderator walked to the depot with me and assured me that if the issue had been squarely put, I should have had a large majority: I am sure of it, from the appearance of the men. (Diary, vol. 9, Oct. 13, 1875)

Newman received their letter a few days later. Though again it was not an official license, it did represent the approval of the whole Elgin Associa-

---

9. In the following diary entries, "conference" and "association" are both used with regard to this body. The action of granting a license is properly the business of an association, and Newman's later entries refer to the Elgin Association, so that I assume the word conference used here refers to the same body.

tion and not simply three members. "It was made clear to me that I was to stay in the West and I decided accordingly. I do not know where or how I am to stay" (Diary, vol. 9, Oct. 1875). Though Congregationalists prided themselves on their independence, in the East their long-standing customary procedures would have precluded an innovation such as this. The western associations were newly formed and changing rapidly. The presence of the Home Missionary Society complicated their deliberations and exerted influence by means of its power to withdraw support from the churches. Consequently, such unusual arrangements as this letter authorizing Newman to preach were common means of getting things done despite dilemmas about official policy. There are three differences between this application for a license and her 1873 attempt. In this meeting she was asked to speak, and it made a difference. The debate was not kept on a theoretical plain, but the people took her self into consideration. In this meeting she was also given a letter rather than a license, but this one was voted by the whole association, not just on the personal recommendations of three of its members. Also in this meeting there was orchestrated opposition from Blanchard which effectively prevented discussion of the issue. Twice he rose quickly to shape the process, once in proposing the committee and the second time to steer the discussion of Newman's account of herself. Apparently, the opposition in the group was much less than that in the Chicago group two years before, but they had a keen political strategist in their camp.

Newman did not have to wait long for a call to a church. "At night Mr. Humphrey brought me a request from Messrs. Brewster and Coffin, endorsed by Mr. Roy, that I should go to Algonquin next Sunday; Mr. Roy adding that it was a run-down church, and that, if I could bring it up I should do more than the men preachers had done. God help" (Diary, vol. 9, Oct. 19, 1875). She began her work at Algonquin the next week.

Algonquin

Emma Newman served the Algonquin church from October 1875 until June 1876, when the deacons voted to close the church. The town lies on the Fox River, about forty miles northwest of Chicago. Farming and stock raising formed the backbone of the economy, and it was a shipping point for dairy products. The river provided power to several grist and saw mills. Ambrose Dodd had started the Congregational church in 1850, in his home. He was still deacon when Newman became pastor. In 1866, the congregation began building a frame church building seating about two hundred, and by 1875, was still weighed down by the financial obligations connected to its construction. In fact, the congregation had not been able to raise a salary for a pastor since the building was dedicated in 1868 (*History of McHenry County, Illinois* 1976, 394). Between 1868 and 1875, two pastors had served short terms at half salary. Much of that time the church had been without a pastor. In 1875, the church reported nineteen members and seventy-five people in its Sabbath School (General Association of Illinois 1876, 62). Algonquin also had an Episcopalian church, a congregation of Free Methodists, and some Lutherans.

Newman's first encounter with the Algonquin church people confirmed the picture Joseph Roy had given her beforehand. Meeting with one of the deacons she formed this assessment: "Dea[con] H[ubbard] spent the evening and we talked over the affairs of a very discouraged church, burdened with a debt of over $1000, and dead as a door-nail. . . . Church members 20, 4 to be depended on, 5 who ought to be out of it; no preaching for a year, because they cannot raise $300, which is all they ever pay" (Diary, vol. 9, Oct. 22, 1875). She spent the next day calling on other church members. "These calls involved some hard walking but it was pleasant on the hills above the Fox River" (Diary, vol. 9, Oct. 23, 1875). She visited Mrs. Hubbard, Mrs. Harbeck, and Deacon Dodd, finding everyone discouraged about the church, "Mrs. Dodd most of all." Her first visits were to the influential women of the congregation, the wives of the deacons. In an era where women were decidedly in the majority in almost every congregation but were barred from official offices, they exercised their influence indirectly through their relationships. It was important to Newman that these women were as discouraged as their husbands were, perhaps more so. Mrs. Dodd's pessimism would prove a powerful factor in Newman's increasing sense of failure at Algonquin.

Her congregation that Sunday numbered thirty-five in the morning and some two hundred in the evening. "Preached, in morn on the touch of Christ to about 35, rather a hard audience, but the Holy Spirit was there and there were some silences that meant much. . . . Extemporized in eve on the strength of the Lord, and held a promise meeting after: about 200 present, but the meeting dragged, it was only by putting my own vitality behind it, that it moved at all well. May the Lord bless the work" (Diary, vol. 9, Oct. 24, 1875). The "Touch of Christ" sermon was, as we have seen, one of her favorites. This was her sixth use of it. The morning meeting was the smaller of the Sunday gatherings. The staunch members of the church and those living close by came to church in the morning. With these people, Newman wanted to establish her theological point of view and her sense of hope for the future.

More people came to the evening service. Added to the morning people were the farmers who had finished their work and those living farther away who had time to travel to church.

Her sermon for the evening, "The Strength of the Lord" (Sermon no. 6), was another of Newman's favorites. The text was Ephesians 6:16, "Finally be strong in the strength of the Lord. Put on the whole armor of God" (AV). She also used the story of David and Goliath from 1 Samuel 17.

Newman used two methods of delivering sermons, reading a full manuscript, and extemporizing or working from a short outline, speaking informally or directly to the congregation. She extemporized this particular evening and apparently never wrote out a full manuscript for the sermon, though she used it many times.

She began the sermon by pointing out that Paul was writing to "an insignificant, despised little church," but that just as Christianity has become the religion of "all strong nations," the strength of the Lord comes in the long run even to such a small church. She went on to ask what the strength of the Lord was for. It was to do right.

> Many remain in a state of suspended development, always asking that life shall furnish what they want. They demand that others shall yield tastes, preferences, principles even to the ruling self: of course, others refuse, and there is friction, storm, unhappiness; the most selfish are the most unhappy. . . . We see this is not the true theory of life: it does not work.
>
> If we may not live for ourselves, what shall we live for? Christ. (Sermon no. 6)

She closed the sermon with Elizabeth Barrett Browning's poem "Work."

This was a morale-building sermon. It might refer to the individual life, but she meant it for the church's life as well, as discouraged small churches needed to take heart, ask for strength from God, and to do Christ's will. With it she used positive, action-oriented hymns such as "Soldiers of Christ Arise," "A Charge to Keep I Have," "Jesus My Strength My Life," and "Awake My Soul Stretch Every Nerve." These hymns had a strong rhythm if sung properly and served to invigorate a congregation before hearing the sermon. Still, this Sunday in Algonquin, she felt she had to supply all the energy while she preached for a meeting of two hundred people.

The next day, the church members met to decide whether they could afford a minister. Newman's report of the meeting revealed the internal workings of the church and some of the financial issues they faced.

> It poured in eve and only 4 came to church meeting. Dea. Dodd threw very cold water said he paid the last minister he invited from his own pocket and should not ask another till he felt able to do it again. Mr. Hubbard Jr., Mrs. Kerne and Miss Seeber were not quite so discouraged, though they hardly saw where hope was to come from. I told them my plan that, if they could get two rich men to guarantee $75 for each of the two first quarters of the year, I would do it myself for the last two, that is, I would take what they could give. They wanted me to stay and they agreed to try; I had suggested Mr. Huntley and Mr. Coffin as the sureties, and they appointed Miss Seeber to visit Mr. H. with me. (Diary, vol. 9, Oct. 25, 1875)

The prior history of the congregation suggests that Deacon Dodd felt himself to be personally responsible for the church. He started the church, paid the minister's salary, and decided who the minister would be. Understandably, he was discouraged. His wife's pessimism was also evident. However, there were others in the church—Newman mentioned two other women here—who were not so discouraged; and there were other members with money to pay the salary. One of the optimistic ones, Miss Seeber, a school teacher, was delegated along with Newman to visit Mr. Huntley. Two single women took the financial and pastoral matters of the church in hand.

After Newman agreed to stay at the Algonquin church Alexander Thain, a neighboring minister and one of her supporters in the association, wrote her an encouraging letter.

Dear Sister,

Some encouraging features of the case are these—

1. Algonquin needs the gospel.

2. The ground is not preoccupied.[10]

3. The people attend church quite well when there is a regular service.

4. There is a large number of young people in the place.

5. I am quite sure that the people in general will receive a lady speaker favorably.

The only difficulty I suppose will be the financial one; and if you can gain the favor and confidence of the people that can easily be overcome. The church is not able but the community is. . . . Although the letter I sent you denies to you the *title of Pastor* yet there is more need of pastoral work at Algonquin than of preaching; and if you go there I hope that you will engage in such work.

I would say to you then—since you ask advice. Be of good Courage, and go forward. Use great plainness of speech in the Word—for they need it and will bear it.

If I can be of any assistance to you at any time feel free to ask me.

Truly Yours

A. R. Thain (Thain to Newman, Oct. 26, 1875)

Newman and Seeber made their way over eight miles to Huntley's house. He readily agreed to guarantee the first quarter's salary. Newman was satisfied. "That settled me for a year," she wrote in her diary. She moved to Algonquin, lodging with the Tillotsons but without board provided. She ate dinner with the Hubbards nearby, but most of the time cooked for herself: beef tea, boiled potatoes and eggs, apples, nuts, bread and butter, and occasionally fish that she caught herself from the Fox River. The room was cold. Someone regularly stole her wood. The scant food and cold room caused problems for her health, especially causing upper respiratory ailments.

The cold rooms were matched by a cold church. Sunday after Sunday she made arrangements for starting the fire in the church early. Each time

10. This meant there were no other denominations active in the area with which the Congregationalists had friendly relations. If they had had a church there, the Congregationalists would have been more reluctant to compete. The Free Methodists, however, differed so much in theology and polity that the Congregationalists, believing there was a clear difference and that they had the superior form, would try to stay. There was a Free Methodist church meeting in the same church building and Newman could not avoid the problems of competition, as well as the need to cooperate with them.

the person responsible forgot, and Newman preached in a cold room. People sometimes left the service before it was over because of the cold. The lack of fire was not only in the stove. Though often more than a hundred people came to church, there was no fire in their hearts that she could detect. On Thanksgiving Day, no one came. She had assumed there would be a service and had not thought to give a special announcement of it. Thanksgiving Day was the most Congregational of all traditional American holy days. These Congregational people were far from their Pilgrim roots and had been neglected too long.

Two or three at a time, Newman visited the people in her congregation. She visited the neighboring people who were not part of the church but whose children were in the Sabbath School, or those who attended occasionally. In the first months she concentrated her visits among those church members she considered excommunicating.

The question of who belonged in the church and who did not was a difficult matter to judge. The Puritan heritage of the Congregational churches led Newman to take the criteria for church membership with the utmost seriousness. Because the original impetus for the Puritan movement in the sixteenth and seventeenth centuries was in part a reaction to the corruption of the church by its ties to the state, for Newman to simply recognize anyone in the community who was baptized and confirmed as a member of the church was problematic.

In the Puritan ideal, the church was the community of the baptized who could give a convincing account of their conversion and also lived their outward life in a recognizably Christian way. In the early years of the Puritan movement, strict standards for conversion and upright life were the norm, but over the next two centuries they became diluted.

Still, Newman expected several things from anyone who claimed to be a church member. She expected above all a particular style of life that included church attendance, prayer, work for the good of the church, the community, and other individuals. She also expected those who called themselves Christians to abstain from activities she and her fellow evangelical Protestants considered to be frivolous or destructive, such as dancing and drinking alcohol.[11]

11. Note that Emma Newman was not an advocate of total abstinence because she mixed her own medicines in alcoholic drinks under certain circumstances.

Concern about church discipline, though generally waning, was particularly lively among Congregationalists that year. The year before, a well-publicized ecclesiastical council in Brookline, New York, considered a case of a member who complained that he had been dropped from his church's membership without cause. Dropping members was less painful than excommunicating them, but the effect was the same. The Brookline Council of 1874, taking a traditional Congregational view, advised that "the idea of membership in a Congregational church is the idea of a covenant between the individual member and the church." According to this council, absence alone did not dissolve the covenant, but any scandalous behavior certainly would (Dexter 1880, 109).

One of Newman's priorities then, as she began her visits to all the church members, was meeting with the four people who she believed were candidates for excommunication. Nowhere in Newman's diary, or in other extant information about the church, is the behavior of any of these people discussed in detail. They may simply have never come to church.

On November 17, a windy day, she visited Lyman Haskins and his daughter, "two of our bad church members, a sad little call, of course only an introduction as I had never seen either of them before" (Diary vol. 9 Nov. 17, 1875). Two weeks later, with a committee of church members, she called on the other "recusant" members of the church, Mrs. Cleveland and Mrs. Adams, as well as paying a second visit to Mr. Haskins. Cleveland declared that she intended to leave the church. In Newman's opinion, "she had never been a Christian." Haskins gave an excuse of his conduct, but Newman noted that "he told one very direct lie, to my knowledge." Mrs. Adams "was violently angry, on hearing that she had been complained against; she will certainly make no confession: I do not think any of them will stand trial" (Diary, vol. 9, Dec. 2, 1875). On December 4, a church meeting of six members voted to excommunicate Mrs. Cleveland, Mr. Haskins, and Mr. Adams. Later that week, Mrs. Adams was voted out by a meeting of ten of the seventeen remaining church members. With repentance and reform of their behavior, they could be readmitted to the congregation. However, their names did not reappear in Newman's diary.

The membership of the congregation (those considered to be in the covenant) numbered about 10 percent of the usual Sunday attendance of one or two hundred. Consequently, the large majority of her congregation would never be subject to such an action, because they did not pledge themselves to the strict standards of church membership.

The dismissal of four members of the congregation came just before a communion service. This was in keeping with the primary theological understanding of Congregational church membership, as those in communion with one another under the rubrics of shared doctrinal teachings and understandings of Christian life. Dexter's *Handbook of Congregationalism*, which Newman followed, stipulated that communion was reserved for those who were members in good standing (Dexter 1880, 85).

In centuries past, where Christianity was also the state religion, excommunication could be a significant threat to an individual's personal welfare. In close-knit communities with long common histories, excommunication could disrupt the social relationships of an individual. In the new and almost unformed communities of the American Midwest, the meaning of excommunication was less clear. Theoretically, from the point of view of the other church members, these people were barred not only from the sacrament of communion, but also from other privileges of the church such as burial in the church cemetery, having one's children baptized, or being married in the church. With three other churches in the neighborhood of differing doctrines and standards, those dismissed would probably not suffer a hardship because, if they valued the sacraments of the church, they could seek these elsewhere.

Three other churches competed with the Congregationalists for the two thousand souls of Algonquin in the 1870s. The Protestant Episcopal church, St. Johns, was the oldest congregation in town. A Lutheran church had seventeen members and served the German population in the area. The Free Methodist society was organized in 1874, a new group with twenty-one members. They had at first used the Congregational church building, but some time in 1874 "were forbidden further use by Rev. Hall."[12] They were again allowed to use the Congregational church in the fall of 1875, when Newman was there. There was ill-will between the Free Methodists and the Congregationalists left from the previous year. In addition, several members of her congregation also found the Free Methodist services interesting and divided their attention between the two.

---

12. However, Rev. Hall was not pastor in 1874—he was the first minister and served in the 1850s (*History of McHenry County, Illinois* 1976, 393–94).

The essential difficulty between the Free Methodists and Congregationalists had to do with sharing the church building—who would have it for the popular customary times and who would have to meet at another time. The Congregationalists owned the building, but were in debt and needed the income from renting the building to another church. The Free Methodists pressed for having their church in the evening, the time when they could expect the largest attendance. Newman found her own congregation divided on the matter.

> Talked with [Deacon] Hubbard at the close of the meeting, he refused to come to church-meeting, said that he had not expected that our meetings would prosper as we showed such want of union feeling, and that my action refusing to give up the church to them on Sunday nights would result in breaking up the Congregational church: that was a cruel speech and kept me awake most of the night—that is the new superintendent [of the Sabbath School], the man I must try to work with for the next six months. (Diary, vol. 9, Apr. 14, 1876)

Mrs. Hubbard, the deacon's wife, said the next day that she would be attending the Free Methodist class. She was one of several people who seemed to have a more fluid sense of denominational boundaries than Newman had. I believe the denominations' failure to provide continuity in pastoral care fostered this fluidity of boundaries. The people went where they could get what they wanted or needed, preaching, education, and solace. Over time, as ministers came and went almost as frequently as the people themselves, the people lost their loyalty to a particular denomination. Theological differences gave way to practical necessity in the minds of the laity.

In Algonquin, two churches, the Episcopal and the Lutheran, maintained stronger denominational boundaries than the others. Their members rarely appeared in Newman's church, nor did her members attend their services. In contrast, there was extensive exchange between the Congregational and Free Methodist churches. While clear differences in liturgical style separated these two groups, social factors played a part in the strength or weakness of boundaries. Newman only once mentioned the Episcopal church, on a Pentecost Sunday morning when a baptism there left her with only ten in her congregation (Diary, vol. 9, May 28,

1876). That same afternoon, the Free Methodists also held a baptism, by immersion in the mill stream. "No meeting in eve on account of an immersion last of the afternoon, by the Free Methodists. I went with Miss Goodson, a rude crowd, baptism close to mill and generally uncouth surroundings, marred the effect, still there was an effect" (Diary, vol. 9, May 28, 1876). Newman's opinion of the Free Methodists, their minister not well versed in the Bible, the baptism in uncouth surroundings with a rough crowd, revealed the division she intended between her church and theirs. Earlier in January, she insisted that the people not "stamp" in response to a temperance speaker.[13] Her purpose was to impart some middle-class respectability along with Christian faith. Whether her congregation shared her cultural view is another question.

Many in Newman's congregation crossed the line easily between the Congregational and the Free Methodist churches, suggesting that they shared cultural norms based on class to a greater degree than they attended to theological differences. Historians of Algonquin and McHenry County have not said much about its economic character. My guess is that the mill owners attended the Episcopal Church and the less prosperous but still well-educated middle-class people attended the Congregational or Lutheran churches, and that the Free Methodists attracted the working class. Quite apart from class interests, people would go to church where their friends were and avoid churches where they did not feel welcome.

The Lutheran church was separated from the others by a strong ethnic and language boundary in addition to any class or theological factors. Consequently, though the Congregationalists also shared their building with the Lutherans, there was no conflict between those groups.

From the records in Newman's diary, one gathers that the most disturbance came from a group within her own congregation. Newman referred to them as "the boys." A group of young men attended her services regularly and were noisy and disruptive. Within a month of their first appearance, she wrote, "The boys behaved badly, no worse than usual, but I will check it—stopped in the middle of sermon and prayed for them" (Diary, vol. 9, Dec. 19, 1875).[14] The next day she asked Constable Snooks to come

13. "I had so strongly insisted that they should not stamp, that they did not dare to applaud at all, till the last, and then I led off in a clap" (Diary, vol. 9, Jan. 10, 1876).

14. Her congregation numbered 175 that evening (Diary, vol. 9, Dec. 19, 1875).

to the next meeting to "keep the peace." "Meeting in eve would . . . have been small, had not the Free Methodist minister failed: some 50 young men filed in looking ripe for fun. I prayed for help and went on; those boys gave good attention; they have never behaved so well since I have been here. Dea. Dodd says that Mr. Andrews wrote a very severe letter to Sq. Philp about their actions, and Mr. P. told him (Dea. D.) that he did not uphold the boys in it. 100 present" (Diary, vol. 9, Dec. 26, 1875). Newman had trouble keeping the boys quiet, but wanted them in church because they needed religious teaching.

During the winter, with the cold and the noise, the attendance at church dwindled. Deacon Dodd became discouraged. Newman wrote:

> This time the key to the church was broken, nobody found it out till time for meeting, and the fire was about as effective as last Sunday, I spoke on the happiness of Christian living to 12 people at first about 6 at last; my boys vanished from meeting, and did not appear in S. S. I asked *the* deacon to come in, but he was blue and bitter and said he meant to leave the church he thought he should get more peace at home, and could do just as much good. Preached to a very uproarious, not very large audience, on God's forgiveness. (Diary, vol. 9, Jan. 23, 1876)

In February, she again reported in her diary that "the church was cold and ruled by boys." Several in the congregation left in the middle of the service. When she left Algonquin in June, the boys were still a problem for her and for the church.

Newman was not the only frontier preacher to report difficulties with unruly congregations of mostly single young men. Many tall tales told about frontier preachers suggest that such rough audiences were common. In the 1870s, the population of Illinois was young, male, and largely single.[15] There are old stories of Peter Cartwright, the Methodist pioneer, preaching with a rifle across the pulpit. Sherlock Bristol, in his published memoirs, tells of successfully thwarting an attempt to break up his meeting. Though he appeared to have handled the situation by oratory alone,

15. In 1870, in Illinois, 56 percent of the population was male, 76 percent was under thirty, and still in 1890, over half the men and women in the state were single (U.S. Department of the Interior, Census Office, 1873, 2; 1895, 1:1).

there is a hint of coercion at the end of the story. "I had one hand in an overcoat pocket, and possibly they thought it had hold of something there" (Bristol 1989, 123–25).

But Newman's male colleagues who preached in her pulpit during the revival and when the congregation had communion did not experience such harassment. I conclude therefore, that these young men were having their "fun" at the expense of a woman preacher, if not harassing her in order to get her to leave, at least showing their disrespect for her usurpation of what they regarded as a male office. That they might sometimes number half her congregation explains the difficulty the rest of the community had in curbing their disruptions (Diary, vol. 9, Jan. 7, 1875).[16]

In contrast, Newman was easily able to handle the theological barbs of the Free Methodist Brother Dunn. An older man, he too tried to disrupt her prayer meetings early in her Algonquin pastorate. "He came to our prayer-meeting, and offered a prayer very heavily spiced with personal allusions; I would not let him break up our meeting, so called on one after another, read hymns etc. keeping the whole in hand, so that he had no chance to speak: he was very angry, and stormed, after the meeting at 'being domineered over by new-comers' " (Diary, vol. 9, Nov. 3, 1875).

Anna Howard Shaw, another early woman minister, also faced the problem of people who use the prayer meeting to manipulate public opinion. Her strategy was to disallow prayer meetings in her church until the perpetrators agreed to stop (Shaw [1915] 1990, 111). Though Dunn continued to challenge her, Newman never allowed him to disturb what she was doing.

One man in the town surprised her by his support. Col. William Henry, an early postmaster of the town, died in early January 1876. Reporting on his funeral, Newman wrote, "I shall miss good Col. Henry; he never seemed shocked at the innovation of my presence as would have been natural in so old a man, 81, but was always interested in all the work, and wishing he could help. His parting benediction, 'God bless you and your work' has helped me many times" (Diary, vol. 9, Jan. 9, 1876).

In addition to preaching and keeping her church organized, Newman

16. During the 1870s, Algonquin, like the rest of Illinois, had more men than women, most under thirty, and single. In January, the church appointed a committee to keep peace in church, but without result.

attempted to start a temperance society in the town. The town doctor, Harbeck, was elected the president, but Newman, her friend Miss Frank Seeber, and Mr. Keyes were chosen to be the program committee that "seems to correspond with the committee on hard work" (Diary, vol. 9, Dec. 13, 1875). Newman recorded only that they succeeded in having one person fined and persuaded another, a Mr. Wanderacek, to stop selling alcoholic drinks (Diary, vol. 9, Feb. 14, 1876). Within two months, a competing organization, the Good Templers Lodge, organized and attracted a large number of the members. In February, Newman's society joined with the Templers' so that the temperance effort in the town would not be divided (Diary, vol. 9, Feb. 18, 1876).

By the end of March it had become clear that the disruptions of the Sunday School and services, the continued competition with the Free Methodists, and the general and persistent discouragement of the deacons and other members of the congregation were at a point of crisis.

> Lem [Hubbard] came . . . was fearfully depressed, and I had to fuss with him to get out the trouble, which came at last to overwhelm me. I was failing here, nobody would pay towards the salary; people complained because the boys acted so in church, and the Kernes, because their children had been reproved for misconducting; Mrs. Kerne and Mrs. Caroline Hubbard had said that they did not like me and never had; the Dodds who had always said that it was idle to try to do anything, were claimed by the disaffected, my friends were hardly able to stand against the tide. Somehow I bore it, I don't know how, made no demonstration of distress to hurt the faithful fellow who said I ought to know how matters were going, but he hated to tell me. Very few things could hurt me worse than that; but I do not know how it is, I will the Lord's will in the matter: if he wishes to break me, I am willing—but I did think He was using me. (Diary, vol. 9, Mar. 20, 1876)

Alexander Thain, the Congregational pastor in neighboring Dundee, advised her to stay. The next week the congregation reorganized the Sunday School. Deacon Hubbard was replaced by Dr. Harbeck as superintendent. Hubbard was a supporter of hers, Harbeck a critic. On Sunday, June 11, the deacons suddenly decided to close the church. "Preached on the right use of God's gifts to about 30. After S. S. Mrs. Kerne told me that the church had voted to shut up the meeting-house. Frank came over after tea and told me about the church-meeting; it seems that the Hubbards, dreading any disagreement, did not go to meeting, except the deacon and he refused to give any opinion or take any part in the discussion" (Diary, vol. 9, June 11, 1876).

Newman considered her work at Algonquin a failure. Since the organization of the church, they had never had a full time minister, and only one had stayed longer than a few months. The pastors who followed her up to 1885 also served a year or less, and sometimes were students from Chicago (*History of McHenry County, Illinois* 1976, 394).[17] The church did not prosper until some time toward the end of the century, though they paid off the debt on the church building the year after Newman left.[18]

Looking back to Thain's first letter to Newman regarding the church, the problems of the congregation went beyond financial worries. Many of the difficulties were rooted in the social structures, or lack of them, in frontier communities. Large numbers of people in the community were single males, and likely to be moving further west rather than settling down; farming or mining economies suffering boom and bust cycles; ties of people with the churches as institutions loosening; and the paucity of denomina-

17. The *History of McHenry County, Illinois* 1885, 394, lists the following ministers for the Algonquin Congregational Church, along with the dates of their service: Rev. C. L. Hall, the first minister, no dates given; Rev. N. C. Clark preached monthly for several months; Rev. N. Shapley served half-time until 1855; Rev. E. C. Berge's, whose pastorate seems to have been the most stable pastorate, 1855–1867, resigned just after the completion of the building; Rev. I. B. Smith, 1867–68, resigned in 1868 because the congregation "failed to raise his salary." Rev. T. Gulespie served half-time, as did Rev. W. W. Cutless, but we do not know for how long. There were also Miss Newman, 1876; Rev. Hill, 1877; Rev. Alfred Wray, 1878; Rev. Andrich, 3 months in 1882; Rev. Huestis, 1 year; and Rev. C. C. Campbell, 1884–85.

18. "The Congregational Church of Algonquin was organized in 1850 by the Rev. I. C. Beach at the home of Ambrose Dodd. Congregationalists met in school houses until 1866 when a hall was rented and services held here until 1868 when a church was built but not paid for and its financial obligations were eventually assumed by S. S. Gates of Crystal Lake and Ambrose Dodd. From there the church prospered. In 1913 the edifice was rebuilt and it is one of Algonquin's leading churches today" (Hoag n.d.).

Lowell Albert Nye (1968, 371) gives a more specific date. "The Congregation was small and faced a heavy debt. A legacy from S. S. Gates and additional funds from Ambrose Dodd and members helped to pay the debt in 1877." This was the year after Newman's pastorate. Freedom from debt did not contribute, at least not right away, to a more stable succession of pastors.

tional support for the churches were all factors faced by Newman in Algonquin. Thain suggested that the encouraging signs included a large number of young people, but they did not all know how to be church members. The ground was not preoccupied, at least by Presbyterians or Congregationalists, but the town had four churches and there was considerable competition among them. The people did attend church, and they did, for the most part, receive a lady speaker, but preaching and Sabbath School teaching alone did not result in a stronger church. Newman's opponent Mr. Dunn was perhaps right when he commented to Newman that "the people of Algonquin had been preached to death" (Diary, vol. 9, Nov. 7, 1875).

Interactions of Geography and Gender

Awareness of the paradoxes of dependence and independence in the ethos of the American West illuminates the interactions of gender and geography in Newman's Algonquin experience. They can further be understood by looking again at the emergence of household models of leadership embedded in the oldest fabric of Christianity. The interdependence of the household acts in counterpoint to both dependence and independence in the formation of human community in the American West.

Glenda Riley, in her book *The Female Frontier* (1988), pointed out that western women extended their sense of household to their whole surrounding and became the mothers of community. Algonquin's Congregational Church, though twenty-five years old, was not yet a community. Newman, following the centuries' old household models of Christian leadership, tried to clarify the boundaries of the community, encouraging commitment to a theology and style of life that would make one recognizably Congregational. Newman nurtured people's faith, but with a sense of challenge. She clarified the boundaries of the church community and held the people responsible for themselves and their church. Newman had extended her own womanly responsibility for community from her congregation to the town. She was not a doting mother, but the *materfamilias*. In the end, the Algonquin people were not ready. As westerners, they still valued their independence from eastern established institutions, including the church. For a little while longer they wanted to live without commitment to an institution that wanted to nourish their souls; at least that was

Newman's view of it. Like any good nineteenth-century mother, she believed their failure was her failure.

If Newman was the *materfamilias*, Ambrose Dodd was the *pater* or patron. Because the church was not supported by the Home Missionary Society and was therefore independent of its restrictions, the church depended
on Dodd almost exclusively for its financial resources. Newman was not
able to foster any sense of independence and responsibility among the
members. With all their celebrated sense of independence, westerners in
towns such as Algonquin, particularly in the difficult economic times of
the 1870s, were often dependent upon either eastern assistance or one or
two wealthy or generous local people to fund their churches. In either case,
this dependence tended to subdue the initiative of the church members. In
her short, seven-months' pastorate, Newman chose an assertive strategy in
upholding rigorous standards of membership, but this left her with negative results. The community was further fractured and less inclined to cooperate. Seven months gave her little time to nurture the development of
"the boys" into mature adulthood, and thus the future base for church
membership remained neglected.

For the next six months, Newman struggled to understand the meaning
of her experience in Algonquin. It had shaken her sense of call. Three
things helped her keep her sense of purpose and view things from a wider
perspective. The first was the Women's Ministerial Association; the second the support of Alexander Thain; and finally, there was the opportunity
to participate in the Chicago Revival of Dwight L. Moody. She remained
in Illinois, visiting her cousins, Charles and Sue Porter in Batavia, and her
friend, Elizabeth Humphrey, in Chicago. Except for a visit to the Centennial Exposition in Philadelphia in September, she lived in Chicago during
the fall, participating in the temperance work of the Dwight L. Moody
organization.

She found the search for her next pastorate discouraging. Questioning
her call to pastoral work, she wrote again to Alexander Thain. Though her
letter to him does not survive, she kept his reply, one of the few letters she
saved for years. He wrote:

> I hardly know what to say in answer to your question. I have had an experi-
> ence which has been vastly beneficial to me, but it was an experience be-
> tween my own soul and God, and I do not know as advice would have

helped me much. . . . I would say, that you appear to be passing through an experience much similar to my own. You will find prayer to be your best relief. Have the courage to look into your own heart, asking the Holy Spirit to assist you, and you will probably find more there than you have ever suspected. Be sure and inquire very closely as to your ruling motive. I found to my surprise and shame that my motive in entering the ministry was not entirely what it should be. I was seeking culture, a certain position etc., rather than the salvation of souls. . . . I will put a test question, not because I consider it to be applicable to you, but because it involves a great sacrifice—feeling as you do. If God should say to you that he does not need you in the ministry—if He should point out some other life work, would your soul rebel? . . . You must look into your heart to ascertain whether your seeming failure at Algonquin was in the preacher, or in the people. You see that I have not answered your question—for I am not wise enough. But I have indicated where an answer may be found—at the feet of Jesus. (Thain to Newman, Oct. 21, 1876)

Thain and Newman shared a theological point of view about God's providence that almost, but not quite, required them to see whatever happened as the will of God. Still, their God required effort. Remarkably, Thain did not discourage her directly by stating that her problem lay in simply being a woman, but he is silent on the matter. He is also silent on the matter of the social, economic, and geographical context in which she worked in Algonquin. For Thain and Newman both, the theological approach was most natural. Their orthodox Calvinism required them to search the soul first when seeking reasons for the events of the world.

But to what degree did context shape Newman's experience? Was her failure at Algonquin due to her or the people? Or was it due to the tentative nature of frontier communities? Algonquin was still new, only forty years old. Some of the founding generation of people remained, but many had probably moved on, as did so many in Western towns. Algonquin gained fewer than two hundred people in the decade of the 1870s (U.S. Department of the Interior, Census Office, 1883).

The American Home Missionary Society Report for Illinois in 1873 noted this continuous movement of people further west, depleting the towns and therefore the churches as they left. "Our churches are fast coming into sympathy with those at the East as to depletion by removals. Our material spreads over the plains and mountains beyond. To strengthen things that remain is becoming a large share of our work" (American Home Missionary Society 1873, 74–75). In addition, the report indicated the difficult economic situation at the beginning of the depression of the 1870s and its effect on the society's work.

> During the latter half of the year, the Treasury suffered severe embarrassment. The Committee had been encouraged to enlarge the scale of their operations. Accordingly, large missionary reenforcements were sent to the frontier portions of the field, and heavy liabilities for their support were incurred. But, in consequence of severe monetary pressure in the Western States, the expected increase of contributions from that quarter were not realized; while the fire in Boston, in connection with other causes, diminished the gifts of the New England churches. The Committee, therefore, were obliged to postpone their plans of enlargement, and to exercise the closest economy in all their expenditures. (American Home Missionary Society 1873, 74–75)

The reports of the American Home Missionary Society in the following decade complain of decreasing financial resources, fast increasing numbers of churches needing aid, and the steady movement of people. The financial problems diminished as time wore on, but the failure of the society to keep up with the movement of the people weakened the Congregational churches in the western states.

The Women Minister's Association

Newman shared a fate similar to many women ministers, especially in the West. They were isolated from one another; they lacked official credentials; and though they had great ability and love for their work, it was difficult for them to find churches willing to take them as pastor. Though many churches were available, served by thinly stretched male missionaries, the American Home Missionary Society steadily refused to support churches that called women pastors.

In Illinois, vocal opposition to women's leadership continued. Newman attended the Elgin Association meeting in Wheaton on October 11, and heard Jonathan Blanchard, the president of Wheaton College, express his objections. "The morning prayer-meeting was shortened because Pres.

Blanchard turned his morning devotions in college into that chapel. In conducting these he told his pupils that women were not to preach, to face an audience, to usurp authority over the men: You wouldn't love such a girl; wouldn't want to marry her: He looked straight at me as he said these words and evidently considered me crushed" (Diary, vol. 10, Oct. 11, 1876). The opposition to women's ordination lasted for another decade. In 1889, Mary Moreland became the first Congregational woman ordained in Illinois (*Woman's Journal*, June 11, 1892).[19] Women did not, even when

19. Mary Moreland was an evangelist in Illinois, ordained in the Wyanet, Il., Congregational Church in 1889. Frances Willard attended her ordination (Haberkorn 1942, 288–94). Moreland was not the first Congregational woman ordained—that was Antoinette Brown in 1853. Louise Baker was also ordained by 1889. It is difficult to ascertain the names and ordination dates of Congregational women because the records are unreliable. The following account of the difficulty is contained in the records of the Women Minister's Association: "As we to-day observe the tenth anniversary of our existence, I think we should be permitted a backward look over the past decade, to note a few of the mile-stones of progress toward a more perfect recognition of woman's ecclesiastical equality with man. The Congregational Church, as the earliest Protestant church in the country, might naturally be expected to lead in according to women higher privileges of advancement; but it is by its aspiring off-shoots that they have been thus honored, rather than by the parent body, which still declines to place the names of women ministers upon its year-book. This fact makes it extremely difficult to procure reliable statistics concerning the woman ministry in this church, which perhaps I cannot better illustrate than by relating a very recent interview with certain officers of that denomination at their headquarters in this city.

"Wishing to present upon the programme of our meeting to-day the precise number of women preachers in their fellowship, I asked to be informed regarding it. The lady in attendance knew there was the name of one woman upon the record somewhere, and courteously presented me with the name of Rev. Mary L. Moreland, Wyanet, Ill., well known to some of us. I asked for more, and the reply came, 'Why, there are no more.' I reminded her of Rev. Ida Buxton Cole, present pastor of the Congregational Church at Dwight, Ill., and also of Rev. Louise S. Baker, of Nantucket. The lady remembered that she had been there, but her name had never been placed on their list of ministers. I turned to a genial officer of the American Board at a neighboring desk, and asked if he could explain why Louise S. Baker, who, after four years of preaching and pastoral labor, was then ordained by the deacons of her church, could not, by a liberal construction of their system, be considered a minister? If seven years of faithful labor in one parish, attending one hundred and seventy funerals, marrying forty persons, and associating in her official capacity with the pastors of other denominations, did not give her name a right to be entered on their year-book, what shibboleth was necessary? His reply was, 'It certainly ought to be there.' I told him I could furnish him other names from memoranda at home; and, as he pored over the leaves of the

ordained, find it easy to get support from the American Home Missionary Society[20] or to serve any but the smallest congregations.

Western women ministers were scattered. In Illinois, twelve women reported themselves to be "clergymen" in 1880 (U.S. Department of the Interior, Census Office, 1883).[21] Few except the Unitarian "Sisterhood" in Iowa were near enough to each other to meet easily. This group of women began their ministry almost ten years after Newman began seeking a license from the Congregationalists.[22] Theirs was an unusual situation. Newman and other ordained women were more likely to be isolated far from contact with other ministers of their own churches whether female or male.

In the 1870s, those woman ministers closest to Boston formed an association. The idea originated with Julia Ward Howe.

Mrs. Howe said: "I had a great interest many years ago in women in the ministry. I was new in the field of women's larger life. I was impressed with the importance of religious life, and believed in the power of association. I believed that women ministers would be less sectarian than men; and I thought that if those of different denominations could meet occasionally and compare notes, it would be of value. But I found it hard to get them together. It was hard also to get women together on other subjects. . . . The purses of women ministers are probably light, and that makes it harder for them to attend conventions." (Blackwell 1904, 91)

---

year-book, his remarks ran in this wise: 'It is all wrong, all wrong. Such names ought to be here. Why, here is the name of a dead *man* minister; and here is another and another'; and he musingly added, 'and not the name of one woman!' I remarked, 'Perhaps they have revised the scriptures to read, "Better is a dead man than a live woman." ' He answered, 'Well, I am glad you came, and something must be done to make this right.' And accepting him as a representative of the more progressive element of Orthodoxy, we may believe there will be a change in this particular." The tenth anniversary meeting of the Woman's Ministerial Conference was held in the Church of the Disciples in Boston on June 1. Mrs. Julia Ward Howe presided. The account of the meeting is found in the June 11, 1892, *Woman's Journal*.

20. We will consider this matter more specifically in the next two chapters.

21. In the entire United States, 165 women reported themselves as clergy (U.S. Department of the Interior, Census Office, 1883, table 34).

22. The Iowa Sisterhood is discussed in an excellent book by Cynthia Grant Tucker (1990).

The first association was a worship gathering held on Sunday afternoons at her house, which Howe called The Woman's Church, featuring women preachers. "Now, I thought, we have got hold of what is really wanting in the Church universal. We need to have the womanly side of religion represented. Without this representation we shall not have the fullness of human thought for the things that most deeply concern it" (Richards and Elliot 1916, 1: 389–90).[23]

Returning to Batavia, Illinois from a trip to the Philadelphia Centennial Exhibition in October 1876, Newman met Howe on the train, who invited her to join the Association of Women Ministers (Diary, vol. 10, Oct. 7, 1876). Though Newman attended only one or two of the association' annual meetings, and although it met irregularly in its first two decades, it did serve as a point of support to women ministers from New England to as far west as the Dakota Territory. Newman's friend Elizabeth Humphrey warned her about the association, saying that "she is afraid to have me go into the women ministers' movement; thinks I shall get mixed up with the Unitarians and Universalists" (Diary, vol. 10, Oct. 8, 1876). Although it is true that the association was dominated by Universalist and Unitarian women, because those two denominations ordained women in greater numbers, the group was nonsectarian throughout its history.

> The first Convention of Women Preachers in modern times was held in Boston at the Church of the Disciples[24] May 29, 1873. The invitation, given without sectarian limitation, called together quite a number of women from various parts of the country,—all engaged in the Christian Ministry. Of these, two or three only were ordained ministers the others being simply preachers, called to this service by a deep interest in the religious well being of the Community, and a belief that this would be greatly promoted by the direct ministration of women in the Christian church. (Women's Ministerial Conference n.d., 1)

Members in the association during the next two decades included Rev. Anna H. Shaw, ordained by the Methodist Protestant Church; Rev. Louise

23. Julia Ward Howe's reflections on the beginnings of the Women's Ministerial Conference. See Richards and Elliott 1916, l: 389–90.

24. The church where Julia Ward Howe was a member, she being the first to call for a convention.

Baker and Emma Newman, orthodox Congregationalists; Rev. Olympia Brown, Rev. Mary Safford, and Rev. Mary Graves, Unitarians; Rev. Mary T. Whitney, Universalist; and other women preaching but not officially members of any particular denomination (Women's Ministerial Conference n.d., 77).

The Chicago Revival

Supported in her discouragement by her friend and mentor Alexander Thain and other woman ministers, Newman spent the months until she received another call in doing "urban work" with Dwight L. Moody's Chicago revival and temperance campaign. Newman attended the opening sessions of the revival in October 1876. "Heard Moody preach on Grace and Sankey sing 'To the hall of the feast come the sinful and fair', and 'Waiting and watching', the latter is just exquisite and Sankey is like the Apostle John. Moody never does me any good but I am glad for the good he does others. The great Tabernacle is good to see, easy to hear in and well lighted a star on high—and the words 'God is Love' in gas jets were very effective" (Diary, vol. 10, Oct. 19, 1876). A month later, Newman joined the ranks of the revival workers. Mr. Humphrey, her friend's husband, congratulated her on her choice of work. "I might get into something in the city, such as preaching to women, which would suit my views, and be within the recognized work of women, but he did not believe my preaching to mixed audiences in country places, would ever amount to anything. I was weak enough to be angry at the coolness which consigned me to work I do not like and am not fitted for, however I thanked him politely, just as if it made any difference" (Diary, vol. 10, Nov. 25, 1876).

Chicago, the site of the Moody revival, had recovered from the great fire of 1871, though not from the depression of 1873. It was a growing city of almost half a million people, a center for rail and water transportation, manufacturing, and agricultural markets. About half the population in 1876 was Anglo-American, largely from New England. The other half were mostly new immigrants from Germany, Ireland, and Scandinavia.

Among these new immigrants, the Scandinavians and German Protestants tended to move fairly easily into the mainstream of the culture with which the Protestant Americans were most comfortable, but the Catholics came to Chicago, Cincinnati, and St. Louis—as they did to cities on the

East Coast, in numbers that were alarming to the descendants of the Puritans. American Protestants were deeply suspicious of what they perceived as a Catholic threat. Protestant views, particularly those of Reformed Protestants such as the Congregationalists, were shaped by centuries of prejudice regarding the Mass and the images of saints as idolatrous and superstitious. In addition, the nativist anti-Catholic movements of the nineteenth century had produced a political rhetoric about the threat of the Pope to American democracy.[25]

Religious prejudice, along with economic class tensions, increased middle-class Protestant uneasiness with Roman Catholic immigrants. Middle-class Protestants wanted to continue to believe that sober, hardworking people would always have work and be able to live. "Every industrious, prudent, skillful and healthy laborer can acquire a handsome competence" by the time he is fifty if he wants to (Robertson 1982, 205).[26] But with the depression of the 1870s, many industrious, sober, prudent people were out of jobs. Because many working-class people followed a religion the Protestants feared, drank alcohol to ease their pain, and generally, Protestants believed, contributed to labor unrest and social turmoil, they inspired a united effort among middle-class Anglo-Protestants in Chicago to convert them to a more familiar evangelical faith and way of life.

Dwight L. Moody clearly connected the revival to the economy. Supported by business owners, Moody claimed the revival would be good for them as well as the churches. "When Chicago has a revival of religion she will be ripe for a revival of business, and we would be able to give a fair show both to God and mammon" (Robertson 1982, 95).[27] The premise behind his preaching was common among evangelical Christians, that eco-

25. This anti-Catholic anxiety can be seen clearly in such classic texts as Lyman Beecher's *Plea for the West* and Josiah Strong's later work *Our Country*. Ray Allen Billington, in his *Protestant Crusade* (1938) discusses the motives and methods of the nativists and their legacy in the late nineteenth century.

26. A more detailed discussion of the socioeconomic aspects of the Moody revivals can be found in Robertson 1982, from which this quote comes. Robertson cited an article in the *Congregationalist* 55 (Nov. 16, 1871): 6.

27. Moody seemed conveniently to forget that the biblical references declared the impossibility of serving both God and Mammon. Newman preached a sermon on the subject, Sermon no. 10, "The Impossibility of Serving Two Masters." Moody never required such a choice. *Chicago Tribune* September 25, 1870, quoted in Robertson 1982, 95.

nomic and social prosperity lay in personal hard work and abstinence from alcohol—and the effective way for a person to stop drinking was to con-vert to evangelical Protestantism. In Moody's preaching there is no evi-dence that he considered the rising Social Gospel theology seriously. For Moody, sin was personal and so was salvation. The state of society rested on individual decisions.

The *Inter Ocean*, a Chicago newspaper supporting the revival and re-porting on every phase of it, also reported news of the world. In the pages of the *Inter Ocean*, the world and Moody's tabernacle never met. Word of war, the Turks against Russia, England, Serbia; the United States against Sitting Bull; word of efforts to raise the price of coal by closing mines; new, huge machines harvesting wheat in the Central Valley of California; and an abundant harvest in Europe did not sway Moody from his simple view of the economy (*Inter Ocean*, Aug. 25, 1876, 5–6).

From October through January, the special tabernacle Moody built was filled almost every night to hear Ira Sankey sing and to hear Moody preach. Attendance reached as many as eight thousand, with standing room only, and the *Inter Ocean* estimated the crowd on the first night at sixteen thousand (*Inter Ocean*, Oct. 6, 1876).[28] Frances Willard collabo-rated with Moody on this series of meetings, and much of the activity focused on temperance. An army of volunteers canvassed the city adver-tising the meetings, Newman among them.

Newman's district was located along Harrison Street, from Halstead west. She found a room to rent nearby, with no fire and a broken window. She ate little, one day subsisting on dry rolls and apples. Despite the cold wind, she bought a city map and began to work.

Proceeded to my district, found stores and went into them thinking it a good time, but left the private houses. Some were indifferent, some interested; found 3 saloons and went in to two: at one they would not take much notice of me; at the other the bar-tender promised to attend the sermon to young men on Wed. night. . . . Went back to my district, and got a nice girl to go with me thinking people would be more civil if they saw one of their neigh-bors, they were not rude, but nobody asked me in, found some Christians,

28. By comparison, the *Inter Ocean* reported on Oct. 6, 1876, that a baseball game be-tween Chicago and St. Louis drew a crowd of four thousand.

some Catholics and one woman who asked if they had to pay .50 tonight. (Diary, vol. 10, Nov. 27, 1876)

During the day Newman visited the homes and businesses of her as-signed district of the city, giving out tickets to the evening preaching, dis-tributing flyers, talking to people, urging them to attend the various functions, and giving charitable assistance where it seemed needed.

The inquiry rooms of the tabernacle were the heart of the revival. Most of the work after each meeting centered in these rooms built into the tab-ernacle, around and below the auditorium seating, where those whose souls were troubled could talk one-to-one with a Christian person trained to help them to conversion. Newman served in the inquiry rooms in the evenings.

> To my very great joy, I was able to help forward the conversion of Mary Berghof. Talked with and comforted a Christian mother, sore-hearted over the death of a child. Went out at nearly 11, hurriedly, and overheard two men talking about want of moral courage: as we all jumped on the horse cars, I managed to quote to one "Be strong in the Lord etc.:" he followed me up the car, eager to talk, and a few words of personal appeal touched him at once; he called to the other and those men listened and talked freely of their own souls and their praying mothers: they were business men from 30 to 35. May God bless them. Went home happy: God is using me. (Diary, vol. 10, Dec. 13, 1876)

In all of Newman's diary accounts of her social work, in the Aid Society in Andover, the various temperance societies in the places where she preached, and in the Moody revival, she never commented on the social context of the individuals she encountered. Her focus was on personal morality and conversions. She was repeatedly disappointed in the people she helped when they slipped back into their old habits. However, she ei-ther attributed it to her own failure of persuasion or their weak wills. She did not read the Social Gospel theologians of the day, and did not in her writing mention the conclusions people such as Frances Willard were reaching regarding the contributions of social injustice to the problems of individuals. She seems primarily to have regarded woman suffrage in the same light, as a tool for moral reform by legislation, rather than a tool for reshaping the social order. In this respect she shared Moody's theology.

However, she retained her orthodoxy. She did not join Moody in his connection of religious conversion and success in business. Newman had a far more complex idea of suffering. She understood that not all suffering could be overcome simply by leading a righteous life. Some suffering was inexplicable and the Christian, she believed, was called to give the suffering person aid and comfort, and to pray for them to understand that only God knew what was best in the situation.

By the middle of December, the energy for the revival was waning. The participation of so many local church members in its daily activities strained the churches. In the end, though attendance numbered in the thousands each night, the majority of those converted were not from the classes the revival aimed to reach, but were the young middle-class professional people like those Newman met on the train. These converts already shared the culture and values of Moody and the revival's supporters.

In his assessment of the revival's results, Darrel Robertson notes that most Chicago immigrants remained Catholic or Lutheran, though there was a sizable—but temporary—increase in membership in the Chicago churches. Nationwide, this revival and subsequent revivals conducted by Moody and Sankey in other cities renewed Protestant emphasis on preaching evangelism and revitalized the hymnody of the evangelical churches. But in summary, Robertson noted, "They had, perhaps unwittingly, made the New Testament Christ of the poor, hungry and socially outcast into a sentimental, moralistic, legalistic and middle-class Savior of the seventies" (Robertson 1982, 308–9). Newman's participation in this revival during an interlude in her ministry strengthened her evangelical views. Though she did not adopt the style of Moody, she remained an ambassador for the same culture.

Newman's Algonquin pastorate was her first sustained immersion in the western context. She brought her New England culture and its three pillars of town, school, and Congregational church into a raw new community, largely male, largely single, faced with competing denominations, and worked to bring about a functioning congregation.

She felt both the freedom of the West and its constraints. Here she found it relatively easy to express her call to preach. She was able to work without the formal credentials required of ministers in more settled areas. However, she faced constraints as well in the lack of support from the Home Missionary Society, because she was a woman, she also faced the isolation she experienced far from other Congregational ministers, and even more the isolation as one of the earliest women doing such work. The Iowa sisterhood of Unitarian ministers was not yet formed, and she was too far from Boston, the center of the Association of Women Ministers to which she belonged, to have much comfort in their society. She was quite literally on her own, free to shape her ministry as she saw fit, but unsupported by the larger ecclesiastical bodies most ministers could count on.

Newman was the mother of her church. She undertook in her public ministry many of the same tasks women performed privately as they built community household by household in the American West. It was a short step from visiting her women companions to visiting her congregation. The experience gained in her social work in the Andover Aid Society transferred easily to her work with the troubled and poor in her congregation and in her neighborhood in Chicago. As Ann Douglas points out, and Ferenc Szasz confirms in his study of Protestant clergy in the trans Mississippi West (Douglas 1978; Szasz 1988), the work of the clergy and the work of women in the West coincided to a remarkable degree, and Newman moved easily into the public mode of the private work she had done all along.

In the next chapter we will discuss further Newman's role in her culture's ritual of appropriation of the land in the home missionary movement. In New Boston, Illinois, secularization, pluralism of denominations, lack of sufficient pastoral care, and ambivalence about women's role in the home missionary movement became significant factors in Newman's work. She also combined the care of body and soul of her people in New Boston in a way she had not attempted before.

"Whoever Takes the Wild Land . . . Makes It Her Own"

> God made this earth to be free to all; and whoever takes the wild land and clears it, and cultivates it, makes it his [her] own—[she's] a right to it.
>
> —Mrs. Metta Victor, *The Backwoods Bride:*
> *A Romance of Squatter Life*

The Wild Land

Given her New England understanding of herself placed in the highest Christian culture, the West was to Emma Newman a wild land. New England people traditionally had ambivalent feelings about the West, and one of the things they sought to do as they moved West was to make the wild land their own. They did this primarily by clearing the land of everything they considered wild, including the native people, and cultivating it, both literally and figuratively.[1] Newman, as a home missionary preacher, did this as well, clearing the wildness from her people's behavior and cultivating New England culture. She also made the wild land *her* own. She forged a personal style of life and work; she brought her whole self to each place and found a way to minister.

Consider what made this land wild. By the time Emma Newman moved west, the line marking the wild land had moved roughly to the Mississippi

---

1. Takaki (1993) offers a good discussion of the ways in which English settlers and their descendants framed western land and people as wild.

River. At different periods in American history, one can draw the line marking the beginning of what a New Englander considered wild land in different places, but in each era the criteria of wildness were similar: space and distance. Space separated settlements from each other; distance marked the path back home. Isolation was common. People often moved west in order to put distance and space, between themselves and their past, their family, or structures of society that they viewed as limiting. Isolation meant freedom. However, it also meant loss: loss of sustaining relationships of all kinds, loss of ties to social order and organization that helped place an individual in a human context and give him or her an identity. Loss of personal identity meant one was in danger of becoming wild.

Another fact of life in the West was the interplay of dependence and independence for both institutions and individuals.[2] Although the freedom of the frontier was its most well-known and celebrated quality, in fact, land, weather, new social and cultural interactions, and the very distances separating people curtailed that freedom. The Homestead Act of 1862 granted each head of household or single individual 160 acres of land, provided they "improved" it sufficiently, that is, made it economically viable, within a certain number of years. People who could never have thought of themselves as economically independent people in the eighteenth century had the chance to be landowners. However, independence and dependence were not so easily separated.

First of all, homesteads were not free land. No matter how Euro-Americans justified appropriation of the land, it was not without cost, moral and economic. No one could quite forget that it was taken, and from someone who was using it, though in a different way. The elaborate argument that the homesteaders, through their superior civilization, were entitled to use the land as they did served only to disguise a sophisticated theft. The fact of the theft rendered them dependent on the military for protection, the first of many dependencies on the federal government.[3]

2. The complex issues of dependence and independence discussed here first developed in my mind in the conversations in the spring 1997 seminar at the Graduate Theological Union on Religion in the American West. The faculty involved were Eldon Ernst, Ronald Nakasone, Fred Rosenbaum, James Treat, and myself. In addition, we shared the work with seven students. I am indebted to all the members of this seminar for sharpening many thoughts presented in this work.

3. Recent works that discuss this dependency on the Federal Government at length are Unruh, Jr. 1979; and White 1991.

The myth of the rugged individual, self-sufficient and strong, developed as Americans romanticized the experience of life in the West. Indeed, in the 1870s and 1880s, the majority of the western population, both male and female, was single and young. Women with children could not live as rugged individuals; the tasks of child rearing required community. Thus it was women, single and married, who tended to instigate the foundation of community structures and institutions in frontier settlements (Riley 1988, 148). They were joined in this effort by many men who recognized stable community structures as beneficial to them.

Homesteaders were also dependent on each other in ways they did not expect. Although the frontier area might be a realm without the usual social constraints of more settled areas, because population was sparse, one had far fewer options for help. People had to trust their neighbors; they were dependent on each other's good will. Sometimes such trust was possible and other times it was not. The creation of familiar forms of social interchange was not always easy, given the distances between people on the homesteading frontier. Schools and churches both fostered community life, but their establishment required resources scattered people found hard to assemble. Though people were free to form schools or churches in their own way, far from the interference of established organizations, they were also without the resources of those established organizations. If they were dependent on help from those organizations, they were often not free to form institutions that would meet the needs of their particular place. Independence and dependence danced together in complex ways.

Emma Newman's roles as a woman and as a pastor complemented each other in the creation of religious community. However, when a church called a woman pastor such as Newman because there were no other ministers willing to come to so small a church or so isolated a place, it risked losing the support of the mission organization upon whom it depended for help with the minister's support, or to whom it owed money for building the church.

The American West also isolated a minister from the denominational centers of power and, because they were so scattered; from the people of the parish. This isolation shaped pastoral style and institutional development. Itinerant preaching reached more people but made it difficult for the pastor to know people deeply. The laity were forced to become more self-reliant, diminishing the social status of the clergy.

However, geographical isolation provided freedom for women to engage in pastoral work in sparsely settled country and allowed them to rise in a tide over the traditional obstacles barring them from pulpits and ordination.

The West required an entrepreneurial spirit, and offered less resistance to new ways of doing things. Western churches took more readily than eastern ones to the innovation of women ministers. Newman's appropriation of the freedom of the West showed itself in her willingness to minister with congregations however small, and in her mixture of physical ministrations with preaching as she tried above all to be useful in the places to which she was convinced God had sent her.

Newman's pastorate at New Boston, Illinois, 1876–1878, provides a venue for considering the way she practiced and combined spiritual care and physical care. In New Boston, we also see her growing understanding of the role of the pastor in the shaping of a Christian community. In New Boston, the interplay of gender and geography in understanding the religious life of a frontier town became more complex.

New Boston

On December 15, 1876, in the midst of her work in Willard and Moody's Chicago revival, Newman received a long-awaited letter asking her to go to New Boston, Illinois, to preach for a very small church, "speaking in terms that showed it to be a very hard place" (Diary, vol. 10, Dec. 15, 1876). Within two days she packed up her trunks and took the train west, first to Dundee, where Alexander Thain now lived, and then on to Aledo to meet Robert Nourse, pastor of the Aledo Congregational church, who apparently had sent her the invitation.[4]

The day after Christmas, Emma Newman moved to New Boston, a town of approximately seven hundred people situated on the Mississippi

---

4. Newman's diary contains an entry that she received the letter. Contrary to her usual practice, she did not indicate who sent it. Nourse preached from time to time in Aledo, according to a report written by Martin Whittlesey, the home missionary superintendent for Southern Illinois. American Home Missionary Society—Sunday School—Department Application, from New Boston Sunday School, Mar. 6, 1877 American Home Missionary Society Papers, Illinois Correspondence File, microfilm Reel #53.

River about fifteen miles west of Aledo. The oldest town in Mercer County, it was laid out in 1834, in a survey by Abraham Lincoln, as a future river port and end of a railroad line. North of the town, Boston Bay, bordered by oak, elm, willow, hickory, and maple trees, provided a beautiful spot from which to fish, or row a boat. The economy of the area depended on sandy farm lands producing corn, oats, wheat, melons, and tomatoes (Moorhead n.d.).

There was a Methodist Church, and a Presbyterian congregation owned a church building but did not have a pastor. Many of the members of the Presbyterian church were Congregationalists, hopeful that Newman would help them start a Sunday School and later their own church. Robert Nourse preached occasionally in New Boston. Martin Whittlesey, the American Home Missionary Society superintendent for southern Illinois, reported somewhat favorably on the possibilities for the Congregationalists, though the field was considered to be "preoccupied" with the presence of the Presbyterians.

New Boston is given up to "infidelity and a material form of Spiritualism." Our Presbyterian brethren over built an expensive house of worship which is still standing there, but their power and hope of doing good seem to be gone. . . . Rev. R. Nourse has preached and lectured for some months—occasionally—at New Boston. Miss Newman takes up her work—on recommendation of myself believing from report that she might be useful there. . . . Miss E. E. N. writes me that this Society is not a church but may become one—and says you must not expect to hear much good news from her for some time. . . . "There is an active M. E. Ch. [Methodist Episcopal Church] here but *these people* will have nothing to do with it saying *it does not* promote manly and womanly living! I am preparing for a discussion at the 'Literary' on the cause of the darkness of the middle ages and I stand alone for the defense of Christianity—The Literary is a Town affair and open to all and well attended. . . . Mine is the only voice ever raised there for the Christian side of any question." God bless this plucky girl. (Whittlesey 1877a)

In the course of her daily notes about New Boston, Newman mentioned the Methodists, the Presbyterians, the Congregationalists, and the Mormons, all small groups. The majority of the people appear to have been irreligious, some atheist.

New Boston presented different challenges than Algonquin. The competition here was not so much with another denomination as with indifference to organized Christianity. Also, in New Boston there was no doctor, so Newman combined her homeopathic practice with her ministry. Because there was a strong Spiritualist movement in the town, people understood and welcomed her combined ministry. Newman stayed in New Boston longer than she had stayed anywhere else thus far, providing time for sustained political activity on behalf of temperance and allowing the question of her licensing to be put once again before the association.

In her first visits in the community, Newman discovered past disagreements between the Presbyterians and Congregationalists in the congregation. Almost as soon as she arrived in town, the Presbyterian trustee, Al Crab, declined to open the church for Newman's preaching. She spoke with several members of the church, all women: Mrs. Gore, Mrs. Van Scoter, Miss Henry, and Miss Calhoun. After these conversations, Newman decided to suggest that if they would form a Congregational society, she would stay and preach for a year; otherwise she would leave at once. They agreed to form the society. Unlike her Algonquin congregation, this one had not yet been organized. To do so, Newman would have to support a schism in the Presbyterian congregation that might leave both groups unable to support either a pastor or the debt for a church building. On the night they appointed for organizing, twelve people, all women, attended. They organized the society, and over the next few weeks the men joined them. They rented the town hall for their meetings.

Newman enjoyed compliments from her congregation in New Boston she had never received in Algonquin, often for the same sermons. Her third sermon was particularly well received and apparently settled the mind of the most influential man about asking her to stay.

Preached on "what we believe" and Christ was with me. Mrs. Gore told me that I was inspired and trials had done me good. . . . The dear little woman had been inspired by that sermon to re-commence family prayer and was full of faith for her husband. . . . Went to talk society with Mrs. Van S.; she amazed me by saying that Mr. Lytle and Roberts both said that last night's sermon was the best they ever heard. . . . The Lord did it, I'm sure I did not. May He keep me from doing some awfully stupid thing to spoil it all. (Diary, vol. 10, Jan. 21–22, 1877)

Secularization—Social Wildness

Emma Newman began her work in New Boston facing the secularized climate of the town. Most people in New Boston did not see church, as Newman understood it, to be necessary. She had to argue for the positive contributions of Christianity to civilization. The 1870s marked a change in American religious history, as a period when unbelief in God became possible and widespread.[5]

Church membership became optional, all the more so the further west one traveled. Newman was faced not with building a church out of people who wanted one but were new in town, but with persuading more than a handful of the townspeople that a church, and a Congregational one at that, was worth having.

Considering first the issue of secularization, let us look more closely at the way in which this aspect of New Boston linked with the gender questions and issues of geography. James Turner, in his book *Without God, Without Creed: The Origins of Unbelief in America,* takes pains to show the ways in which evangelical Protestant ministers and theologians helped to bring about the possibility of unbelief by their adoption of scientific methods to defend the truth of the Bible. He writes,

> It was, after all, theologians and ministers who had welcomed this secular visitor into the house of God. It was they who had most loudly insisted that knowledge of God's existence and benevolence could be pinned down as securely as the structure of a frog's anatomy—and by roughly the same method. It was they who had obscured the difference between natural and supernatural knowledge, between the tangible things of this world and the impalpable things of another. By the mid–nineteenth century they had, really, no effectual model of knowledge except science. (Turner 1985, 193)

This process contributed to a change in mentality in America. Religion was moved to the realm of the feelings and intuition, making it inaccessible to reason, and therefore irrelevant to thinking people.

Two months after beginning her work in New Boston, the Literary Society invited Newman to participate in their meetings. "A question on the

5. Turner (1985) offers a good discussion of this change.

cause of the darkness of the Middle Ages came up in such a way that I was obliged to move that it be discussed at length, and thereby threw down the gauntlet to all the leading gentlemen, as mine is the only voice ever raised there on the Christian side of any question. I am frightened, but I must stand to my guns; my duty is plain" (Diary, vol. 10, Mar. 2, 1877). The debate was held two weeks later. In a literary society in Andover, Newman might have to defend a notion of Trinitarian Christianity against a Unitarian argument, but in New Boston she had to defend Christianity itself against the idea that it was not only irrelevant, but also possibly harmful to society. More people belonged to the Literary Society than to the churches. The Home Missionary superintendent, Whittlesey, regarded the organized Literary Society and the unorganized Spiritualist group as equally threatening to the cause of the evangelical churches.

Whittlesey's observation that there was a large Spiritualist influence in the town suggested that the problem of unbelief was serious. Spiritualists characteristically wanted to prove scientifically that religious experience was real. Spiritualists were particularly interested in the possibility of communicating with the spirits of the dead. They also experimented with the effects of the mind or spirit on the body, and the idea of mental healing. New Thought, a movement of interest in mental healing that included Christian Science and later the Unity School of Christianity, also claimed scientific verification for its belief that the body could be healed by the mind alone. Newman, with her interest in magnetism, was in this sense related to both groups.

The historian Tamar Frankiel links the Spiritualist movements to other movements such as Pentecostalism, where in the midst of a society calling for increased conformity, "those who oriented themselves by means of an inward spirituality offered vigorous alternatives for empowerment through intense or unusual experiences" (Frankiel 1997, 79).[6] Spiritualism spread rapidly in the American West; it was particularly popular in California. However, even in a small Illinois town, it could fill a vacuum left by the ab-

---

6. That Frankiel notes these movements going underground in the first half of the twentieth century suggests a point I would like to make in the next chapter. Women participated in the leadership of these Spiritualist groups and were interested in religion and healing. This connection also goes underground during the early twentieth century and reemerges in the understandings of ministry among many women ministers after the 1970s (Frankiel 1997).

sence of traditional organized religion. It was a do-it-yourself religion. Spiritualist groups did not need a trained leader, only interest in the phenomenon.

Though Whittlesey mentions the Spiritualists in his correspondence with the Home Missionary Society regarding New Boston, Newman does not include them at all in her discussion of the religious state of the town. The owner of the hotel where Newman lived was as interested as she was in magnetism, but he was a member of the Congregational society and her account of his theology proved him to be acceptable, if a little vague on the specifics of Christian doctrine. "Mr. Roberts spoke very thoughtfully on his idea of God, as the power that rules the world, and his confidence in that power" (Diary, vol. 10, Jan. 21, 1877). None of the people who attended prayer meetings caused difficulties like those caused by the Free Methodist Brother Dunn in Algonquin. In her sermons and diary entries regarding those who were not members of the churches in town, she did not single out Spiritualism as a difficulty in converting them. As we have seen before, she remained most interested in the character of people's outward lives as a sign of the state of their souls. Where Whittlesey described Spiritualism, Newman simply found secularism.

The link between Spiritualism and secularization was also strong because both attracted lay people who had lost interest in organized religion. They desired their faith to seem as certain as science, and wanted spiritual experience to be available to any seeker regardless of mystical bent or favor by God. The controversy in the Literary Society in New Boston over the reasonableness of Christianity corroborates Turner's conclusion about the relation of the two movements. "So powerful seemed scientific knowledge that many believers gladly signed over to it rights of eminent domain over God. This was the animus wishfully embodied in Spiritualism, but not in Spiritualism alone" (Turner 1985, 190). Newman's defense of Christianity rested on the evidence of the heart. Her clearest presentation of it is found in her final sermon in New Boston, discussed at the end of this chapter.

As Turner suggests, once people considered unbelief to be possible, it would have been difficult for Newman to make a compelling case for creating a church to a person who had chosen unbelief. She would have to move into more sophisticated theological territory than she typically inhabited. Her emphasis on Christian lifestyle and simple acceptance of Christ as savior could not provide an unbeliever with sufficient reason to accept Christ. One could clearly live a moral life without joining the church. Newman argued that the evidence of the difference made by Christianity was evident to the heart, in the stronger presence of love, hope, and faith (Sermon no. 87).

Newman was pragmatic. For the most part she stood in the long-standing tradition of orthodoxy. She was soundly Trinitarian. She stood in the evangelical tradition as well, emphasizing conversion, decision and commitment, and piety. In that tradition, the heart provided a more sure path to truth than reason. Her theology also shared the liberalism of Bushnell and Beecher. She tended to be optimistic about human nature, saw doubt as primarily misunderstanding, and was always hopeful that words of encouragement would touch the individual heart. The world was saved individual by individual. Nowhere in her sermons is there any indication of the stubborn persistence of sin in corporate and individual life. She did not preach about hell and heaven, but about the habits of a Christian life and character. Only occasionally did she preach on theological doctrines.

I call her pragmatic because she did not follow any one theological stream of her time, but used them as they best fit her purpose, shaping people's practical character, and thus shaping overt social behavior. Bushnell and Beecher, whose works she read more than any others, failed to provide a sophisticated analysis of the role of the heart in discerning truth, leaving later generations with an intellectually soft theology unable to stand up to the rigors of scientific challenge. In Newman's time, Spiritualism, even as it explored weird phenomena, aped science in its method. Newman did not try to reason about faith; she had no more intellectual resource than Bushnell provided. But she did use the resources of his theology, and challenged the agnostics in her congregation to account for the workings of the heart (Sermon no. 87).

For Newman and the home missionary movement, the existence of the church in the West was a necessary sign confirming God's favor on the settlement enterprise. It was not simply a sign of their success in debate.

Appropriating the Wild Land

The American Home Missionary Society would have several objections to supporting a church in New Boston. For one thing, it was not a growing town.

Between 1870 and 1880, the town lost two hundred people.[7] Newman stated in the application for Sunday School aid that the population was "standing still." Most of the Home Mission supported churches were in areas that could expect a large influx of people likely to join Congregational churches.

The fact of the "preoccupation" of the field by the Presbyterian's was a further problem. Though the Plan of Union that governed the cooperation between the Presbyterians and Congregationalists in home missionary territory had not been in effect since 1861, the society was always reluctant to compete with the Presbyterians. The American Home Missionary Society and the Presbyterian Board of Missions issued a joint statement as late as 1874.

> We therefore most earnestly recommend to all Presbyterians and all Congregationalists, especially to all our brethren in the ministry, and more particularly to all missionaries . . . to study first of all the things that make for peace . . . to be careful so as to advise and act with respect to all unorganized communities that, if possible there may be but one strong and harmonious church organization at first, whether it be Congregational or Presbyterian; to avoid the wicked waste of funds in the support of two feeble churches, both of which must be weak, and which might become involved in bitter, protracted and unholy strife. (Goodykoontz 1939, 352)[8]

The depression of the 1870s left the society unable to support the missionaries it already had in the field. They made appointments sparingly,

7. In 1870, the population of the New Boston township was 1758. In 1880, it was 1526 (U.S. Department of the Interior, Census Office, 1883, vol. 1, table III).

8. The American Home Missionary Society considered it a rule of its operations that it would not start a church in a place where there was another "evangelical" church. This did not include Episcopalians, Baptists, or Methodists. With these churches, Union congregations were impossible. The society considered that with the Episcopalians it was impossible to design a worship service that would suit everyone; with Baptists the issue was restricting communion to those baptized as believers by immersion; and with Methodists the Congregational perception of their enthusiastic worship and uneducated ministry prevented cooperation (Goodykoontz 1939, 353). In fast-growing communities, the society would be less concerned about competing with sister evangelical Protestants. In the case of New Boston, Illinois, the Presbyterians already had a church, though they did not supply a minister. The Congregationalists had joined the Presbyterian Church in the beginning; therefore, the American Home Missionary Society would be reluctant to support a separate Congregational church.

and only in the most promising locations. But more than that, Newman was a woman. Correspondence from the Home Missionary Society files of 1877 indicates that there was a difference of opinion on the acceptance of women home missionaries within the society. Any application for aid had to be recommended by the local superintendent. Joseph Roy, superintendent for Northern Illinois, favored women preaching and supported Newman, but having suffered an injury in a railroad accident, was unable to perform his duties that year. Martin Whittlesey, who acted for him in northern Illinois, was against women preaching.

The Home Missionary Society faced a paradox in its work, and its actions with regard to the New Boston Church were characteristic of the dilemma it faced. It saw itself as the vanguard of a cultural army, and it used specifically military terms for its project. Without its work, the West would decay into a wild society without moral roots or religion. So, at least, it said when it tried to raise money. However, it was reluctant to support the beginnings of congregations at the point where they needed support the most. It did not like to fail, or to report to those who had given hard won money that some of their donations had gone for nothing. Therefore, the society supported mostly the safe bets, so there was an acute lack of pastoral care on the frontier among the Congregationalists and Presbyterians.

Secularization was abetted in the American West by the chronic shortage of clergy. This shortage plagued all denominational groups, including the Roman Catholics. The home mission literature of all of them contained lament after lament of the places where pastoral ministry or preaching was needed and they had no money, or no people, to supply it.

Congregationalists, whose theological and ecclesiastical roots lay in the Geneva Reforms of John Calvin, regarded preaching as the most important aspect of pastoral work. In common with most of the church movements dating to the sixteenth century, the word of God—the Bible and preaching—was the heart of Christian experience. Western ministers found it was easier to preach than to provide pastoral care because an itinerant preacher could serve several communities at once. The Home Missionary Society, needing to conserve its resources, encouraged the practice. "It is worthy of notice, also, that a greater proportion of them [the missionaries] than heretofore have occupied fields each of which embraces several congregations; so that the Society has been able to extend its ministrations over a wider area and to a much larger number of communities than during the previous year" (American Home Missionary Society 1873, 59). But the itinerant preacher could not supply the kind of pastoral care that bound the community together through visiting, sitting with those who were troubled or grieving, and simply being available enough to become known. Although the church has lamented from its very beginnings that there were too few leaders and workers, the failure of the American churches to supply the West with pastors allowed for the easy acceptance of a secular view of life and the growth of religious movements that required very little structure and formally authorized leadership.

In early April 1877, the New Boston Congregational society applied for aid from the Home Missionary Society for its Sabbath School. Whittlesey wrote to the Home Missionary Society president offering qualified support for the application. He did this despite the fact that, for the first time, he had to face the prospect of a woman pastor in one of the churches for which he was responsible. On the one hand, he needed her; on the other, everything in his training was against it.

The question of women's leadership in the home missionary movement was an open one at this time. We have already seen that the Illinois Congregational associations were reluctant to face the question head on. The American Home Missionary Society was also ambivalent. Newman had received encouragement from Joseph Roy. Martin Whittlesey, supervising the work in Roy's area during his absence, indicated in his quarterly report that the New Boston church was an important part of his work for the first three months of 1877. His first mention of Newman does not contain any apparent problem regarding her being a woman, except for the Presbyterians and the conflicts over use of the church building. On the contrary, he seems impressed.

In March, the chief work was a survey of new ground—first in Mercer Co. where, at New Boston, a Miss Emma E. Newman, has commenced work among a population, supposed to be not reached by any religious society.— Rev. R. Nourse of Aledo has been at New Boston on Friday evenings occasionally for a year. His hearers have been a class of Spiritualists, a Materialist who looks with contempt on Meth. Church service and who can not be drawn in to the Presbyterian House of worship. That house new and expensive stands unoccupied. The Moderator of Presbytery refusing it to a "woman," the Masons have tendered her their hall—or hired one. She now has a small growing audience and a Sabbath-school of fifty-five pupils. (Whittlesey 1877b)

But in a private letter sent a few days later, Whittlesey expressed his reservations. Whittlesey wrote:

> Emma E. Newman is quasi recognized, by the Elgin Assoc. Her name is in the Minutes for '76—but she is not ordained.
>
> Probably she cannot be sustained by money got at New Boston—(She is a cousin of Wendell Phillips) If application were made for aid by the A.H.M.S.—would the fact that she is a woman embarrass the application? And cause its refusal?
>
> Yet if this woman *can prove* herself useful,—in "the present distress"—prove her *divine call*,—I have no objection to the Lord using her—in that way, I shall be glad of it. Please tell me how this matter strikes you brethren. There is a breaking down and caving in on the woman question—all around—(save in the New Testament—as I read it). If the Society feels like courting this ancient maiden (somewhere between 28–40)[9]—I will open this door. But my inclination is to try her—on the independent line—and to say "Don't trouble the old lady" "our good mother, the A.H.M.S." with these new fangled notions. (Whittlesey 1877c)

It was a strategy similar to that used by the Elgin Association in giving her a letter stating that they did not mind if she preached, but that this was not a license. They left the question of policy unasked and undebated. Whittlesey simply reported her work in the official venue, without raising the woman question publicly. Newman was both welcome and expendable. If she wanted to stay, no one would object, though according to all the policies of the society she could not count on any support. But if she succeeded, the resulting church could later be given to a man supported by the Home Missionary Society.

The reply from the Home Missionary society was equally ambivalent. They clearly did not want to lose an effective preacher, but until everyone else decided to authorize women's ministry, they were not going to set the precedent. "Dear Br. We don't feel called upon to settle the woman question . . . until we have all the men disposed of. If any church prospers with

---

9. Newman was thirty-nine.

female preaching and can support her, we won't object. It may settle the matter with Paul. But in our distributory other brothers many, many of whom agree with you and me and *Paul* on this subject, think it best for the Society to keep in the old paths for the present" (Carr 1887). This ambivalence provided Newman and other women like her a space within which to work.

As the mother of the nineteenth-century family was responsible for providing the gathering center for the family, so the woman pastor provided the gathering center for the church. The connecting family rituals of common meals, common work, and even common prayer had their place in the churches and served the community as such rituals served the family within the home. The household origins of Christianity supplied layers of tradition regarding the pastor's task that in the nineteenth century became explicitly connected in the minds of female ministers.

Like Peggy Pascoe, Richard White, in his recent history of the American West, suggests the idea of an imperial vision of the home, extending women's "natural" sphere into the realms of education and business (White 1991, 351). Newman's work can be seen as part of this imperial extension of domestic values into the life of the larger community.

The Rev. J. F. Ware is responsible for the statement that "a woman's work is good to do because it is woman's work, because if she will not do it, it becomes in the lowest sense menial or is left undone." As this dictum is preceded and followed by a tirade against those women who refuse to "take the honorable tasks and self-denials that, as wives and mothers, devolve upon them," it becomes clear that Mr. Ware means by "women's work," not the work that each individual woman is fitted to do, but the work, that women have usually done.

Certainly, housework, including the work and care that secure a cheerful, happy home is very good to do; if a woman has taste and faculty for it she will do it well and the blessing of well-doing will appear in her life. But many women have neither taste nor faculty for such work and the providential arrangements of their lives do not call for it. Most of them have worked at it, more or less, however, with pitifully poor results, leaving undone those things for which they were fitted, and for doing which the world would have thanked them. Was the distasteful, poorly executed work "good to do" because it was "woman's work?" Let unhappy homes and insane asylums answer. (Newman 1872, 109)

The idea that not all women were providentially intended for marriage and motherhood was important justification for an orthodox woman minister. That the fruits of her labor justified her work had less importance.

Newman conceived her highest duty to be serving God by serving the needs of the souls and bodies of the people in her church. She knew she was clearly not called to marriage and motherhood. However, she conceived marriage and motherhood as a calling as sacred as hers. In her Andover Aid Society work, she was distressed because Mrs. Goodwin had not provided a common meal for her family. Mrs. Goodwin had accepted this responsibility when she married and had children. Newman's implication was if she was not fitted for it, she should not have married.

The fact that Newman shared the ideal of female moral leadership and the understanding that women's work included the growth and care of spirit and body, allows the coherence of her preaching and her medical work to become clear. Few pastors in the late twentieth century dare to touch their parishioners as Newman did; we have separated the medical world from the spiritual. In addition, people have moved apart physically. Pastors have to be taught to touch carefully and with constraint. People do not consent to be touched so freely as in Newman's day. Attending to body and soul, Newman served as mother of her congregation. The boundaries of the home over which she presided expanded to include her whole community.

After a year in New Boston, Newman for the first time ventured the question of ordination to Whittlesey, who said she should not ask for it, that the Home Missionary Society would not allow any money to go to a woman when there were men who could not find work. "I suppose that means where there is any money a man must have it" (Diary, vol. 11, Jan. 12, 1887). She also consulted Thain, who advised her that he did not think the association was ready to make such a move. "He is in my favor, and a good judge, so I shall act on his opinion, but it is a dreary thing to be a woman and neither to have nor to want 'the safe sweet corner of the household fire, behind the heads of children' " (Diary, vol. 11, Jan. 19, 1878). This little phrase was used often enough to be found in more than one place in late nineteenth-century literature about the role of women. An anonymous work by a woman advocating women's return to the home uses it as well. "The 'safe sweet corner of the household hearth behind the heads of children,' is almost a forgotten and certainly a very much neglected place."[10] Although Newman did not see herself as revolutionary, upsetting the centuries-old icon of the male minister representing Christ to the congregation, she clearly was conscious of choosing a different and lonely path, one that shocked people. The depth of her appreciation of Col. Henry of Algonquin, who was not shocked, hints at her sense of difference.

Toward the end of her work in New Boston, a Baptist minister moved to town and began gathering a congregation. The Presbyterian church still did not have a pastor. The Congregationalists were not interested in the Band of Hope, a new group with a holiness style, or the Methodists. But Newman's people were evidently interested in the new Baptist preacher. Newman decided that she would not stay if the Baptists organized a church. She recorded two reasons in her diary. One, that she would not stay in the difficult climate of New Boston if she was going to be unable to accomplish anything, and second, she had some sense, despite their favorable comments to her, that the congregation would prefer a man. "They are wondering . . . whether the society would not prosper better with a man to manage it. I am willing to step out and told Mrs. G. that I would write to Mr. Whittlesey to ask for a man if they wanted me to" (Diary, vol. 11, Apr. 13, 1878).

Sectarian rivalry was a serious problem in many towns in the American West, as we have seen. In New Boston, despite the denominations' official policies of cooperation, the people of the various churches did not intend to cooperate. The Presbyterian elder, Crab, did not want to open the church to a woman preacher. His objection was stated as a matter of church policy: "Said he 'liked to see people come in by the door' " (Diary, vol. 10, Jan. 2, 1877). Newman was not ordained, and Crab viewed her appointment as irregular. The other elder in the session, Davis, was also only willing to recognize a Presbyterian minister "in good regular standing" (Diary, vol. 10, Jan. 20, 1877). This, by Presbyterian policy, could not be a woman.

By June 1878, it was clear that Miller, the Baptist minister, had gathered most of the church-going people into his congregation, so Newman took leave of her third church.

10. I have searched in vain for several years to find the origin of the phrase. Every use I have seen places it in quotation marks.

Pastoral Care of Body and Soul

Ordained or not, Newman did make a place for herself as a woman in New Boston by combining with her preaching and traditional pastoral activities a more extensive homeopathic practice than she had in Algonquin, where there was a doctor in town. The case of Mrs. Lytle, Mrs. Van Scoter's daughter, illustrates the way Newman integrated the two professions; in doing so she followed an old model of ministry that did not survive the professionalization movements of both medicine and pastoral ministry. It reemerged in the late twentieth century with the dramatic rise in the numbers of women clergy, though not followed by women exclusively. We will discuss this further in the last chapter.

If the New Testament can be taken at all as a source of information about the concerns of the early churches, then physical healing was a primary factor in ministry and closely connected with spiritual well-being. Healing was one of the most significant aspects of Jesus' ministry, and male and female deacons visited the sick, as did the elders, laying hands on them, the same sign used to confirm authority in church leaders. Before the sixteenth century, healing was a primary focus of women's ministry, especially in women's monastic orders. One of the most well-known medieval women, Hildegard of Bingen, was a mystic and theologian, but also a healer. She wrote a treatise on medicine, as well as her works of theology. In the growing anxiety of the Renaissance and Reformation eras, women who practiced healing often fell under suspicion as witches, but even as medicine became increasingly scientific, women continued to serve as doctors, midwives, and healers. The care of the sick and dying remained within the *oikos*, where it had, in the earliest centuries of Christianity, already become part of the work of church leaders. Only as medicine and pastoral care became professionalized in the late nineteenth century did the *polis* become the main arena for healing. In the Roman Catholic Church, women religious continued to combine spiritual and physical healing, but in Protestant circles, except for midwives, such work was confined largely to a woman's immediate family. As a Protestant minister and healing practitioner, Newman simply brought this household work into the public sphere as part of her pastoral concern.

Besides homeopathy, Newman was interested in magnetism and mental healing, especially in using these practices to cure headaches and other minor illnesses. Rubbing was part of the application of these treatments, a kind of massage designed to restore a healthy flow of electricity in the body. Often Newman applied the treatment without touching the patient, but simply moved her hands, a few inches away, over the patient's body in one direction. Newman's notes on the technique of magnetic cure suggest that the treatment was as effective if the practitioner did not touch the patient as if she did. "Draw out the diseased nerve-aura with hands used as a sponge to sop it up. Hold hands on the seat of the ailment for a minute or two, then draw off with downward passes and shake vigorously to throw off. Repeat, not ever more than half an hour. Wash hands. Either repeat the 'laying on' or the downward passes, with concentrated idea of pouring stimulating curative influence along the nerves" (Newman, "Notes on Sinnett's Directions for Magnetism"). Theoretically, the magnetism from her hands helped to align the magnetism of the patient's body.

In addition to treatment of the magnetic field of the patient, both patient and practitioner needed to sustain positive thoughts about the prospects for healing. Newman, in her use of the theorist Warren Evans,[11] was interested in an orthodox Christian interpretation of the theories of magnetism and mental healing, attributing the healing to God. Her practice of both techniques was a combination of traditional Christian healing practices of prayer and laying hands on the sick with the use of herbal and homeopathic chemical remedies.

Homeopathic theorists held that disease originated within the body itself and healing involved inoculating the body with a substance that causes symptoms like the disease. According to this theory, the body was active, stimulated to heal itself. In contrast to homeopathy, the allopathic physician viewed disease as originating from outside the body. The allopathic physician did not use medicine that produced like symptoms, but medicine that produced the opposite symptoms. In allopathic theory the body was passive and best healed by removing the disease. Allopathic physicians favored such techniques as purgatives, bleeding, and surgery, often termed heroic medicine. Neither of these kinds of practitioners

11. Newman used Warren Evans' book *Manual of Mental Healing*, a copy of which I have been unable to locate. Her notes on another of his works, "Esoteric Christianity and Mental Therapeutics," are preserved in her notebook entitled "Things in General."

knew much about the causes of any disease they treated. Neither could claim more success than the other.

Physicians were not yet licensed, though there was increasing professionalization of medical practice. It was largely up to patients to choose the kind of treatment they thought most likely to cure them or alleviate their suffering. Newman's combination of medical practice and pastoral care in this case illustrates the permeable boundaries of both professions at this time. It also illustrates the way in which women moved in both professions despite formal exclusion from structures of education and authorization. Newman's physical nursing originated in a traditional female knowledge and role, caring for family members. She began her adult life caring for her mother, and learning from Howarth, the homeopathic physician in Andover, about making medicines and which to use for what diseases. Newman also learned by treating her own numerous ailments, especially upper-respiratory troubles, problems with her ears, and the kind of liver and digestive ailment that kept her ill much of her time in New Boston.

In Newman's society, the sickroom was open to women. From simple chores such as washing bedclothes and making teas, to more complex treatment of symptoms, people assumed women had skill and to some degree knowledge about nursing. Her society was also undecided about the most effective kind of medical practice. Allopathy and homeopathy were equally sought, some patients preferring the heroic treatments of allopathy, others the more gentle treatments of homeopathy.

Newman became acquainted with her patient and parishioner Hortense Lytle upon her arrival in New Boston in January 1877. She treated Lytle's physical and spiritual ailments until Mrs. Lytle's death at the end of August. Newman's engagement with Lytle involved both physical care and the care of her soul.

New Boston did not have a resident physician; one had to come by boat. Roberts, the owner of the hotel where Newman lived, practiced magnetism. Newman favored magnetism, but also had her homeopathic remedies available. The two of them, and perhaps others, served most of the town's medical needs.

Newman's initial contacts with Lytle were pastoral:

Made a long call on Mrs. Lytle talking with her of her own spiritual life: she is rather a small pattern of a woman, selfish and sick, and, most unwarrantably, thinks herself superior to her very bright husband, yet there is something interesting about her, and I hope Christ will develop her. . . . Took tea with Mrs. Lytle and had a long talk with her in which she told me the history of a selfish life: she wants to be a Christian, but she does love herself more than anything else in heaven or earth. (Diary, vol. 10, Feb. 14 and March 1, 1877)

A few days later, after preaching a sermon on seeking Christ, Newman noted that Lytle seemed solemn. By the beginning of April, she was clearly ill.

Newman diagnosed Lytle's illness as one of the soul. Newman had already noted her "selfishness" as the main characteristic of Lytle's spiritual malaise. One of the mental healing theorists Newman studied also raised the issue of selfishness in the production of physical disease. Newman preserved a quote from Evans' *The Mental Cure* in her commonplace book: "Disease is often only a state of supreme selfishness" ("Things in General"). Related is the fact that Newman considered selfishness to be one of her own faults. "God had work for me, the last work I should have chosen when I reach Heaven I shall know why it was best. My selfishness and impatience called for a severe discipline and they had it," she wrote in her autobiographical sketch.

Aside from the basic psychological truth that one sees one's own faults best in others, what can we make of this diagnosis of selfishness? For Newman selfishness had a theological explanation and was a disease of the soul; but as a mental healer, she believed diseases of the soul were the cause of diseases of the body. "The lungs in their action respond to the intellect. An act of faith inaugurates a change in the action of the lungs. So, also, fear, and every abnormality of the mind, affect the action of the heart and lungs in the direction of disease . . . Mental cure is magnetism in its higher spiritual applications and uses. The system of mental healing must ever be kept within the domain of a genuine Christianity."[12] For Newman, the spiritual disease of selfishness could be cured only by Lytle's conversion. Newman's and her other physicians' physical remedies would not cure her illness, only ease her discomfort.

---

12. From Evans' "Esoteric Christianity and Mental Therapeutics," quoted in the notebook "Things in General."

At the end of June 1877, during Lytle's illness, Newman preached about selfishness in a sermon titled "The Unselfish Theory of Life" (Sermon no. 57). She took her text from Second Corinthians 5:15: "He died for all, that they which live should not henceforth live unto themselves, but unto Him who died for them and rose again" (AV). She began the sermon with the question of the meaning of life, and the various ways that question has been answered over time. Newman suggested that the question itself was a selfish question, that the individual wants it answered in such a way that her or his own life seems significant. The theories offered by various philosophies do not satisfy, and "we are bewildered."

> We turn to instinct, and we find its first direction to be an utterly selfish one. The babe cries for what it wants, and will not give it up till forced: it demands poison and milk with the same persistence, it cares nothing for any claim but its own, it must be constantly over-ruled by superior wisdom, if it is to live at all. . . . The body and the mind grow, but, often, the soul seems to meet with an arrest of development, and to remain in this stage throughout life, its main idea being varied forms of this one theme: "I will have what I want, if I can in any way get it." (Sermon no. 57)

Newman attributed the conflicts, storms, and great unhappiness of human existence to this instinct of selfishness. But she also considered another instinct, one given by God.

> When we see a mother, worn with nursing a sick babe, yet caring gently for the older children, ordering the house with ready thought of everyone, curbing the impatience of her own strained nerves, that she may be the keeper of peace for the family, have we not all admired that quiet heroism? The martyrs of the family and the sick-room bear more than those of the axe and the stake, and often we hardly know it, but when attention is called to that firm, loving unselfishness, even those who do not wish to imitate it, know that it is better than their own lives. (Sermon no. 57)

Newman shared with her generation the assumption that women were supposed to be models of Christian virtue. The mother in this sermon fit the ideal in her unselfishness, putting her own needs aside patiently, heroically. The mother became a saint, or even a Christ figure. The cult of domesticity provided the ready image of the self-denying mother as personification of unselfishness.

Unselfishness was, in Newman's sermon, the surest way to happiness in this life. At least an appeal to people's natural selfishness indicated that unselfishness promoted a better life, and to prepare for the future, unselfishness was the surest way toward heaven. "Christ . . . constantly teaching that life was given for unselfish uses, accompanied his words by life and death which, all could see were not for himself" (Sermon no. 57). The essential thing about living would not be to answer the question of life's meaning, but to follow Christ's lead. Newman also closely correlated unselfishness with usefulness. A life devoted to others meant doing useful things for people. Unselfishness was active and visible.

Though selfishness was a theme running through Newman's thought, her view of it was personal, confined almost entirely to the family. She did not address issues of social selfishness. That personal selfishness that Newman identified within herself and within Mrs. Lytle was sufficient explanation for the ills of the world.

Lytle's physical problems were in the urinary tract and bowels, congestion and obstructions. She consulted both allopathic doctors for heroic treatments such as purgatives and operations, and Newman and Roberts for homeopathic remedies and magnetism. Newman's record of one day illustrates the way they all worked together.

> Spent the whole day helping to take care of Mrs. Lytle who was in great distress; her husband also hung over her all day; Mrs. Gore took Freddie away, Mrs. V. circulated about as was necessary, and everything was as favorable as it could be. I gave her sulphur, Mr. Roberts rubbed her, Dr. Bras insisted on giving her castor-oil and whiskey, which she took with much hesitation, retained for some time, and finally vomited with great agony. Nothing seemed to do her more than momentary good till Mr. Roberts came and rubbed her for a long time, after that, she was quiet. She is very nervous and screamed and groaned and writhed most of the day. (Diary, vol. 10, May 14, 1877)

Sulfur was supposed to cause fever and heat. A homeopathic practitioner used it in diluted form to treat fever by stimulating the body to heal itself from fever. Diluted in alcohol, the remedy also had a sedative effect.

In contrast to the mild treatments of Newman and Roberts that day,

Lytle also received "heroic" treatment from her allopathic doctor, a dose of castor oil and whiskey, a powerful purgative. Her symptoms suggested blockage in her digestive system. The allopathic remedy would therefore be one that would cause her to vomit the offending substance.

In June, Newman noted some problems with other members of the family. Freddie Lytle, a small boy, was restless and disrupted the church service. Mrs. Lytle complained that he would not sleep, and Newman lent Mrs. Lytle the hammock in which she usually slept so the child could sleep near his mother. This seemed to quiet the boy. Newman also noted that there was some unspoken trouble between herself and Mr. Lytle. Newman did not think systemically about this family. Despite all her experience with the burdens of family illness, Newman did not connect these family disturbances to Mrs. Lytle's illness, but treated them as individual problems.

At the end of July, Lytle was much worse. The allopathic doctor still came to see her, though he had to come by boat from some distance. Newman postponed her vacation so that she would not leave the family in a difficult moment.

> Went over to see Mrs. Lytle, found her very weak, stayed but little while but promised to return in afternoon when her nurse would have left. She can hardly live many days, and I promised not to leave while I could be any comfort to them. Mrs. Lytle slept very little, but her bowels which both her allopathic doctors had pronounced hopelessly obstructed, moved as much as could be expected with her little eating and the case began to look hopeful. I prayed with her in the night and she spoke freely of her trembling Christian hope, saying that she thought, if she was to live, it would be her delight to do good, and she hoped never to live such a selfish life any more, but she felt ready to die, and would prefer to go then if she could not get strong again. (Diary, vol. 10, July 31, 1877)

Newman had a pastoral concern for the salvation of Lytle's soul. Newman had talked to her many times about her selfishness, as well as other spiritual matters. Over the course of the weeks, Lytle became more interested. Newman marked a Bible for her to study. Here Newman reported the beginning of a change in her patient. A week later, Lytle had a vision.

> Returning [from Boston Bay] met Mrs. Gore, who had been searching the woods for me, to tell me of a sudden ecstatic experience of Mrs. Lytle, "her

conversion" they called it; a vision I think it must have been, of Christ coming through a parted veil taking her in His arms and saying to her "You're safe," repeating it three times. The weak little woman had so longed for something tangible that this seemed the condescension needed; such gentle love. Prayer meeting was one of thanksgiving, 6 present. Sat up with Mrs. Lytle, she was feeling the re-action from her excitement, and suffered much. She wants to be baptized, but has scruples about having the ceremony performed by me, because I am not ordained. (Diary, vol. 10, Aug. 8, 1877)

As the doctors were called over long distances for emergencies of physical well-being, the nearest ordained Congregational minister was called for this emergency of spiritual well-being. Rev. Nourse came from Aledo, fifteen miles away. We do not know if there was no ordained minister in New Boston at the time, for instance the Methodist, or if the family preferred a minister they knew. Because Rev. Nourse had been preaching from time to time in New Boston before Newman's arrival, he would know the people.

He came on August 9 to baptize Mrs. Lytle. "Mrs. Benedict came for me saying that Mr. Nourse had come. . . . Mrs. L. was able to attend to the whole service, which, including the baptism and communion was somewhat long for an invalid, and looked wonderfully animated. . . . Mrs. Lytle expected the doctor in the night and was prepared to insist on an operation, so we all felt that we might see her no more" (Diary, vol. 10, Aug. 9, 1877).

Lytle lived three weeks more, and Newman recorded no more concern about her soul, though she visited her every day and continued to try to make her as comfortable as possible.

Newman's pastoral work shifted to the family when Lytle died on Sunday, August 26, 1877. She was present to help them through the trial of an autopsy.

Mrs. Gore came round before I was up in the morning to say that Mrs. Lytle had died at 30 min. A. M., and to ask me to go over as soon as breakfast, which I did. I found that the post-mortem examination was to be held at 9, and that it would be a comfort to them, if I would stay. Of course, I stayed, though I did not go into the room except once when Mrs. V. [Van Scoter, Mrs. Lytle's mother] wished to go, and I accompanied her. It seemed to me a terrible necessity, for the good of humanity that it should be done, and a needless aggravation to have any one but the four doctors witness the operation. I hope I can be cremated. Went over by invitation in eve, to pray with them, but there were some uncongenial people in, and everybody was very tired, and it seemed best not. (Diary, vol. 10, Aug. 26, 1877)

Newman presided at the funeral, which was delayed because the coffin Lytle particularly wanted had not arrived.

> Went over at 3, but found that the coffin had come untrimmed, and there must be a delay of half an hour; went back to my study and was very glad . . . as the delay was over an hour. Spoke very simply and earnestly, not at as much length as I should have done, had not a heavy thundershower threatened; it came before the close of even the shortened services making the house absolutely dark, so that lamps were lighted; we could not leave for the rain and the singers were kind enough to sing several tunes. When the violence of the rain had ceased, such as could well ride went up with our friends to the cemetery and waited while the grave was filled in. I gave the benediction, and we left the poor tortured little body there. (Diary, vol. 10, Aug. 28, 1877)

Newman was struck by the weather during this funeral. She noted it in her commonplace notebook from which she drew illustrations for subsequent sermons. "At the funeral of a lady who had suffered long and terrible pain, a heavy thunder-storm threatened the town, absolutely darkening the air. The scene was one of awe. In the darkness and distress, I rose to pray, and began, 'We thank Thee, our Father, that there is no power, in this world, or in any other world, that thy children need ever to fear' " ("Things in General"). Others at the funeral remarked about it as well. "Called on Mrs. Gore and the Lytles, was glad to find the latter gratified with the incidents of the funeral; the darkness had been grateful to their feelings the delay pleased them, as Horty had said that she would like to be buried at sunset, and they thought my remarks just right. Mrs. V. specially thanked me for having spoken with no unmerited eulogy of the dead" (Diary, vol. 10, Aug. 29, 1877).

Newman's pastoral work rested upon her community's sense of the interrelation of all things, their understanding that God's presence was marked by natural phenomena, as well as by symbolic acts and words. Newman incorporated the darkening rain storm, a coincidental occurrence, into her work of helping a grieving community make sense out of death and the life that remained to them. In the romantic tradition, influenced by Ralph Waldo Emerson, and particularly in the writings of naturalists such as John Muir, this interconnection of all things becomes explicit. But this tradition itself rested on older Puritan habits of searching the environment for signs that would indicate a visitation of the grace of God in times of trouble. It was Newman's duty to point out signs of God's presence in the ritual of comforting the bereaved.[13]

Emma Newman's most important theological message to her congregation was not, I think, contained in her preaching. It lay in her pastoral care. Newman herself did not ever say this was so, nor did she ever delineate the theology underlying her pastoral care, but she had unspoken, perhaps even unconscious assumptions behind her work. Although she preached about the love of God, she demonstrated it far more powerfully when she sat up through the night with a sick parishioner so that the family could get some rest. Although she preached about trusting God, she demonstrated it more effectively by trusting God herself. Though she preached about the incarnation of God in Jesus Christ, she declared it more effectively by visiting isolated people and praying with them and simply talking to them.

Her homeopathic and mental healing work proceeded from an understanding that the divine spirit was available to heal the body. She practiced healing as an application of spiritual truth by physical means. She was a child of Reformed Christianity with its emphasis on the Word of God, but as a child of American pietist evangelicalism, she also knew intuitively that the incarnate Word is not expressed by words alone, but also by deeds.

Christianity and Society in New Boston

In addition to her homeopathic and mental healing work, Newman was more politically active in her ministry in New Boston than she had been in previous places. She stayed longer, and thus had more time to work on such matters. She organized a small speaking tour for Susan B. Anthony to

13. I am grateful for a conversation with Archie Smith, Jr., in which we explored this aspect of pastoral care in relation to his book *The Relational Self: Ethics and Therapy from a Black Church Perspective* (1982), and the ideas of process theology. Process theology developed after Newman's time, but she uses many of the ideas that process theologians made explicit.

visit New Boston and some neighboring towns in the spring of 1878, putting up a quarter of the necessary money herself. Anthony's lecture on April 9 was well attended. "Had a lively discussion with Miss A. who charged that ministers were cowardly and afraid of their people because they did not preach on woman suffrage. Mr. Matthews, Miss F[raizer]'s brother in law, upheld her" (Diary, vol. 11, Apr. 10, 1878).

Newman also started a temperance society in the town. Both women's rights and temperance were movements rooted in a Victorian anxiety about the fate of the family in times of rapid change.

> The future of the family was a matter of great concern, for, in a sense, the sentimentalists were carving out a new and more ambitious role for this most basic of human institutions. It was to serve as a moral counterweight to a restless, materialistic, individualistic, and egalitarian society. The family was, in fact, to serve many of the functions formerly reserved for the church. Religion, which had been disestablished in the public sphere during the upheavals of the eighteenth century, would now be reestablished in the private sphere of the family and placed in the keeping of women. For this reason, more than any other, most sentimentalists opposed the movement for women's rights, for they perceived it as a threat to the very institution upon which they counted for moral redemption. (Strickland 1985, 5)

Newman brought the two movements together in her ministry, seeing suffrage as essential if women were to preserve family and community from the unbounded selfishness of the day. Newman moved from practicing usefulness in the private family sphere in her youth to public but nonprofessional usefulness in her work in Andover Aid Society, and finally to public, professional work in the church. Her personal transitions match the same transitions in women's leadership in the nation as a whole. Women's first leadership roles outside the family belonged to the voluntary societies existing beside but outside the churches. After the Civil War women increasingly stepped from leadership positions in these societies into public leadership in the churches. With the church reestablished in the family, the old household models of Christian leadership based in teaching, healing, and the sacred meal came again to the fore. Because the church also remained a public institution, women's leadership within it became harder for church people to deny.

Though Newman's work was natural to her, she could not avoid being an object of curiosity and even hostility. Still, Newman had far more local support for her work in New Boston than she had in Algonquin. The interdenominational quarrels in New Boston were not as hard to bear as serious quarrels within the congregation in Algonquin had been. But she was, as a single woman living in the local hotel, vulnerable to gossip.

The hotel owners, the Roberts, were soon good friends. Mr. Roberts was interested in animal magnetism, and he and Newman both treated the people of the town. Newman's friendship with Roberts provoked gossip at one point, and an attempt at blackmail, though Newman had been unaware that gossip about herself and Roberts was general in town. A Mr. Eames, from out of town, contacted them, claiming to have a letter written from one to the other that would compromise them both.

> The Eames who wrote of a letter, he pretended to have found actually dared to come here to a dance on Saturday night, and stay through the day on Sunday. Mrs. Ballard came in, in the morning, to tell me that he was here. I went for Mr. Roberts, who was not then at home, but at night he asked E. again for the letter and met the same evasive answer: then we both went down to the office and confronted the wretched fellow. I told him that I supposed he meant black-mail, and that I never should pay him one cent. I explained the only note I ever wrote Mr. R., and one of the men sitting by in the office said that he was the clerk who sold me the tickets for Mr. and Mrs. R. He finally agreed to send me the letter, provided that I would give him a receipt for it. (Diary, vol. 11, Mar. 19, 1878)

The incident did not become a scandal, but indicated the vulnerability of a single woman in such a situation. The general gossip died down, but was fanned again by Miller, the Baptist minister. Though her congregation seems not to have taken it seriously, this incident was a factor in Newman's decision to leave New Boston.

Newman did not succeed in forming a Congregational church in New Boston; there is not one there to this day. Unlike her work at Algonquin that she considered to be a failure (and where the church still exists, now a United Church of Christ congregation with almost fourteen hundred members), she seemed to have had no regrets about her work in New

Boston. Certainly she did not feel it necessary to search her soul to the degree that she did after leaving Algonquin.

By the end of May 1878, Miller's Baptist congregation was growing, Newman's congregation numbered just fifteen, and she concluded it was time to move on. "Mr. Stowell made me a call in eve, feeling much better; he says that more are to be immersed next Sunday, and the new Baptist church is fixed fact, but will mostly be supported from the country; he hinted at our continuing in spite of it, but I would hear none of it. I shall miss the good man much" (Diary, vol. 11, May 29, 1878).

On Sunday, June 9, Newman preached her last sermon in New Boston to a congregation of fifty. "Lay awake nearly all night. God bless my people." She titled the sermon "Life Made Glad by Trust in Christ" (Sermon no. 87).[14] The text was from the account in Luke of the two disciples on the road to Emmaus. "We trusted that it was He which should have redeemed Israel" (AV). She added a later verse as well. "He expounded unto them the things concerning Himself" (Luke 24:21 and 27 AV). This sermon was at once her answer to the agnostics, her encouragement to her struggling congregation, and her counsel to herself concerning the future.

Henry Ward Beecher used this same text for a farewell sermon to his Plymouth Church congregation in Brooklyn, New York, in 1863, as he left for an extended trip to Europe. It is the final sermon in the first volume of his *Sermons* (1868). His approach differed considerably from Newman's sermon preached twenty years later, but Newman had spent many hours reading Beecher's sermons aloud to her mother and fellow boarders, and I suspect it is not an accident that she chose the text for a farewell sermon. Beecher did not spend much time on the meaning of the resurrection, or on the mysterious presence of Christ with the disciples on the road. He used the text to discuss his relationships with the congregation and to defend his orthodoxy, to show that he believed in the grace of God manifested in Christ, though he did not always mention Christ in his sermons. Beecher seemed to use the occasion to review his work and place it in an

14. Because this is the only sermon on which Newman did not record the date and place where she gave it, I cannot be absolutely certain that this was her last sermon at New Boston. However, the sermons are numbered in the order in which they were written, and the number before this one was given as the Sunday before, June 2, 1878, I am reasonably certain that this is the one she gave on her last Sunday in New Boston.

orthodox light. Newman, by contrast, focused on the disciples' inability to see Christ, and urges her congregation to "see" all that scripture has said about Christ, in a sense proving the validity of Christianity. Newman was not leaving behind a rich and powerful church, but a small and struggling one, beset by doubts and indifference.

Newman began the sermon by discussing the despair of the disciples after Christ's death, a despair of doubt and bitter disappointment. She then outlined the ills of the world, reasons enough for anyone to give up hope.

Shall we then despair? Unless some higher wisdom comes to our aid, we must despair. Some noble minds have stopped here. They say, "You have beautiful dreams, but we cannot go beyond the evidence of our senses. We see suffering and crime, we see little children dying, because of others' sins, but we never see your ruling Love. We hear cries of distress of horror and of fear, the unanswered appeal of a world suffering often innocently: we never hear a voice proclaiming justice. If there be a God, there is no place for His interference. There is no escape from necessity." They take that dreary waste, bound in affliction and iron, to be all of life, and they work in it, consciously honest and unselfish, in a way that undermines their whole reasoning, showing higher life in their own souls than their own theories could ever have put there. (Sermon no. 87)

To those in her congregation who were feeling abandoned and uncertain about the future of the church, or who were suffering in some other way, she reminded them that Christ did not come to bring their personal happiness, but that joy in life consisted in the presence of Christ in whatever circumstances they find themselves. "But we ought to have the great joy. Christ, walking with us while we know Him not, waits to unfold to us the things concerning Himself. We may be very stupid in understanding, as the two disciples were, but, if we listen, we shall know something, and, if we believe that, we shall know more" (Sermon no. 87).

She closed with an affirmation of trust that sustained her own faith, and left her congregation with encouragement to faith beyond the reach of human reason. "Little by little we shall find that His plan is far higher than we had thought, that He is carrying it on in ways beyond our comprehension and that we can safely rest in the wise God. We begin to see that He is doing much better with us and for us than if He had followed our plans, and given us the things we cried for in the dark" (Sermon no. 87).

She finally rested her argument on the evidence of the quality of the lives of those who truly trust in God, not just those who call themselves Christians. As we saw above, here she stood firmly on the theological ground explored by such theologians as Frederick Schleiermacher and Horace Bushnell. Quality of life was not necessarily perceivable by the senses, but rather by the heart. These lives are "more strong, more helpful, more glad than other lives because Christ rules [them] and His peace and His power abide in [them]" (Sermon no. 87). With this word, she left New Boston.

History usually remembers success. Congregations concentrate their memories on the times the church outgrew its building or achieved other notable successes. But far more common in the lives of small towns and their churches were years of struggle. Poorly paid pastors came and went almost as fast as the congregation itself changed with older members moving on west and newcomers settling in their place. New Boston was beginning to settle down somewhat, but Newman still labored with a congregation that was not certain of its future. The setting was characteristic of the West, with a growing indifference to organized religion, several churches competing for a small number of members, and an openness to the ministry of a woman, especially when no man would take the church. For a while, Newman stayed and tried to make this wild land her own.

She engaged in a customary style of pastoral visitation and preaching aimed at shaping a more pious and faithful community. She brought to bear her ideal "highest Christian culture" from Andover orthodoxy, and she engaged in defending the faith from those in the community who saw no point in religion. However, unlike her Home Missionary Society superintendent, she did not see the Spiritualists in town as a particular threat. In fact, she shared with them the belief that spirit and body were intimately connected, and she did not hesitate to add healing to her pastoral work. "If we think of the office of pastor in its full sense of offering care for the members of a congregation and community in the crises and the joys of life and of guiding their Christian growth, as well as of strengthening the institutional base, it began to find expression across the continent in the work of the Builder" (Osborn 1991, 98). In contrast to the Revivalist who could experience the thrill of multiple conversions in every place, the Builder had to bring the sheep into the fold one by one. In the process, the Builder pastor had to develop lasting relationships, many deep and lasting friendships, in order to accomplish the foundation of a church. In addition, the Builder's preaching changed. "Preaching came down to earth, slowly untangling itself from its involvement with abstract doctrinal quarrels among Christians to deal more directly with the practical problems of everyday living and the certainty of dying" (Osborn 1991, 98).

Newman was a Builder, and as a woman worked to "make the wild land her own." She developed a seamless pastoral style that included both the body and the soul of her people. She entered the public arena in the cause of temperance and the defense of Christianity, working to establish the "highest New England Christian culture" to the frontier. She was finally defeated in New Boston by the number of competing denominations struggling to recruit the same small group of souls. Her gender aided her in providing her access to the homes and lives of her parishioners on a more intimate plane than that available to her male colleagues. However, it also hindered her because she continued to be regarded as intrinsically inadequate to the work. Through her struggles and successes, we are given a clearer picture of the complex history of the Protestant churches in the West.

"Dial Is Our Only
Self-Supporting Church"

Dial is our only self-supporting church, and the pastor, Miss
Emma E. Newman, does most of the supporting. It is small and
weak.

—General Association of Kansas

Because a volume of her diary is missing, we do not know what Emma
Newman did when she left New Boston, or how she came to be in Kansas.
Records of her preaching indicate that she served from October 1880 until
May 1881 in several small communities clustered around Fairview in
McPherson County, Kansas. The gap in the diary requires us to piece
together fragments of her trail. At the end of her pastorate in New
Boston, Illinois, Emma lived with her cousin Charles for a while, visited
Hattie Chadbourne in Vinton, Iowa, and lived for several months in
Chicago, before returning to Andover at the request of her Aunt Fay in
the summer of 1879. There, volume 11 of her diary ends. The next volume
begins on March 8, 1883. The evidence of her activities during this three-
and-a-half-year period can be found in her notations of the places and
dates of her sermons and in the records of the Congregational Church in
Kansas.

The earliest evidence of her presence in Kansas are sermons preached in
1880 in Delmore, Durham Park, Galva, Ashland, and Fairview, all between October and December. This represents a wide geographical range.
Fairview, Delmore, and Galva are within a day's ride of McPherson. Ashland is forty miles south of Dodge City. From the dates on her sermons, it is

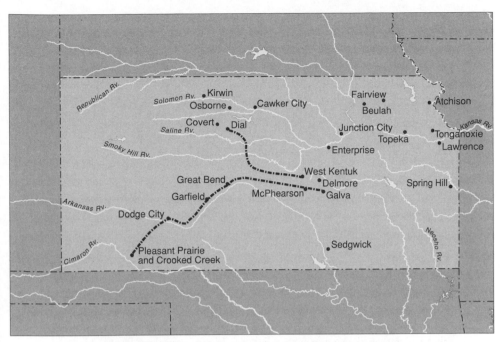

Emma Newman's Preaching in Kansas, 1879–1889
(Dotted lines show Newman's 1883 journeys by horse and buggy)

clear that she traveled from Fairview to Ashland and back between October 1880 and January 1881, a distance of four hundred miles, but all accessible by railroad.

In 1881, she preached in Fairview, Hardscrabble, Delmore, Olive Branch School House, Garfield, and Gere. Olive Branch School House was also near McPherson. Hardscrabble was within a day's journey of Delmore. Gere was near Great Bend, and Garfield was between Great Bend and Dodge City. The Olive Branch School House may have served an African American community. In early April 1883, Emma spoke to a Mr. Roseberry in Great Bend, a Black minister, about her Olive Branch people, and was glad to hear that a Mr. Spearman had been converted (Diary, vol. 12, Apr. 4, 1883). In 1881 she moved south again to Meade County.

Beginning in February 1882, Newman preached for a year at Crooked Creek, near Dodge City, working with a Rev. Feemster. The *Kansas Telephone*, the Congregational newspaper of the state, contains reports of her working in that area, and her diary resumes with entries from her last few weeks in Crooked Creek.[1] In March 1883, she returned to the McPherson County neighborhood. She lived in Galva for a few months, looking for a permanent place. In September 1883, the church in Dial, Osborne County, called Newman to be their pastor. She stayed there four years.

In her work in Kansas, Newman moved to the very edge of the frontier. She no longer served churches located near railroad lines. In southern Kansas, she was close to the well-traveled Santa Fe Trail, but in her move to Dial, she left even that convenience behind. In Kansas we find a fully

1. The *Congregational Year-book* listed her as pastor in Pleasant Prairie in Meade County in 1881, though according to her own preaching records, none of her sermons was preached there until 1882. It is possible that some sermons from this time are missing; however, the manuscripts are numbered carefully and there are no breaks in the collection until after she left Kansas. I am not sure what to make of the discrepancy between her own records and those of the Congregational Association. Crooked Creek, within a few hours' travel of Pleasant Prairie, was without a pastor in 1882, according to the Year-book, and seems also to have been supplied by Newman. She preached occasionally in Gilbert and Belle Meade, also nearby. From the dates on her sermons, we can conclude that she was an itinerant preacher, based in one larger community, but preaching at several smaller neighboring stations. Even before her appearance in the *Congregational Year-book,* she was preaching in Kansas. In 1880, she preached in Durham, Ashland, Fairview, (whether this was the Fairview near Atchison in Brown County or the one in Smith County is difficult to tell— if it is in Smith county, Newman's move to Dial is not difficult to explain), Delmore, and Rearick's School House. All of these were located in western Kansas, but represent hundreds of miles of travel among them. By the next year she had added to her preaching venues Hardscrabble, Gere, Sedwick, and Enterprise along with the Ashley and Olive Branch school houses. These also required her to travel long distances among them, though she seems to have stayed several weeks in each place.

The *Kansas Telephone* noted her presence in the Meade County neighborhood several times. In March 1882, one article stated, "The churches of Crooked Creek and Pleasant Prairie in Ford and Meade counties have extended a call to Miss E. E. Newman, a licentiate from Illinois and she is now engaged in preaching to them" (2:2). Pleasant Prairie reported no other preaching services within thirty miles. By January 1883, the *Telephone* indicated that she was having some success. "Crooked Creek church in Meade County, has just received three on profession of faith. Miss E. E. Newman ministers to this church" (3:3). In the August issue of the *Telephone,* the notice of the Southwestern Association meeting contained the report that the association had assigned an exegetical essay on II Corinthians 5:1–4 to be presented by Emma Newman. Newman's own account in her diary was not hopeful. Her work in the neighborhood was discouraging because there were so few people, so far apart. One Sunday, her congregation consisted of two people from the neighborhood and four cowboys who came over from Collins (Diary, vol. 12, Mar. 25, 1883).

westernized Emma Newman. She no longer looked to Boston for the model for her work, but adapted her pastoral work to the western conditions of distance, isolation, uncertain economic development, lack of resources, and weak community structures. She benefitted from the comparatively egalitarian views of the frontier that welcomed those who would work hard without much regard for their gender, class, or race. This is not to say that she did not face unique difficulties as a woman pastor. The notion of women's leadership in the church remained a novelty. But in Dial, Kansas, she found a church that regarded her no differently from her male colleagues, and within a year requested that the association ordain her.

Her journey to Dial was lengthy and difficult. She traveled about 170 miles from Galva to Dial in Osborne County (a distance of a hundred miles as the crow flies), in a wagon pulled by a horse named Kate. The trip cost her a bit less than six dollars. Just how difficult the journey was is best told by Newman herself.

September 24, 1883. Clear and cold. Packed in misery being quite too sick to do the work that must be done. Drove down to Mr. Ebaugh's to get the rest of my salary: he had not collected it

September 25. Took leave of West Kentuck without one regret, except that I had not done more good. A late start made me drive late, and I was homesick at not finding for miles a person who could speak English to direct me. Some pretty views and good weather to be thankful for. Passed the night with a Mr. and Mrs. Pickering, kind people, who refused payment. 30 miles. Collected $3.25 on the way making $21 received from W. Kentuck.

September 26. Tedious driving round making double the distance because the cattle-men had fenced up the section line roads and all others. Spent the night with delightful people Howard by name in a good large house. 30 miles.

September 27. Kate breaking down badly. Roads tedious, because the small settlers were shutting up the angling roads and there were many miles to go round. Ellsworth Co. is one to be avoided. Night at Wilson.

September 28. Tedious day, but better roads. Kate very weak. Was directed wrong, apparently with malice, lost the way, and had a very hard time in finding it. God showed me. Night with a Mrs. Keith. Kate had water-colic from drinking too fast after a long dry time.

September 29. Kate really not able to travel, but I was obliged to get through. She did not go more than two miles an hour and I drove her eight hours. The last two miles a north wind struck us in the face and completely discouraged her. This is the first bad wind we have had this week, being greatly favored with good weather. Reached Mr. McAllister's[2] about sunset to find that they had misunderstood the letter sent them and had not given notice [that she was preaching].

Sunday September 30. Preached to 24 on repentance[3] in this house, a sod dug-out of one room. No small children, so one can take comfort. Made the people promise to come out next Sunday for a prayer meeting. (Diary, vol. 12)

With the church less than two years old and some of its members discouraged already, Newman began her by now customary visiting and preaching. She also visited the outlying communities to provide occasional preaching. Her major tangible accomplishment at Dial was getting the church building built. Though the community of Dial was hardly even a town, consisting of the McAllister's farm, serving also as a way station and post office, and the Coates farm across the road, building the church marked the place as both an official community and as a part of American Protestant culture.

Kansas as Cultural Context in the 1880s

There were two wests in Kansas at the end of the nineteenth century. In the eastern part of the state there was plenty of rain, the tall grass prairie was fertile, the woods provided sufficient fuel and building material, and the early arrival of railroads fostered the development of cities. This part of Kansas had much in common with Ohio or Illinois, and cultural developments followed similar patterns.

The western part of the state was arid. Here the assumptions of prairie homesteading were suddenly called into question during a series of dry years from 1877 until 1884. The settler's life in western Kansas was diffi-

---

2. The community of Dial in Osborne County consisted of the McAllister's farm and that of the Coates's, about a mile away. Mrs. McAllister took in overnight guests traveling between Osborne and Russell and the family kept the post office. There was no church building at that time.

3. Unfortunately, this sermon is not in the collection at the Huntington Library.

cult, isolated, and precarious. The homesteading system worked well in eastern Kansas, but western Kansas was too dry to make a 160-acre farm economically viable. Nonetheless, by 1880, Kansas had almost one million people, mostly farmers or people making their living from agriculture, and was more sparsely settled in the western counties.

The Congregational church had found itself at home among a sizable New England population around Lawrence and Topeka, in eastern Kansas. In a long struggle, their Yankee culture's antislavery views had prevailed over the proslavery territorial government. Kansas became a state in 1861, after any Southern opposition to its admission was temporarily gone from the United States Congress.

Western Kansas, the setting in which Emma Newman did her most extensive pastoral work, was not settled until after the Civil War, less than twenty years before Emma arrived. The line marking western Kansas as a geographical region lies near Wichita, where the land begins its rise to the Rocky Mountains. Here the tall grass prairie gave way to the short grass prairie with some yucca and cactus. The weather was unpredictable, with very hot summers and very cold winters. Rain came sporadically, and was not uniformly spread, raining hard in one place, but not at all in another place nearby. There were few trees.

Prolonged drought and the consequent decline of farmers to pay off debts led to economic difficulties at the end of the 1880s. Farmers in western Kansas found it took far more than five years to make a farm profitable. In addition, lack of trees made lumber for building and fuel hard to come by.

The western settlers lived in sod houses that were prone to collapse in the rain and alive with bugs, though well insulated from both heat and cold. Although springs, streams, and rivers provided easy sources of water in the eastern prairies, western settlers had to dig wells. Later, windmill pumps provided water from deep aquifers. In 1880, increasingly expensive and complex irrigation projects began to control the flow of water to western Kansas farms. In Newman's day, widely scattered water sources increased the isolation of homesteaders from one another and suppressed the development of towns. In the long run, wheat farmers prospered on the arid plains with the spread of irrigation, but in the 1880s, cattle ranching was still the predominant means of livelihood in western Kansas.

Situated along the Arkansas and Solomon Rivers, the Kansas territory was an easy thoroughfare for travelers to the Rockies and beyond. The Santa Fe Trail crossed Kansas as early as the 1820s. Settlement followed the river valleys first; the railroads followed the earliest settlements along the rivers. Both the Union Pacific and the Atchison, Topeka and Santa Fe Railroads took their transcontinental routes through Kansas. Given the direction of the rivers and then the railroads, it was easy to move east and west in Kansas, but difficult to move north and south.

There was very little urban development in western Kansas. There were only six cities in the western part of the state in the late nineteenth century: Wichita, Hutchinson, Great Bend, Dodge City, Garden City—all located on the Arkansas River—and Salina. And all of them were located on the railroad lines. As the railroads progressed across the state, the towns at the end of the lines became magnets for cattle drives moving from Texas and Mexico to the eastern cities. The cattle boom lasted until the middle of the 1880s, when farmers began fencing the range to prevent incursions by other settlers and by longhorn cattle from the open ranges in Texas that carried splenic fever, dangerous to more domesticated cattle (Miner 1986, 175–76). The state issued a quarantine in 1884 to prevent the spread of disease from the Texas range cattle to those in Kansas.

Newman's first work in Kansas was in the cattle country of the southwest. Her church in Crooked Creek was only a few miles from Dodge City. After preaching in Meade County for a year, the neighboring minister, a Rev. Feemster, who she assisted, decided that the effort of sustaining a church at Crooked Creek was too much. The entire county had a population of only 246 people in 1880, certainly not enough to sustain two Congregational ministers. In early March, he announced that there would be no more Congregational preaching at Crooked Creek. Newman gave her last sermon there on Sunday, March 25, 1883.

Walked to church, carrying kindling: no one went from the house. I had just made the fire when 4 cow-boys came over from Collins: Frank Waite came over later and Huldah Smith about the close. Of course I did not have a regular service, but talked awhile. At the close Frank offered to take me over: I asked him to wait till I warmed myself and improved the rare opportunity. He said he had been thinking more of religion and his duty of late; then I pressed him to decide at once telling him that the opportunity was an answer to my prayer, and that God asked him to decide and he yielded. I did not dare pray with him as I wanted to do. God knows. He has given me my wages and I am over-paid. (Diary, vol. 12, Mar. 25, 1883)

At the end of March 1883, Newman left for McPherson County, where she had preached in 1880 and 1881 and hoped to find another church.

Newman had by this time become westernized. Though she considered herself an ambassador for her New England culture, her two decades of work in the West had changed her. The processes that led people to dilute or even abandon ideals and habits common in the East worked on Newman as well. Her first mention of the problem of the West came as early as 1872, in a comment on a sermon preached at an association meeting in Missouri. "Went to meeting again in eve. Sermon on true wisdom, with much more thought than the morning one, but, Mr. Campbell said, not so effective here" (Diary, vol. 6, Nov. 10, 1872). A year later, on hearing a scholarly sermon by Prof. Thayer in Andover, the difference struck her. She commented that she was "so far westernized that the style sounds strange to me." She changed her own preaching accordingly, increasing the number of illustrations and decreasing the amount of intellectual discourse on theological points. Her sermons became shorter. She spoke from an outline rather than reading a manuscript. Her illustrations about farm life developed from mere mention of farms as property in a sermon on the Prodigal Son preached in Big Woods, August 10, 1873, to an understanding of the spiritual danger involved in the consuming work of homesteading in a sermon to the Dial church, November 1, 1885. "We have taken our portion, strong hands, quick brains, the power to gain whatever we have and have used it for our own pleasure. If our riotous living has been in the form of good hard work, so much the worse to waste the good work; we have nothing that will last if we have not character" (Sermon no. 15). This was added when she wrote the outline form to use in Dial from the larger manuscript sermon she had used thirteen years earlier.

Although as early as 1878, toward the end of her time in Illinois, she was feeling at home in the West, she still found her Boston manners to be in the way. "Westerners say that eastern people are always glad to get back again: I experienced that mysterious gladness when I found myself in the congenial neighborhood of sample rooms and wholesale liquor dealers, and, when my delighted eyes rested on the mystic legend 'Star of the West

Sugar Cured Bacon,' my felicity was complete" (Diary, vol. 11, Oct. 2, 1878). In April, she wrote, "I must try to become more of a Westerner, since the Lord keeps me here; I am not so useful to the people, because my roots are in Boston" (Diary, vol. 11, Apr. 11, 1879). Still, the decline into "barbarism" disturbed her. From her surprise that her congregation in Algonquin did not think to hold religious services on Thanksgiving Day, to her concerns about dancing among the young people in the communities she served, she regarded herself as engaged in battle to preserve New England (Newman would say Christian) values of moral earnestness, middle-class propriety, and hard work. Though her work involved creating and sustaining community, she and her peers did not understand fully the problems of creating community among people scattered over large distances.

The distance, physical and psychological, between the American Home Missionary Society offices in New York and the ministers in the western churches contributed to the decline of religious institutions in the West. The line of communication between the office and the missionary was almost never face to face. The state mission superintendent, whose word weighed more than the missionary's, often filtered correspondence between the New York office and the churches. The superintendent's agenda involved supporting the churches and missionaries while minimizing the funds drawn from the society's coffers. Thus the needs of the local congregations were both exaggerated and minimized. One wonders if the New York people ever truly understood the work they were trying to do. Small country churches needed sustained support, and perhaps could never pay a full salary for a minister. The work in the West did not proceed according to society expectations and they had little desire to reward what to them seemed like failure.

Little by little the Home Missionary Society shifted its emphasis in the West from rural churches to urban ones, where growth was more certain. Erling Jorstad suggests that the post–Civil War period marked a low point in religious influence in the American West, and that in some rural areas there was no church until well into the twentieth century (Jorstad 1977, 976). Among Congregationalists, the resources of the Home Missionary Society never stretched far enough to supply pastors to the smallest places. These small churches were the ones most likely to call women such as Newman to their pulpits.

The Congregational Church in Kansas

Sylvester Storrs, the American Home Missionary Society superintendent for Kansas, addressed the problem of numerous small chrches unlikely
ever to become self-supporting in his annual report to the General Association of Congregational Churches in Kansas in 1884. In this message he
was "preaching to the choir," but hoped to galvanize the enthusiasm of the
Kansas Home Missionary Society to support its own churches generously.

> But have *great mistakes* been made in organizing *country* churches? The
> greater number of them were organized by missionaries whose main work
> was in towns, but who looked beyond and established out-stations to ac-
> commodate those who could not well attend meetings in town. In the new
> counties nearly all were poor. Many of them were not in condition to go to
> town; had not team but a yoke of oxen, and some none at all. These out sta-
> tions were located from four to twenty miles away, and the frontier mission-
> aries have traveled from four to twenty, and even forty miles on the Sabbath
> to fill their appointments, frequently preaching three times, to carry the
> Gospel to the poor. Sunday Schools were organized and maintained and
> after some progress had been made, the people asked for a church organiza-
> tion where, perhaps, with their present facilities for traveling, the request
> would not have been made.
>
> The heavy expense of the frontier work has not been so much because
> the country churches had to be looked after, as in the inability of the people
> to pay—the absolute *poverty of the country*. We should remember that this is
> the first year of good crops for seven years, yet the country is improving and
> the settlements are permanent. (Storrs 1884, 35)

Storrs went on to point out that the proportion of conversions in country
churches exceeded those in the cities where the societies believed their
money was best spent. He also pointed out that most of the city folk came
from the country, and it was in the country that the future civic leaders
were being raised.

The next year the new superintendent Addison Blanchard[4] noted the
growing commitment of the American Home Missionary Society to the

---

4. This is not the same as the Blanchard, president of Wheaton College, who opposed
granting women license to preach.

support of urban mission work among immigrants and the consequent decrease in their interest in rural missions.

> It is time even now that we begin to look forward towards self-support in our missionary work as a State. Anyone who is at all familiar with the rapidly growing demands of the work among our immigrant population in the older states will appreciate that this may be forced upon us sooner than we think. . . . If we are to develop an enthusiasm for the work given us in this State, we must be learning to look less and less to glorious Massachusetts and more and more to consecrated hearts and consecrated wealth here, to a piety indigenous in Kansas. (Blanchard 1885, 4)

This challenge to the Kansas churches was of practical relevance to Emma Newman.

The Congregational Church in Kansas had its origin in the emigration of New Englanders to Kansas in the early 1850s to try to claim it as a free state before southern immigration could make it a slave state.[5] The American Home Missionary Society began work in Kansas in 1854. Already, the Home Missionary Society undertook to mark the religious territory, first to mark it as Christian in opposition to the Indians who had just been pushed out, and second to mark it as Congregational, or New England Protestant in opposition to a Southern Christianity that tolerated slavery. Later, the society refined its sense of territory, and tried hard to counter Roman Catholic immigration with new Protestant churches. They saw the threat of barbarism in all of these non-Protestants.

As the conflict between proslavery and abolitionist citizens in Kansas heated up, New England settlers came in colonies, groups establishing towns together, for mutual security against violence. By 1874, there were over one hundred Congregational churches and four thousand members in Kansas. The Congregationalists established Washburn College soon after their arrival, its purpose to train young men for professions, especially the ministry in Kansas.

The issues facing the Congregational churches in the 1880s were related to a rapidly increasing and highly mobile population. In the reports

---

5. A summary of the first decade of Congregationalism in Kansas can be found Richard Cordley 1876.

of the General Association of Kansas and in the *Kansas Telephone*, the Congregational newspaper, the three most pressing concerns were the slow movement of the churches toward self-support, the rapid turnover of pastors, and the number of churches that closed due to pastoral neglect. The dependency fostered by support from the Home Mission Society and the economic struggles of the people made churches reluctant to cut their ties to the society that provided the support of their pastors. "Stand on your own feet! Control your own church! As a polity Congregationalism secures its results through a consecrated independence" (Haskell 1884, 46). Thus pled the leaders of the General Association of Congregational pastors and churches in Kansas.

However, the number of churches without pastors, or supplied by pastors without full credentials, was large. Many churches were unable to attract ministers to their isolated rural settings, and so they merged with those of another denomination, or closed their doors altogether. Many churches closed because people moving into an area during a boom time left just as quickly when the economy soured. Towns came and went frequently in western Kansas.

Addison Blanchard wanted the best ministers for the home mission work and the ministry of self-supporting congregations in Kansas. "What kind of men are needed?" he asked. The answer was, those able to do union work, who have strength of character, breadth of sympathy, great wisdom, and supernatural powers; those with clarity about the great doctrines of Christianity; those able to work without supervision, able to attract the unaffiliated and unappropriated and the largely skeptical young people, "We cannot wait for Congregational immigration" (Blanchard 1885, 6–7). The best ministers, however, were not attracted to Home Missionary Society salaries, and so the Kansas churches languished. In addition, the society made a shift in the 1880s to support urban work in the Eastern cities as well as rural and urban work in the West. This further diminished the society's interest in the smallest rural places, where success was least certain.

All Protestant denominations faced the same dilemmas. The isolation, low pay, small congregations, and other discouragements of western Kansas church life made clergy of any kind scarce. Though the population was growing fast, it was scattered. Many small churches formed, rather than a few larger ones. In such a time, a seminary-educated woman with experience as a preacher and willingness to live on very little was welcome to help, but the Home Missionary Society remained reluctant to support the innovation.

The Home Missionary Society expected to see two particular, tangible signs of the missionary's success, in addition to a steadily increasing number in the congregation: erecting a church building and self-support. Constructing a church building was a signal that there were enough permanent residents in a place to assure a future for the congregation, but still the mobility of the population and uncertain economies dependent on weather and the agriculture commodities markets made erecting a building risky if the congregation had to borrow money to do it.

Newman knew what a drain the church building had been for the Algonquin church, yet she encouraged the Dial church to build though the congregation was split by controversy about the location of the church and whether or not they could afford the project.

In addition to serving as a sign of stability, a building also proved an important marker of the presence of a community. The local Dial newspaper agreed to its importance. As early as February 1884, the *Osborne County Farmer* noted with some sarcasm the difficulty of beginning the project of building a church. Phunny Pheller, the pseudonymous author, did not say whether he was a member of the church.

> The Congregational church of this place needs a church building. The members are going to get together and try to settle their petty difficulties, and we are all going to stop playing spoiled baby, and go to work as a body of Christian brothers and sisters should do, and not be a standing menace to the religion of Christ, and a stumbling block to his people; a reproach to the gospel, and the laughing stock of the ungodly. We sincerely hope they will close up ranks, and stand firm as a united band of Christian men and women, whose power for good must and will be respected if nothing more. (*Osborne County Farmer*, February 28, 1884)

The congregation took up the idea of building in January, calculating how much it would cost to build a sod church. The figure came to forty-four dollars, with thirteen dollars for a stove and pipe and an unknown amount of cement (Diary, vol. 12, Jan. 6, 1884). In March, they further elaborated on the plan. "They want to make the shell cost $150 and to wait till we can raise the money enough to finish before beginning to build. I was almost discouraged with them, they will not push" (Diary, vol. 12, Mar. 26, 1884).

On April 3, 1884, the date of the church annual meeting, the congregation discussed the matter of a site for the church. "Then we all went out to look at sites, and came in to ballot. Mr. Coates' corner was chosen after several ballots, much to my surprise: I did not know that one member of the church thought it best, though it is the prettiest. It seems the deacon, while saying that the church should go west, had been working to have it on his own ground" (Diary, vol. 12). The property was across the road from the Dial Post Office and Mr. McAllister's farm. Lucius Coates and his wife Josephine deeded the property to the church for two dollars (*The People Came* 1977, 120). McAllister and Ewing purchased the lumber a few days later. The *Osborne County Farmer* reported that the size of the building was to be sixteen by twenty-four feet.[6] No more was done on the church until the summer. In June, Newman went herself to the Rose's to borrow tools to begin construction. The men began on June 21 by cutting stone for the foundation.

In a single day, two men became disgruntled with Newman and the building project. "Mr. Wilson got angry at an innocent thing I said to him: it looked as if he were finding an excuse not to work at the church, as he had agreed to do." Deacon Coates was equally sensitive. "[He asked] if I meant him in praying that people might be moved to help build from higher motives than the increased value of their farms. *I did not.* I seem to have been singularly unfortunate yesterday" (Diary, vol. 12, June 22 and 23, 1884). Work continued another day and then broke off until after the harvest.

When Newman returned from her vacation in late summer, another minister had been to preach once at the Dial church. Deacon Coates was looking for a man to be minister. At the Northwestern Association meeting in October, Newman concluded that the man who had preached did not have "the faintest idea of coming to Dial." Because the deacon could find no alternative, the church asked Newman to stay. She agreed pro-

6. "The Congregationalists have purchased the lumber for a new frame church building 16 x 24 feet. It will be erected on the South-west corner of Lucius Coates' land" (*Osborne County Farmer*, Apr. 10, 1884).

vided they finish the church building. By February 1885, the church walls were up, but they were blown over by a storm before the roof could be put on. By early April, the walls were replaced, the roof was nearly shingled, and the new pulpit installed. By August 1885, the church was ready to be plastered inside.[7] On October 1, 1885, the *Osborne County News* reported that "the new Congregational church of Dial will be dedicated on Sunday the 4th day of October. Supt. Blanchard will be at Dial on the 1st of October Thursday and will hold services that night, also Tuesday and Saturday nights and on Sunday the church will be dedicated free of debt." Building the church building brought out all the tensions in the small community, yet almost everyone worked on it, men and women alike. Though their conflicts were sometimes with their pastor, in the end they wanted Newman to be ordained when the building was dedicated.

The other tangible result desired by the Home Missionary Society was self-support. This was sometimes the more difficult of the two to attain. The quote that begins this chapter, "Dial is our only self-supporting church, and the pastor, Miss Emma E. Newman, does most of the supporting" (General Association of Kansas 1884, 15), speaks volumes about the state of all the churches in the association and their dependence on the society. Newman's church, denied support by the American Home Missionary Society because its pastor was a woman, and receiving only a small amount from the far poorer state society, depended on Newman's own fund raising efforts among her friends and her contribution of a large portion of her own income to sustain the church. Newman was their patron. Having her church listed as self-supporting only disqualified it further from receiving any aid from the home missionary societies.

The Church and the Construction of Community

In this environment, where success was deceptive and always bought by hard work, where people lived far from each other, where danger, illness, and loneliness were common, the church served a significant social need. One reason a church of twenty members like Dial boasted an average attendance of over one hundred on Sundays lay in the social venue provided

7. The course of the building of the church can be followed in Newman's Diary for 1884–1885 and in the *Osborne County Farmer* for the same period.

by the service. Coming to worship gave people a time to see and visit with their neighbors, as well as worship in a common way, providing a sense of shared meaning to their otherwise isolated lives.

For Newman, the social use of church membership was not theologically important, though for her the church was her society, the framework in which she had most of her relationships. The issues of her people's understandings of church and community showed clearly in two interrelated incidents in her Dial work: Hattie McAllister's desire to join the church, and Jack Ewing's transgression of the church's expectations of proper social engagements.

Hattie McAllister was the youngest daughter of Silas and Mary McAllister, founders of the Dial church. On Saturday, March 7, 1885, Hattie B. McAllister and Herbert Fletcher, another young person, presented themselves to the preparatory meeting[8] to be considered for admission to the church. The vote was favorable and the two young people were admitted to the church the next day (Record Book of the Dial Congregational Church, Mar. 7, 1885). The event capped a long discussion between Emma Newman and the young people.

Newman was familiar with Hattie because Newman's sod house stood on the McAllister's property and she took her meals with the McAllister family. Newman knew that Hattie and her mother did not get along. Because Mary McAllister was often ill, Newman allowed Hattie to stay with her on days when her mother was particularly uncomfortable. It was awkward for Newman to oppose Hattie's admission to church membership because she depended on the McAllisters for many necessary services, to say nothing of their company. Still, Newman notes many instances of Hattie's insensitivity and misbehavior in her diary. Hattie and Herbert Fletcher had laughed at Mr. Knouse's singing in church (Diary, vol. 12, Oct. 27, 1884). They had attended a dance together. Hattie also had an ill temper. When she studied the church covenant, she concluded that living up to it would be too difficult for her (Diary, vol. 12, Jan. 8, 1885). Meanwhile, Herbert, a timid young man, seemed to Newman to be an "earnest Christian." However, he too found church membership burdensome. He wanted to put off joining the church so that he could take Hattie to dances (Diary,

8. The preparatory meeting was also meeting for a lecture about the meaning of the Lord's Supper in anticipation of the communion service the next day.

vol. 12, Dec. 28, 1884). "Hattie came in to ask if I would admit her to the church on her promise only to go to decent dances, was provoked at my showing her that that was not a Christian spirit, then she said she only wanted to join the church to please Herbert—which was doubtless true. Disagreeable child" (Diary, vol. 12, Feb. 2, 1885).

The two young people wanted to be part of the adult world, but were not ready to give up their pleasures to meet Newman's strict standards of church membership.

> I had a final talk during the week with Hattie about joining the church; she appeared better than she had ever done before about it, and it was decided that she should join. Yet she and Herbert went over to Mr. Cole's visiting [on Sunday] and it appeared afterward H. set up his new stove. They seem to want to do right when something else does not come up. I am greatly troubled whether to take them into the church or not. Prayer meeting in eve was fully attended and very solemn. Herbert spoke, which he had not done lately. (Diary, vol. 12, Mar. 1, 1885)

The other adult church members were not so troubled as Newman by these young people, who were both examined and received as church members the next Sunday.

The same ambivalence over the standards of behavior for church members surfaced with regard to the adults. Newman struggled with what she thought of as the attenuation of religious feeling and practice in the West. In talking with another young woman, May Rose, Emma noted that she "has a real sense of sin, not common with these shallow Westerners" (Diary, vol. 12, Nov. 10, 1884). Though the area had been settled some years and the wild cowboy behavior common in the southern part of Kansas was not found among these farmers, the wild West loosening of moral restraint allowed dancing to emerge from hiding, enjoyed by the young people and condoned by their elders.

The dilemma was probably shared by Silas McAllister, Hattie's father. He presumably approved of Hattie's admission to the church, despite knowing that she enjoyed dancing. However, on the same day that Hattie and Herbert were approved to join the church, Silas brought charges against one of the members, Deacon Jack Ewing, for allegedly holding a dance for the young people on the same night as the prayer meeting.

Newman was one of a generation of ministers raised in the old forms of New England church life, where people's social standing was related to their church membership. In the new West, people's characters were not judged so strictly, and being a member of a church was not necessary to the enjoyment of company with on's neighbors. The matter of Jack Ewing and the dance held at his house on the night of the prayer meeting illustrates these dilemmas not only for the pastor, but for the other church members as well.

Mr. Ewing was one of the first deacons in the Dial church. He attended prayer meeting regularly. His wife was a willing organizer of the Woman's Board of Missions of the Interior Auxiliary started by Newman. The Ewings were among the six working members of the church, the others being Silas and Mary McAllister, Lucian Coates, and Mr. Cole. When the Sunday School was organized in March 1884, Jack Ewing was elected superintendent.

The first hint of tension between Ewing and McAllister came in the summer of 1884, over the collection of pledged funds for Newman's salary. "Jack Ewing was here yesterday; I suppose they asked him for his subscription, and he claimed to have paid it by building on this house last fall. Poor Jack! That threw Mr. and Mrs. McAllister into the depths of despair anent the church. I do not know what to do with the whole lot of them" (Diary, vol. 12, July 13, 1884). In August, he wanted to close Sunday School "to allow himself an hour more in the morning." A month later he made the proposal to the congregation to disband the Sunday School, but nobody agreed (Diary, vol. 12, Aug. 31 and Sept. 7, 1884). With the vote going against him, Ewing could have dropped out of the life of the congregation; however, the next week he was in church with his family "in a penitent and religious mood."

Tensions broke out again while Ewing and others were working on the church building. "There was a difference of opinion about some lumber and Jack was provoked into saying that he would not work any more." "Tried hard to mollify Jack couldn't" (Diary, vol. 12, Nov. 27–28, 1884).

The first serious complaint against Ewing was made in January 1885 by Deacon Coates. "He said that Jack had sold a mortgaged cow, but, though he had not legal right to do so, he claimed to have sold it to pay the debt and to have done no moral wrong. The other charge was that he had gambled; this was not under the deacon's knowledge, and he had not yet spoken to J. about it" (Diary, vol. 12, Jan. 31, 1884). In March, Newman in-vestigated the complaint that Mr. Ewing had a dance at his house. That Saturday, Silas McAllister brought the matter before the entire church by making a public complaint.

> Silas McAllister complained of Brother J. B. Ewing that he held a dance at his house on the evening a prayer meeting at Deacon Coates which he had promised to attend if he could. I make this complaint at the first opportunity without time to talk it over with Brother Ewing he being out of town wish-ing to make it clear to the community that the church does not approve his action. If Brother Ewing shall repent and confess his sin I intend to with-draw the complaint. (Record Book of the Dial Church, Mar. 7, 1885)

Newman talked with Ewing the next day after the communion service. "He explained the whole matter as a perfectly innocent one, and, on urg-ing, promised to make that explanation at meeting to-night." But he failed to do so then. In fact, Ewing did not explain the matter publicly for a month.

> Since Silas McAllister presented his complaint against Bro. J. B. Ewing he and the pastor talked to him. He said he had not a dance at his house but a play party that he advised the young folks not to come that night on account of the prayer meeting that he had intended to attend it himself. After this explanation Silas McAllister withdrew his complaint. Brother J. B. Ewing withdrew from the church which he had a right to do under agreement made at the time the church was organized. (Record Book of the Dial Church, Apr. 5, 1885)

Newman ended her account of the day with "Poor Jack." Some time within the next year a reconciliation took place. There is a gap in Newman's diary between April 1885 and May 1886, so the details are un-known. In May 1886, Jack Ewing and his family were early for church, and Ewing was again teaching a Sunday School class.

The problem for Newman was not so much dancing but the temptation people faced of substituting that form of community gathering for one of prayer. In addition, she was the one charged with talking to Ewing, and his conflict with McAllister was carried out in the public arena of her church. Community norms were sorted out in the venue of the church, the pastor being responsible for communicating between the parties and for shaping the mores of the community. During this conflict, Newman preached on the matter of community, but not on the matter of dancing.

She titled the sermon "Sincere Living" (Sermon no. 79). The text was from Job 35:13, "Surely God will not hear vanity, neither will the Almighty regard it" (AV), but the sermon was based on the first chapter of James. In the sermon Newman addressed the issue of hypocrisy, reminding the congregation that one's outward behavior should match one's inward or expressed convictions. Although hypocrisy might be seen as simply self-deception, in reality it harms community life. "We ask God to bless this town, in which we live, but just so far as we set a bad example, or neglect to set a good one, in anything whatever, we do not really want God to bless the town, so much as we want to have our own way and do as we choose, certainly if we wanted the blessing most, we should be willing to give up any indulgence rather than to stand in the way of it, should we not?" (Sermon no. 79).

Newman went on to describe the destruction of community that followed people's judgement of their neighbors. "The fact that a given man does not like us, does not confuse the distinctions of right and wrong, so as to make everything that he does wrong, and every little slanderous story about him true. We owe just judgement to our own self-respect, as well as to others, and God expects us to use it" (Sermon no. 79).

In the same sermon she addressed Ewing, who had held an entertainment for the young people on the evening of a prayer meeting, and McAllister, who complained about his neighbor but did little to further the religious life of his own daughter. Her concern was above all for the community. She preached this sermon twice in Dial. The first time was before the trouble between Ewing and McAllister began. The second time was two Sundays after Ewing made his explanation, McAllister withdrew his complaint, and Ewing withdrew from the church for a time. The personal trouble between these two men was disrupting the church. Building came to a halt.

Alexander Thain had once reminded her that the people needed pastoral care even more than they needed preaching. This sermon grew out of her hours of pastoral counsel with the two men in their quarrel with each other, not only for their own sakes, but for the good of the community. Thain had also reminded her that though she did not have the official title of pastor, not being ordained, she was in reality the pastor, and should feel authorized to do that work.

Working within the parameters of woman's responsibility for the relationships among those in the household, Newman took as her task to repair the breach in church fellowship. The two men were, in a sense, trying to define the boundaries of the community, testing by act and reaction the location of a community response. that could guide their behavior. They wanted to shape community norms comfortable to them. Newman stepped in to provide a link or create an interaction between them. She had particular norms in mind and intervened to repair the breach between them but also to uphold her sense of morality. In the end her creation of the link preserved the church household or *oikos* intact, and smoothed the way for them to finish building the church.[9]

Emma Newman's Quest for Ordination

After so many years of labor without the formal authorization for it, Emma Newman was the first clearly recognizable woman to appear in any official list of Congregational ministers. She is listed in the *Congregational Year-book* of 1882, in the reports for the year 1881, as serving the church in Pleasant Prairie, Meade County, Kansas. She was reported as a licensed minister, but with an asterisk by her name indicating "that these persons, while reported as supplying churches, are not reported to be approbated by, or under the care of, any Congregational organization" (National Council of the Congregational Churches of the United States 1884, 265, 115).

In March 1883, the Southwestern Association met in Garden City. Emma Newman was leaving Crooked Creek and Pleasant Prairie, but expecting to preach elsewhere in Kansas and so applied for a license. Though she had worked among them and participated as any other minister would have in the business of the association, the body declined to act on her request.

The old story. Towards the last minute, the committee handed me a note, saying that they thought it not best to examine me. I applied at noon, for ad-

9. I credit an important conversation with Archie Smith, Jr. for helping me clarify my thought on this incident. My thanks to him.

mittance to the association with my papers: the committee on new members reported that there was no business before them. I read my essay on "Woman's Work in the Church" and there was a discussion on it, largely occupied with (indirect) advice to me to marry, and discussion as to whether Paul was a bachelor. Mr. Prior of Great Bend criticized rationally. (Diary, vol. 12, Mar. 21, 1883)

Newman's next request for a license was to the Northwestern Association in Kansas. She suffered an accident with her horse and buggy in the summer of 1883 and while recovering from her injury, she continued to preach at Fairview, the site of her accident, hoping to be called as their pastor should the minister they wanted not be available. In August, she traveled to Great Spirit Spring near Cawker to soak in the mineral water. Cedarville, a nearby Congregational church, was without a pastor and Newman preached there while taking her treatments at the springs.

While in the area, she corresponded with Floyd Sherman and Charles Kellogg, two of the pastors in the northwestern part of Kansas. Soon she received an invitation from Sherman to attend the meeting of the Northwestern Association in Cora and apply for a license to preach. She arrived at the meeting September 19, 1883, and was unanimously voted a regular license (Diary, vol. 12, Sept. 20, 1883).[10]

18 Sept. [Traveling to Association Meeting] Tedious day of traveling and waiting enlivened by the appearance of Sec. Storrs at night.

19 Sept. The Barden House at Bur Oak proved a good hotel. Sec. Storrs, Mr. Platt, the new S. S. Sec. and I had a good ride of some 26 miles to Cora and I began to feel better. The main thing in P. M. was an excellent sermon from Mr. Sherman: text, "The very God of peace sanctify you wholly" etc. After session, I had my examination before the committee, not a severe one. Was pleasantly entertained in the best sod house I ever saw.

20 Sept. Sermons and essays especially one on tithing by Mr. McHenry with a good discussion. The association voted unanimously to give me a regular license. Left at noon for a very hard ride in the wind, 25 miles. (Diary, vol. 12, Sept. 18–20, 1883)

10. Interestingly enough, Newman made no records of the proceedings as she had done for earlier meetings of this kind.

As far as I know, hers was the first regular license to preach granted by an association of Congregational churches to a woman. With this license, on a rainy Sunday, October 21, 1883, Newman accepted the call to be pastor of the Dial church.

Newman, as a licensed minister, was initially elected to the pastorate of the Dial church for one year, because her license was held only for a year at a time. In January 1884, she was received as a member of the Dial church, a sign she meant to stay, and the same Sunday the church gave her authority to administer the Lord's Supper while she had the pastoral care of that church (Record Book of the Dial Congregational Church, January 5, 1884). Though there was little practical need for her ordination, symbolically Newman's lack of it meant both she and her congregation suffered from diminished recognition and standing in the larger denomination. In addition, Newman had to repeatedly renew her license, whereas ordination was permanent.

In March, the church requested the association to ordain her. "It was moved and carried that it is the desire of the church that Miss E. E. Newman be ordained and that Rev. Sherman be conferred with as to the best time and place for such an ordination" (Record Book of the Dial Church, Mar. 1, 1884). Because the Northwestern Association had licensed a woman with little trouble, how would they react to a request to ordain her?

April 15, 1884. The council [at Kirwin] was called for two o'clock, waited till three for a quorum, then adjourned till the next morning: there were but 7 members present while ten were necessary. Sermon in eve by Mr. Richards a little commonplace.

April 16. Organization, etc. as usual. A quorum of the council present and more, but, as Mr. Storrs would not come till Thursday, they adjourned to wait for him. That looked black for me, their waiting for Mr. Storrs to tell them what to do.

April 17. The council went to work at last, after a long siege in organizing, which showed that I ought to have had the letters in the hands of the country churches more than three weeks ago, and that some of the ministers were deplorably ignorant about Congregational usages. After the council was in order, a resolution, written, I think by Mr. Storrs, was moved by Mr. Sherman to the effect that it was not expedient for the weak and inexperienced churches to ordain a woman. Then ensued a lively debate; Mr. Osborne said it was foreordained and predestined that women should preach; several delegates spoke on my side; Mr. Kellogg, my strongest advocate, called on the other side to show their hand. Mr. Sherman made a cautious well considered speech, saying that women would be ordained in the future, but he thought the time had not quite come. Mr. Eckman ridiculed the idea of ordination by this council. Mr. Storrs objects for all time. Mr. Kellogg made a very able speech in my favor, and the resolution was voted down by a majority of one. An hours recess for dinner had taken place during this debate; after the vote Mr. Eckman and Mr. Storrs objected to taking any more of the time of the association, and the regular exercises went on. A paper from Mr. Richards, Mr. Storrs Home Missionary talk and the communion. Then the council re-assembled and, as it was clear that there would no quorum in the morning, dissolved! (Diary, vol. 12, Apr. 15–17, 1884)

Sylvester Storrs, who led the opposition, was the American Home Mission Society superintendent for Kansas. That society had, upon Newman's application to be commissioned as a home missionary supported by them, replied that the society was not ready to adopt the policy of commissioning ordained women as its missionaries (Diary, vol. 12, Dec. 18, 1883). Almost all of the churches in the Northwestern Association were dependent upon American Home Missionary Society money, and therefore all were reluctant to go against Storrs' advice, though from their ease in licensing her, one might conclude that they were not against ordination for women. Just prior to the meeting, Sherman had received a letter from Joseph Clark of the Home Missionary Society headquarters in New York indicating that he was also uncomfortable with the idea of ordaining a woman. He wrote,

Dear Bro. As to the question of Miss Newman's ordination, we are not acquainted with the candidate, and have no opinion, therefore, to express. Whether the fact of her being a woman could be regarded as an objection, is a question of personal taste and judgement, and we shall cheerfully leave it to the council.

Miss Newman has twice been urged upon us as minister of a church seeking our help—We have tried to treat the application without prejudice—but we had decided each time that the safer way for us was to refuse the grant. This was the "real reason." We are simply *not ready* to apply our funds to churches so [peculiarly] officered. (Joseph B. Clark to Rev. F. E. Sherman, April 8, 1884)

The council neatly avoided a vote by making sure there would be no quorum. In May, Newman and her church thought of calling another meeting of the council to finish their work, but Charles Kellogg, a neighboring minister, advised her against it, in a "good brotherly letter."

Without the approbation of the Home Mission Society, but with a regular license to authorize her work, Newman went about building up the small, new Dial church. When the church dedicated its new building in October 1885, the Kansas Home Missionary superintendent was there. The State Home Missionary Society had already shown itself more friendly to the support of a woman minister. The church made its second request for a council to ordain their pastor. "At a meeting for the Dial Congregational Church a motion was made and carried that it is the desire of this church that a committee be appointed to call a council to ordain Miss E. E. Newman to the ministry of the Gospel and to fix a time for such ordination and it is the opinion of the church that said council be called at the time of the dedication of the church at Dial" (Record Book of the Dial Church, Aug. 10, 1885). The matter failed again for want of a quorum, but the Dial church changed the form of its call to Newman to one of the more usual kind, to a permanent pastorate terminable with three months' notice from either side. The church also agreed to haul her wood in the coming winter.

The problem of not having a quorum may have been due to the distances and travel conditions of the day, so that people did not arrive on time. However, it was also a convenient way for the association to avoid an actual vote on the ordination of women.

The Home Missionary Society had great power in the decisions of the associations in the West regarding who would be ordained and who would be called to which church. The stated policy of the society was to follow established Congregational usage in these matters. "The American Home Missionary Society has ever regarded the ecclesiastical bodies as the appropriate judges of the standing of their own ministers, and of the wants of the churches in their connection. Accordingly, the commission issued to each missionary requires that his commission be acceptable to the ministerial body of his denomination, within whose bounds he is appointed to labor" (American Home Missionary Society 1873, 97–99). Nevertheless, the Home Missionary Society in a place like the Northwestern Association of Kansas held enormous power. Because almost every church was in some way dependent upon the society for support, they were reluctant to act contrary to the desires of the society.

For this reason, Newman was never ordained, although one other congregation requested it. Newman resigned from her pastorate at Dial on September 1, 1886 (Record Book of the Dial Church, June 6, 1886). There are gaps in her diary from April 1885 to May 1886 and after a very few entries from May 1886 to December 1887. Therefore, it is difficulty to tell why she left. There is no indication either in her diary or in the church record that she was or they were unhappy. Clearly, it was not a sudden resignation, as she gave three months notice. The year 1886 was one of growth for the Dial Church, increasing from ten to twenty-four members (Minutes of the General Association of Kansas 1887, 51). The previous year had also show an increase in membership. Newman never referred in any subsequent extant materials to her reason for leaving Dial. A year after leaving the Dial church, Newman served a small congregation near the Blaine Post Office in Pottawatamie County, Kansas. We know this from the records of the Kansas Association calling a council to consider her ordination, as reported in the October 1887 *Kansas Telephone* (13:1). She would have stayed at that church if she had been ordained. However, she was not and soon left in favor of a man. She continued to be licensed, however, though later in the 1890s, when she applied to transfer her license from Kansas, the Kansas association reported that they thought she had become a Christian Scientist.

Newman spent 1887 and 1888 in Lawrence, working as a mental healer, and left Kansas in 1889, to care for her aunts in Andover. Hannah Fay died that year, and Newman was left to care for Margaret Newman (Aunt Mardie). While in Andover, she continued to practice as a mental healer and homeopathic practitioner, but she did not preach.

In 1895, when her aunt no longer recognized her, she hired a woman to care for her, and Newman left for California. She settled in Sierra Madre, near Los Angeles. At first she was preoccupied with another nursing situation, taking care of a younger cousin who had come to California with tuberculosis. Newman spent a few months in 1896 trying to start Congregational church in the neighborhood where Ammie Semple McPherson built her Angelus Temple. Though Newman never succeeded in getting more than a Sunday School started, the people eventually formed the Garvanza Congregational Church in 1905, which survived into the 1950s.

The Professionalization of Medicine and Ministry

When Newman left Kansas she was only fifty-one. Why then was she never again fully active as a minister, and why was her healing work from then on practiced mostly with her family and friends? The least significant factor might serve in itself to explain this. The accident she had with her horse and buggy in the spring of 1883 left her with external and internal injuries that troubled her ever afterward. She may simply have been physically worn out. However, she did try to resume preaching in California. The same Home Missionary Society objections to a woman doing the work were there. They classified her as an "accredited worker," but there was never a church open for her to serve. The male ministers had priority.

I believe she was caught in the professionalizing process in both medicine and ministry at the end of the nineteenth century. This is the main factor in her retirement from active work in these areas that she considered to be her calling. Medicine and theology were two of the oldest professions, as academic disciplines reaching back into the origins of the medieval universities. Both had a body of knowledge and customary ways of practice that marked them out as separate kinds of work, both had always required study and training. Until the late nineteenth century, entrance into both professions was fluid. Anyone who professed to have done the study necessary and who had learned the arts necessary to the practice could begin work in either profession. Increasing numbers of people studied theology in seminaries, but many still studied and practiced with established pastors until their competence was recognized in a call to their own church. Indeed, in the West, a seminary degree could hinder a candidate. This was not only true of Congregationalists. Cynthia Tucker notes the "poor showing" of Harvard graduates in the West (Tucker 1990, 125). It was more complicated for a woman, but the process was essentially the same.

As the end of the century approached, more and more professions had specialized schools and required particular courses of education and training. The right to practice was increasingly regulated by government or other institutions. Institutions such as the American Medical Association and the church denominations took over the regulation of their professional practitioners and excluded those who did not conform to their norms, including the tacit requirement of being male.[11] Women, whose more informal medical practice extended into the community from the

11. A helpful discussion of this professionalization process as it affected women in the 1890s can be found in Glazer and Slater 1987.

family, were relegated once again to practice within the household. In the Congregational churches people without formal seminary education found it more difficult to find placement as a pastor. Because few theological seminaries admitted women students, doors remained closed to them.

In addition, as mainline Protestants embraced the scientific world view, they separated healing and religion. They left healing to the physicians, the scientific professionals. Although Protestants might offer prayer for the sick, they abandoned such ceremonies as anointing or laying hands on those who were ill. The mainline Protestants could not understand Christian Science, Spiritualism, or New Thought as anything but heresy. After the turn of the century, they sought to distance themselves also from the rising Pentecostal movements, uneasy about the free play of emotion in Pentecostal worship, pointing out the cases where faith healing was a hoax. Although rituals of healing continued to be available to Roman Catholics and to some degree the Episcopalians, and more informal rituals could be found in smaller Christian sects, the major Protestant churches turned toward more rational ways of comforting the ill, such as building hospitals, sending missionary doctors to the poor, and continuing to counsel people to avoid alcohol and tobacco. With the rise of psychiatry, the mainline churches came to understand their pastoral care as clinical work, and the cure of the soul proceeded from a scientific, therapeutic model.

In those churches where healing was still practiced, women's ministry continued to flourish, though not always through ordination. In their early years almost all Pentecostal churches counted some women in the vanguard of their movement. Christian Science continued to appeal to women, and many Christian Science practitioners were women. Though the number of women ministers in the Congregational church rose steadily throughout the early twentieth century, they were not a prominent part of the leadership of the churches as were the Pentecostal women or the Christian Scientists.[12]

I believe that Emma Newman found her interest in healing moved to

12. Two sources provide documentation of this slow but steady rise in the numbers of women clergy. Mark Chaves, in *Ordaining Women*, shows that it is the case for all Protestant denominations taken together. Marilyn Hedges-Hiller, in an unpublished paper on Congregational clergy women, also showed it to be true of the Congregationalists by themselves. (Chaves 1997, 15; Hedges-Hiller 1992).

the sidelines in the Congregational church, even found it was viewed with suspicion, and so she either did not or could no longer practice publicly as a mental healer. Her homeopathic practice also moved to the sidelines of medical practice in general. With the rise of scientific medicine in the second half of the nineteenth century, homeopathy waned. Allopathic treatments became more reliable, and pain relief and antibiotics discovered in the twentieth century changed people experience and perception of medical professionals. Homeopathic practitioners refused to put their theories to trial, and allowed themselves to be dismissed by the allopathic doctors as naive at best, or quacks at worst. By the time she moved to California, the professionalizing process in both medicine and ministry was well along, and in the growing urban centers of Southern California, Los Angeles and Pasadena, Newman found herself unneeded in both arenas.

Only in the 1980s, a hundred years later, did the mainline Protestants begun to reconnect religion and healing. The medical profession has become aware of the limits of treating the body alone, and professionals in religion and medicine have made new approaches to one another. Mainline Protestants seem recently to have become disembarrassed by the role of faith in healing the body, and rediscovered the power of prayer and community support. Coincidentally, in the 1980s, there was an upsurge in the number of women ministers in the mainline Protestant churches. Whether the two movements connect to each other is a matter for further investigation.

The Household Model of Church
Leadership and Women's Ministry

To understand Emma Newman, it is not enough to understand developments in American Protestantism. One must also investigate Christianity as a religion. As I discussed in the first chapter, I believe that women's ministry in nineteenth-century America had as its foundation patterns of leadership embedded in Christianity from its origins in the household sphere in the Greco-Roman world. These patterns were submerged when Christianity became connected to the political life of the empire, when it became the vehicle for the unity of society and took on secular power. As we have seen in Algonquin, New Boston, and Dial, Christianity on the frontier was no longer functioning as the vehicle of unity. It was one among many choices. The Congregational churches still understood themselves as representing the religion of their culture, but their attempt to mark the West with that culture succeeded only to a degree. As one moved west, things became more and more secularized, and there was more room for different religions.

As in the Mediterranean world of the earliest centuries of Christianity, on the American frontier, the church spread from the base of the household, not from a political act from on high. Each of the churches we considered started in a house. The women were the ones who wanted a church enough to work for its establishment, though the men were listed as the founding deacons, trustees, and pastors. The places in which we find Newman working are not the centers of population or power. Dial was an outlier of Osborne, the county seat. New Boston was a secondary town to Aledo. None of the places Newman served were considered important by the men running the institution. However, she was there. Their indifference made her free.

But the explanation lies also with the women. She was participating in the process of making the frontier into a home for her church and her culture. She served as a *materfamilias*. She provided for the comfort and spiritual guidance of her family, no matter how small. She engaged them in relationship with her and among themselves. She healed and nursed them in their illnesses. She kept the family altar, made sure family prayers and offerings were made, and taught the people the things necessary for community, as well as individual salvation. She transacted business on their behalf with the patrons of such activities. Indeed, she served as a patron herself, supplying her own support from time to time. And she served the poor, or those unfortunately outside the safe circle of the church. In visiting, preaching, teaching, prayer, admonition, founding churches, healing, and charity, she performed most of the functions of the earliest church leaders. That these functions corresponded so well with many of the functions thought to be natural to women by nineteenth-century Christians served to define a growing place for women's ministry in the American Protestant Churches.

Though proving such a thesis as this will require much more research than I have as yet been able to undertake, I have seen enough in Emma Newman's life to convince me that the emergence of women's ministry in the nineteenth and twentieth centuries in Christianity is not an accident, but a flowering of patterns of leadership embedded in the very structures of the Christian religion.

It is only when and where Christianity has waned as an official vehicle for cultural and political unity that its original forms come to the fore. Although mainline Protestants tend to mourn this waning of political influence as a loss, I would contend that it presents the historian, and possibly also the Protestant Christian, with a stronger and more deeply rooted base from which to understand the strengths of American Christianity and women's roles within it. These household bases of leadership in early Christianity also, I would argue, provide a more substantial basis for understanding the developing structures of any of the nineteenth-century missionary churches, most especially those found in the American West.

Newman's diary ends with the entry for June 22, 1897. That day she rose at five and took a horse up into the mountains outside of Sierra Madre. There is very little information about the rest of her life.

We know that she married Nicholas Emmerson in 1901. Emmerson followed Newman as pastor of the Dial church and they had corresponded for over a decade. Newman was sixty-three and he seventy-eight (Marriage License, Los Angeles County, 1901). Emmerson's' wife Jane died in 1900, and in 1901, Emmerson and Newman decided to marry. Emmerson's first thought was to bring Newman home to Kansas to live. The farm on which he lived with his son and daughter-in-law was to belong to them after his death and they planned to care for him until then. They objected to his plan to bring a new wife, fifteen years younger than himself, into the house as well. They did not want to assume any obligation to care for her also, so Nicholas Emmerson sold the farm to his son and moved to Sierra Madre.[13] By Emmerson family accounts they had a happy marriage. Some time in 1905, Emmerson returned to Kansas in poor health to live with his daughter and her husband in Osborne. Apparently Newman was not able

---

13. The account of Nicholas and Emma's marriage is from memories of the Emmerson family shared with me in several conversations with Earl and Ula Emmerson of Osborne, Kansas. Earl Emmerson is Nicholas Emmerson's grandson. I am grateful also to the Emmersons for photos of Emma and Nicholas.

to care for him, and remained in California. He died in November of that year.[14]

Newman continued to live in Sierra Madre. She supported the cause of Home Missions. An obituary in the *American Missionary* quotes a part of a letter she wrote to the Congregational Home Missionary Society in 1915. "I am a poor widow, seventy-seven years old. I wish to give $500 to your branch of our Master's work, but I need the income of it for so many, or so few, years as I yet live here" (*American Missionary*, April 1922, 22). The article continued by expressing appreciation for her support of the Home Missionary Society, "for whose work she had sacrificed so much in the days of her strength," an ironic word from the society that had at every turn declined to support a woman. The society received her $500 and paid her a quarterly dividend until she died. She lived quietly and attended the Sierra Madre Congregational Church regularly. One manuscript obituary described her later years in this way:

> So long as she was able, Mrs. Emmerson entered heartily into the community life of her new home, and even during years of invalidism she found many chances for helpfulness. Hers was a quaint and vigorous personality, intolerant of shams and often impatient with conventions, but clear of mind and generous of heart. Her friendships were many and lasting, for the one thing she asked of life was the opportunity to work. Her deep interest in the "woman's movement" which made such progress during her lifetime, was far more on what she hoped women would give than on what they might receive. ("Emma Newman Emmerson" obituary)

Emma Newman died on July 16, 1922, of chronic endocarditis, from which she had suffered for three years.

In this book, I have attempted to reframe the history of women in American religion by seeing Newman not as exception, but as representative. Until now, most work on the subject has treated women's leadership as exceptional. Susan Hill Lindley's book, entitled *"You Have Stept Out of Your Place": A History of Women and Religion in America* (1986), illustrates the point exactly. This is a fine book, the only attempt made so far to tell

---

14. Conversations with Earl Emmerson and unpublished history of the Emmerson family by Earl Emmerson, supplement 1, 8.

the complex story of women in American religion as a single narrative. However, the title indicates the theoretical stance of seeing active women as exceptions. When they appear on the scene, they have stepped out of place. I have tried to argue here, following a lead suggested by scholars such as Anne Braude, that women in American religion were stepping into place, and their stories are falling into place for historians. Newman becomes representative of a larger movement of women, a movement taking place outside the frame of the exceptional stories that have lately been the mainstay of women's religious history in America, but which is, I think, the central story.

Newman's life contains certain transitions in her religious experience and institutional participation. Upon graduation from Abbot Academy, she joined the church. It does not matter that we do not know if she had a religious conversion experience or simply decided that it was time. This represents her transition to adulthood—a transition outwardly the same for men and women. Both had equal rights to church membership and almost equal rights within the church.

At the same time, Newman took up a new set of duties both within her household and in the church. She moved from dependence on her elders to a position of responsibility for her mother and she took up her share of the charity and teaching work of the church. Her participation in both arenas of duty prepared her with knowledge of nursing and healing, as well as skills in group leadership developed in the context of the Aid Society. Like most of these voluntary societies, it was related to the institutional church, but not officially part of it. It was a venue located partly in the household and partly in the public realms, and it offered a wide range of leadership opportunities to women. She also took seriously her duty to improve her mind by reading and attending lectures in theology. Although she would not think of larger possibilities while her mother was alive, almost immediately after her mother died, she made another transition, this time to public leadership in the church.

Nineteenth-century Protestants had a variety of ways of understanding someone's call to public ministry. Despite the differences, two items were common to all of them: the person needed to be certain that there was some inner sense that God had called him or her, and the person needed to be called out by the church. The inner call could be spectacular, a vision, a voice, or some arresting event. It could also be quiet, growing conviction.

Newman, whose family was filled with ministers, would have been familiar with the parameters of this inner call. She appears to have heard it first in conjunction with the more public call from the church in the form of her friends' urging her to preach. She tested the waters and looked for signs from God to confirm that the course was right, but once convinced she proceeded with persistence and energy. Given her preparation, this transition seemed natural. Given the mood of the churches regarding women, it seems much less natural. Yet I want to argue that it was representative of a widespread movement among women and that it is representative of characteristics in American Protestantism that have yet to be explored fully.

This transition to public leadership caused Newman so little internal conflict because of the embedded household models of leadership in the church and because the roles of clergy and women overlapped, especially in the West. In the unformed communities of the American West, where the new separation of church and state could proceed unhindered by tradition, the initial egalitarianism of the early church began to show itself. The church's origins deep in the *oikos*, or household, reemerged from under layers of patriarchal tradition built up over the centuries.

It is also no accident that Newman found need in the West to serve the community not only as a spiritual leader, but as a physical healer as well. This was not an unusual combination for clergy of any kind in the West, but was particularly characteristic of women. Even in the East, many of the familiar early women ministers either became doctors or practiced some kind of medicine in addition to preaching. Anna Howard Shaw became a physician, the Unitarian Iowa Sisterhood combined medicine and ministry, and Newman's mentor Dr. Clisby was a member of the Women Ministers' Association. As much as foreign missionaries, male ministers on the frontier also found it useful to know something of medicine. Both clergy and women stood in the forefront of efforts to build community stability in the western towns. They supported libraries, public schools, and civic responsibility. They also used the church to develop "society" or social connections that both served to organize the community and to foster friendship and cooperation. Both women and clergy moving west concerned themselves with transmitting culture from East to West. A clergy woman shared these concerns, as well as those more particular to the church and the household. She found no conflict between her role in the church and her place as a woman in this cultural enterprise. Consequently,

I argue, this study of the intersection of gender and geography in the analysis of Newman's life illuminates this shared space of women and clergy and helps to explain the hospitality of the West to women ministers.

Emma Newman integrated preaching, pastoral care, and healing in her work. Together with a geography in the West that called forth practical and innovative strategies from everyone who came there, and the practical nature of women's roles in society, women were doing many things they did not usually do. To have a woman run a business or preach was not so much of a surprise, even though for most women, the work they did in the West was no different from that they did in the East, only more difficult.

Women experienced both independence and dependence in the West. Although there were openings for women to work on their own and to invent new roles, because of the isolation of the frontier, they were dependent on their families and immediate neighbors more than in the thickly settled East. They had fewer resources to make life easier. Newman forged together these aspects of her pastoral work into one because there were insufficient resources to specialize, and because there were fewer conventions to suggest that practicing all three in conjunction was inappropriate.

Newman's theological work was done in the context of all three modes of pastoral work: preaching presented her theology verbally, pastoral care demonstrated her theology by example, and her healing work demonstrated her understanding of the link between body and spirit in Christian faith and practice. The resulting theological stance I would name pragmatic evangelicalism. In the tradition of Finney, Newman was primarily concerned with faith put to use. Her theology as presented in her sermons was loosely orthodox and for the most part romantic. However, all her sermons aim at shaping her people's behavior as much as their belief. She urged temperance, Sabbath keeping, integrity of relationship, concern for modeling one's life after the example of Christ, and calling one's family, town, and nation into conformity with Christian moral principles. But she also taught that God had particular concern for each individual, and so in her homeopathic and mental healing, she taught that faith opened the doors to physical and psychic healing. She deliberately joined faith and healing. She deliberately argued against those mental healers who skewed evangelical Christian belief or discounted it all together.

This pragmatic, evangelical theology integrating healing, pastoral care and preaching had a brief life at the end of the nineteenth century in the hands of clergy such as Newman. It was broken apart by the professionalization of ministry in the mainline churches by the turn of the century. As medicine, ministry, and social work developed professional schools, demanded credentials, and increasingly operated in the context of professionalized institutions, not only did women find it more difficult to practice them, but integration such as Newman practiced became impossible given the barriers raised between practices. Within Congregationalism, healing went underground. Though certain streams of Christianity in America retained the relationship between healing and pastoral work, notably in the rising Pentecostal churches and the more liturgical traditions such as the Roman Catholic and Episcopal churches, the integration of the two modes of care did not resurface until the late twentieth century, coincidentally with the dramatic rise in women's ordination and the appeal of new religious movements originating in the West, particularly California. The question of whether there is a connection among these movements is the stuff of another study. The constellation of gender and geography may still be at work.

I want to offer a parting word, not to my academic colleagues, but to my friends and colleagues in the churches. Where the late-twentieth-century mainline Protestant church is surely called to rethink its models of ministry, Newman's work might be seen as a sketch for recovering a more whole way of working. The psychological, entertainment, and business models of ministry have contributed to the decline of mainline Protestantism, though they are by no means the only factors. Granted, the need to develop its theological foundations from a more complex and current perspective, but Newman's integration of the body and the spirit in preaching and pastoral care reminds us of the richer nature of community life in the church, the household of God. In order to make ministry professionally respectable we may have explained away too much, and as we became distanced religiously from our bodies, we lost our connections to our souls.

References

Index

References

Abbott Academy Emma Newman File. n.d. "Mrs. Emmerson Was a Pioneer for Her Sex." Phillips Academy Archives, Andover, Mass.

Aguirre, Rafael. 1984. "La Casa Como Estructura Base del Cristianismo Primitivo: Las Iglesias Domesticas," *Estudios Eclesiasticos* 59: 27–51.

Ahlstrom, Sidney. 1976. *A Religious History of the American People*. Garden City, N.Y.: Doubleday and Company.

Ahlstrom, T. R. 1990. "Andover Religion: Puritans in the Age of Expansion." M.A. thesis, Andover Newton Theological School.

Allis, Frederick S., Jr. 1979. *Youth from Every Quarter: A Bicentennial History of Phillips Academy, Andover*. Hanover, N.H.: Univ. Press of New England.

American Home Missionary Society. 1873. *The Forty-Seventh Report of the American Home Missionary Society*. New York: American Home Missionary Society.

Basso, Keith H. 1996. *Wisdom Sits in Places: Landscapes and Language Among the Western Apache*. Albuquerque: Univ. New Mexico Press.

Beecher, Henry Ward. 1868. *Sermons*. New York: Harper and Brothers, Publishers.

Beecher, Lyman. 1835. *A Plea for the West*. Cincinnati: Truman & Smith.

Big Woods Congregational Church. 1950. "115th Anniversary of the Big Woods Congregation and Dedication of the Church Building." June 25. Chronology prepared by H. M. Triplett. Chicago Historical Society Collections, Chicago, Ill.

Billington, Ray Allen. 1938. *The Protestant Crusade, 1800–1860: A Study of the Origins of American Nativism*. New York: Macmillan.

Blackwell, Alice Stone. 1904. "Women Ministers at Mrs. Howe's." *Woman's Journal* (June 4): 91. Clipping found in the Women's Ministerial Conference (Universalist). Records, 1873–1914, bMS 199. Andover-Harvard Theological Library of Harvard Divinity School, Cambridge, Mass.

Blanchard, Addison. 1885. *Kansas Home Missionary Society Report of the Superintendent*. Ottawa, Kan.: Kessler and McAllister.

Boylan, Anne M. 1978. "Evangelical Womanhood in the Nineteenth Century: The Role of Women in Sunday Schools," *Feminist Studies* 4 (October): 62–80.

Braude, Ann. 1997. "Women's History *Is* American Religious History." In *Rethinking U.S. Religious History,* edited by Thomas Tweed, 87–107. Berkeley: Univ. of California Press.

Breisach, Ernst. 1994. *Historiography: Ancient, Medieval, and Modern,* 2d ed. Chicago: Univ. of Chicago Press.

Breckus, Catherine A. 1998. *Strangers and Pilgrims: Female Preaching in America 1740–1845.* Chapel Hill: Univ. of North Carolina Press.

Bristol, Sherlock. [1887] 1989. *The Pioneer Preacher.* Urbana: Univ. of Illinois Press.

Brooten, Bernadette. 1982. *Women Leaders of the Ancient Synagogue.* Chico, Calif: Scholars Press.

Calvin, John. [1559] 1950. *Institutes of the Christian Religion.* 2 vols. Reprint, translated by Ford Lewis Battles and edited by John T. McNeill. Philadelphia: Westminster.

Carr, D. B. 1887. To M.K. Whittlesey, April 10. American Home Missionary Society Correspondence. Microfilm of materials from the Amistad Research Center.

Chambers-Schiller, Lee Virginia. 1984. *Liberty a Better Husband.* New Haven: Yale Univ. Press.

Chaves, Mark. 1997. *Ordaining Women: Culture and Conflict in Religious Organizations.* Cambridge: Harvard Univ. Press.

Clark, Joseph. B. 1884. To Rev. F. E. Sherman, April 8. The American Home Missionary Society Papers. Microfilm reel 334 #5485.

Commemorative Biographical and Historical Record of Kane County, Illinois. 1888. Chicago: Beers, Leggett and Company.

"The Cooper Family in Eastern Maine." 1886, 1889. *The Bangor Historical Society Magazine* 2: 40–41; 5: 46.

Cordley, Richard. 1876. "Congregationalism in Kansas." *Congregational Quarterly,* New Series, 18: 367–86.

Culley, Margo, ed. 1985. *One Day at a Time: The Diary Literature of American Women from 1764 to the Present.* New York: The Feminist Press.

Dexter, Henry Martin. 1880. *A Handbook of Congregationalism.* Boston: Congregational Publishing Society.

Douglas, Ann. 1978. *The Feminization of American Culture.* New York: Knopf.

Douglass, Jane Dempsey. 1984. "Christian Freedom: What Calvin Learned at the School of Women." *Church History* 53 (June): 155–73.

Eliade, Mircea. 1954. *The Myth of the Eternal Return, or Cosmos and History.* Translated by Willard R. Trask. Princeton: Princeton Univ. Press.

Evans, Warren. 1869. *The Mental Cure.* Boston: William White & Co.

Filson, Floyd V. 1939. "The Significance of the Early House Churches." *Journal of Biblical Literature* 58: 105–12.

Frankiel, Tamar. 1997. "Ritual Sites in the Narrative of American Religion." In *Retelling U.S. Religious History*, edited by Thomas A. Tweed, 57–86. Berkeley: Univ. of California Press.

Gastil, Raymond D. 1975. *Cultural Regions of the United States*. Seattle: Univ. of Washington Press.

General Association of Illinois. 1876. *Minutes of the General Association of Illinois*. Jacksonville, Ill.: Daily Journal.

General Association of Kansas. 1884. *Minutes of the General Association of Congregational Churches and Ministers of Kansas*. Lawrence, Kans.: Republican Journal Steam Printing Establishment.

———. 1887. *Minutes of the General Association of Congregational Churches and Ministers of Kansas*. Lawrence, Kans.: Republican Journal Steam Printing Establishment.

Glazer, Penina Migdal, and Miriam Slater. 1987. *Unequal Colleagues: The Entrance of Women into the Professions 1890–1940*. New Brunswick: Rutgers Univ. Press.

Goodykoontz, Colin B. 1939. *Home Missions on the American Frontier*. Caldwell, Id.: Caxton Press.

Haberkorn, Ruth Ewers. 1942. "The First Ordained Congregational Woman Minister in the United States." *Journal of the Illinois State Historical Society* 35, no. 3 (September), 288–94.

Haskell, J. G. 1884. "The Duty of Self Support." In *Minutes of the General Association of Kansas*, 442–51. Lawrence: Republican Journal Steam Printing Establishment.

Hedges-Hiller, Marilyn. 1992. "A Trickle of Ordained Women." Unpublished paper.

History of McHenry County, Illinois. [1885] 1976. Evansville, Ind.: Unigraphic Inc.

Hoag, Jack. n.d. "Algonquin." Illinois State Historical Library, Springfield, Ill. Federal Writers Project Files Box 1.

Jorstad, Erling. 1977. "Protestantism." In *The Reader's Encyclopedia of the American West*, edited by Howard R. Lamar, 976. New York: Thomas Y. Crowell and Company.

Kagle, Stephen. 1988. *Late Nineteenth-Century Diary Literature*. Boston: Twayne Publishers.

Klauk, Hans-Josef. 1981. *Haugemeinde und Hauskirche im frühen Christentum*. Stuttgart: Verlag Katholischess Bibelwerk GmbH.

Lawrence, Robert. 1856. *The New Hampshire Churches: Comprising Histories of the Congregational and Presbyterian Churches in the State*. Claremont, N.H.: Claremont Manufacturing Company.

Lindley, Susan Hill. 1996. *"You Have Stept Out of Your Place"*: A History of Women and Religion in America. Louisville: Westminster John Knox Press.

Lloyd, Susan McIntosh. 1979. *A Singular School: Abbot Academy*. Andover, Mass.: Phillips Academy.

Maffly-Kipp, Laurie F. 1997. "Eastward Ho! American Religion from the Perspective of the Pacific Rim." In *Retelling U.S. Religious History*, edited by Thomas A. Tweed, 127–48. Berkeley: Univ. of California Press.

Marsden, George M. 1980. *Fundamentalism and American Culture: The Shaping of Twentieth-Century Evangelicalism: 1870–1925*. New York: Oxford Univ. Press.

McKeen, Philena, and Phoebe McKeen. 1880. *A History of Abbot Academy, Andover, Massachusetts, 1829–1879*. Andover: Warren F. Draper.

McLoughlin, William G. 1978. *Revivals, Awakenings, and Reform*. Chicago: Univ. of Chicago Press.

McNeill, John T. 1951. *A History of the Cure of Souls*. New York: Harper and Brothers Publishers.

Mead, George Herbert. [1934] 1962. *Mind, Self, and Society*. Chicago: Univ. of Chicago Press.

Miner, Craig. 1986. *West of Wichita: Settling the High Plains of Kansas 1865–1890*. Lawrence: Univ. of Kansas Press.

Moorhead, Robert W. n.d. "Rural Tour from New Boston North to Rock Island County Line." Federal Writers Project. Box 1. Aledo File. Illinois State Historical Society Library.

Myrdal, Gunnar. 1944. *An American Dilemma: The Negro Problem and Modern Democracy*. New York: Harper and Brothers.

National Council of the Congregational Churches of the United States. 1884. *Congregational Year-book*. Boston: Congregational Publishing Society.

Newman, Emma. n.d. Diary. Vols. 1–16. Huntington Library, San Marino, CA. Manuscripts. Emma Newman Collection. Boxes 2–3.

———. n.d. Letters. Huntington Library Manuscripts. Emma Newman Collection. Box 1.

———. n.d. "Notes on Austin Phelps' Lectures on English Style." Huntington Library Manuscripts. Emma Newman Collection. Box 4.

———. n.d. "Notes on Sinnett's Directions for Magnetism." Huntington Library Manuscripts. Emma Newman Collection. Box 4.

———. n.d. "The Other Side of the Boardinghouse Question." Huntington Library Manuscripts. Emma Newman Collection. Box 5.

———. n.d. "Recipes to Cure Certain Illnesses." Huntington Library Manuscripts. Emma Newman Collection. Box 5.

———. n.d. Sermons. Huntington Library Manuscripts. Emma Newman Collection. Box 5.

Sermon no. 1 "The True Work of Life."

Sermon no. 2. "Exhortation to Leave Wrong and Turn to the Right."

Sermon no. 3. "The Touch of Christ."

Sermon no. 4. "Freedom Through the Truth."

Sermon no. 5. "Growth in Grace."

Sermon no. 6. "The Strength of the Lord."

Sermon no. 9. "The Coming of God's Kingdom."

Sermon no. 10. "Ye Cannot Serve God and Mammon."

Sermon no. 12. "The God of Patience and Consolation."

Sermon no. 13. "Good Gifts, God's Gifts."

Sermon no. 14. "Home Missions."

Sermon no. 16. "Kindness and Forgiveness."

Sermon no. 17. "Trust in God."

Sermon no. 57. "The Unselfish Theory of Life."

Sermon no. 79. "Sincere Living."

Sermon no. 87. "Life Made Glad by Trust in Christ."

————. n.d. "Things in General." Huntington Library Manuscripts. Emma Newman Collection. Box 4.

————. 1871. "Notes on Austin Phelps' Lectures on Homiletics." Huntington Library Manuscripts. Emma Newman Collection. Box 4.

————. 1872. "Woman's Work." *Woman's Journal* (April 6): 109.

Nussbaum, Felicity A. 1988. "Toward Conceptualizing Diary." In *Studies in Autobiography*, edited by James Olney, 128–39. New York: Oxford Univ. Press.

Nye, Lowell Albert, ed. 1968. *McHenry County, Illinois 1832–1968*. Woodstock, Ill.: McHenry County Board of Supervisors.

Osborn, Ronald. 1991. *Creative Disarray: Models of Ministry in America*. St. Louis: Chalice Press.

The People Came. 1977. Osborne, Kan.: The Osborne County Genealogical and Historical Society.

Pomeroy, Sarah. 1975. *Goddesses, Whores, Wives, and Slaves: Women in Classical Antiquity*. New York: Shocken Books.

Record Book of the Dial Congregational Church. 1881–1914. Kansas Historical Society. United Church of Christ Collection. Topeka, Kansas.

Richards, Laura E., and Maud Howe Elliott. 1916. *Julia Ward Howe, 1819–1910*, vol. 1. Boston: Houghton Mifflin Company.

Riley, Glenda. 1988. *The Female Frontier: A Comparative View of Women on the Prairie and the Plains*. Lawrence: Univ. of Kansas Press.

Robertson, Darrel Marvin. 1982. "The Chicago Revival, 1876: A Case Study in the Social Functions of a Nineteenth-Century Revival." Ph.D. diss, Univ. of Iowa.

Royce, Josiah. 1913. *The Problem of Christianity*. New York: Macmillan.

Schlesinger, Arthur M., Sr. 1967. *A Critical Period in American Religion 1875–1900*. Philadelphia: Fortress Press.

Secretary of the National Council. 1874. "The Annual Statistics of the American Congregational Ministers and Churches Collected in the Year 1873." *Congregational Quarterly* 16: 108–112.

———. 1875. "The Annual Statistics of the American Congregational Ministers and Churches Collected in the Year 1874." *Congregational Quarterly* 17: 109–113.

Shaw, Anna Howard. [1915] 1990. *Anna Howard Shaw: Story of a Pioneer*. Cleveland: The Pilgrim Press.

Shedd, William G. T. 1871. *Homiletics and Pastoral Theology*, 8th ed. New York: Charles Scribner and Company.

Smith, Archie Jr. 1982. *The Relational Self: Ethics and Therapy from a Black Church Perspective*. Nashville: Abingdon.

Smith, Daniel Scott. 1974. "Family Limitation." In *Clio's Consciousness Raised*, edited by Mary Hartman and Lois Banner, 119–36. New York: Harper and Row Publishers.

Smith, Henry Nash. 1950. *Virgin Land: The American West as Symbol and Myth*. Cambridge: Harvard Univ. Press.

Spelman, Elizabeth. 1997. *Fruits of Sorrow*. Boston: Beacon Press.

Storrs, S. D. 1884. "Report of the Board of Directors of the Kansas Home Missionary Society." In *Minutes of the General Association of Congregational Ministers and Churches of Kansas*, 30–37. Lawrence, Kans.: Republican Journal Steam Printing Establishment.

Strickland, Charles. 1985. *Victorian Domesticity: Families in the Life and Art of Louisa May Alcott*. University: Univ. of Alabama Press.

Strong, Josiah. 1885. *Our Country: Its Possible Future and Its Present Crisis*. New York: American Home Missionary Society.

Szasz, Ferenc Morton. 1988. *The Protestant Clergy in the Great Plains and Mountain West, 1865–1915*. Albuquerque: Univ. of New Mexico Press.

———. 1982. *The Divided Mind of Protestant America 1880–1930*. University: Univ. of Alabama Press.

Szasz, Ferenc Morton, and Margaret Connell Szasz. 1994. "Religion and Spirituality." In *The Oxford History of the American West*, edited by Clyde A. Milner II, Carol A. O'Connor, and Martha A. Sandweiss, 359–92. New York: Oxford Univ. Press.

Takaki, Ronald. 1993. *A Different Mirror: A History of Multicultural America*. Boston: Little Brown and Company.

Torjesen, Karen Jo. 1993. *When Women Were Priests*. San Francisco: Harper and Row.

Toulouse, Mark G., and James Duke, eds. 1997. *Makers of Christian Theology in America*. Nashville: Abingdon Press.

Townsman, Aug. 25, 1922. Obituary of Emma Newman. Phillips Academy Archives, Andover, Mass.

Tucker, Cynthia Grant. 1990. *Prophetic Sisterhood: Liberal Women Ministers of the Frontier, 1880–1930*. Bloomington: Indiana Univ. Press.

Turner, James. 1985. *Without God, Without Creed: The Origins of Unbelief in America*. Baltimore: Johns Hopkins Univ. Press.

Tweed, Thomas A., ed. 1997. *Retelling U.S. Religious History*. Berkeley: Univ. of California Press.

U.S. Department of the Interior, Census Office. 1873. Consensus Reports of the Ninth Census. Washington, D.C.: Government Printing Office.

———. 1883. Consensus Reports of the Tenth Census. Washington, D.C.: Government Printing Office.

———. 1895. Consensus Reports of the Eleventh Census. Washington, D.C.: Government Printing Office.

Unruh, John D., Jr. 1979. *The Plains Across: The Overland Emigrants and the Trans-Mississippi West, 1840–60*. Urbana: Univ. of Illinois Press.

Vanderpool, Harold Young. 1971. "The Andover Conservatives: Apologetics, Biblical Criticism, and Theological Change at the Andover Theological Seminary, 1808–1880." Ph.D. diss., Harvard Univ.

Victor, Metta. 1860. *The Backwoods Bride: A Romance of Squatter Life*. New York: Beadle & Adams.

Walker, Williston. 1906. "Changes in Theology Among American Congregationalists." *American Journal of Theology* 10: 204–18.

White, Richard. 1991. *"It's Your Misfortune and None of My Own": A New History of the American West*. Norman: Univ. of Oklahoma Press.

Whittlesey, Martin. 1877a. To American Home Missionary Society. American Home Missionary Society Correspondence. Microfilm of Amistad Research Center Collections. Reel 53. March 6.

———. 1877b. "Secretaries of the A. H. M. Society Report for Quarter Ending April 1, 1877." American Home Missionary Society Correspondence. Microfilm of Amistad Research Center Collections. Reel 53. April 1.

———. 1877c. To D. B. Carr. American Home Missionary Society Correspondence. Microfilm of Amistad Research Center Collections. Reel 53. April 5.

Women's Ministerial Conference (Universalist). n.d. Records, 1873–1914, bMS 199. Andover-Harvard Theological Library of Harvard Divinity School, Cambridge, Mass.

Woods, Leonard. 1885. *History of the Andover Seminary*. Boston: James R. Osgood and Company.

Wright, Louis B. 1955. *Culture on the Moving Frontier*. New York: Harper and Row, Publishers.

Yeates, Marion. 1994. "Beyond Trifles." *Journal of Women's History* 6 (Summer): 150–59.

Index